THE COMMONWEALTH AND INTERNATIONAL LIBRARY
Joint Chairmen of the Honorary Editorial Advisory Board
SIR ROBERT ROBINSON, O.M., F.R.S., LONDON
DEAN ATHELSTAN SPILHAUS, MINNESOTA
Publisher: ROBERT MAXWELL, M.C., M.P.

LIBRARIES AND TECHNICAL INFORMATION DIVISION
General Editor: G. CHANDLER

HOW TO FIND OUT ABOUT CANADA

3

HOW TO FIND OUT ABOUT
CANADA

Edited by

H. C. CAMPBELL ed

Chief Librarian, Toronto Public Libraries

6

5 ## PERGAMON PRESS

OXFORD · LONDON · EDINBURGH · NEW YORK
TORONTO · SYDNEY · PARIS · BRAUNSCHWEIG

7

1967

Pergamon Press Ltd., Headington Hill Hall, Oxford
4 & 5 Fitzroy Square, London W.1
Pergamon Press (Scotland) Ltd., 2 & 3 Teviot Place, Edinburgh 1
Pergamon Press Inc., 44–01 21st Street, Long Island City, New York 11101
Pergamon of Canada, Ltd., 6 Adelaide Street East, Toronto, Ontario
Pergamon Press (Aust.) Pty. Ltd., 20–22 Margaret Street, Sydney,
New South Wales
Pergamon Press S.A.R.L., 24 rue des Écoles, Paris 5e
Vieweg & Sohn GmbH, Burgplatz 1, Braunschweig

Printed in Great Britain by A. Wheaton & Co. Ltd., Exeter

(3306/67)

Contents

List of Illustrations

Acknowledgment for the use of specimen pages from reference works is here-
by made for the following: Figs. 2, 5, 6, 7, 13, 14, 15, 18, 22, 28, Queen's
Printer, Ottawa; Figs. 3, 17, 33, R. R. Bowker Co.; Figs. 27, 30, University
of Toronto Press.

B*

Introduction

IF YOU want to find out about Canada, three things are necessary. You must travel her land, meet her people, and read her books. From the early sixteenth century this has been the pattern followed by countless thousands of individuals from all parts of the world, all eager to find out what the country has to offer.

In spite of the changes in travel and communication that the twentieth century has brought, the same steps are still necessary. Radio and television now allow one to travel the land and meet the people in a fashion that was not possible earlier, but even with these the full task is not done, and it is still necessary to read her books and to know something of her writers, poets, novelists, and song writers.

The desire to know about Canada is not something that is felt only by those who live outside the country. Thousands of Canadians have never seen a good many parts of their own country. There is therefore no lack of interest in finding out about Canada among the people who make up the nation. This is particularly true for more than one million who have come to Canada from the countries of Europe and Asia in the last 20 years. Post-World War II immigration reached a peak in 1957, when in the one year over 257,000 persons landed in Canada to take up settlement. Few of them had more than a slight knowledge of the country and its people when they arrived.

This knowledge was often based on meagre newspaper and magazine accounts which told something, but not much, about the vast, free, open, and largely uninhabited land, and cities with such names as Montreal, Toronto, Vancouver, and Winnipeg. For generations many people have emigrated to Canada with little real idea of the country beyond the bare awareness of its existence. But they probably knew of some other person, often a relative or friend, who had gone to Canada and had written back to say that the country had a future and the prospects for a home and employment were good.

While it is possible to find out a good deal about Canada from books and periodicals, it is also necessary to make the acquaintance of some of the many national and provincial organizations that can supply an up-to-date account of what is happening in the country.

A knowledge of the location of the various professional and specialist associations in Canada is not easy to acquire, even though most of them are listed in the telephone books of their respective cities. Guides to as many such associations as possible have been included in this work.

Other sources of valuable information are the current daily, weekly, or monthly newspapers published in many languages in all parts of Canada. Only a few of the major daily newspapers are listed here. Unfortunately only one comprehensive index to the contents of a Canadian daily newspaper (*Le Devoir*, Montreal) is published. Thanks to the efforts of the Canadian Library Association, the National Library, Ottawa, and the University of Laval, there is a partial index of the contents of some Canadian periodicals in both English and French.

A further source of information about Canada consists of the travel and tourist publications distributed widely inside and outside of the country. These are not included in this book, since it is presumed that they and similar publications will be referred to as a matter of course by those wishing to know something of a general nature about the Canadian scene.

The largest single source of published works of reference about Canada becomes very apparent as one goes through this volume. It is clear that this position is occupied by the Government of Canada with the University Presses of Toronto and Laval taking second place. Then follow a number of commercial book and periodical publishers, mostly situated in Montreal or Toronto.

On the whole, reference books on Canada are not distributed

too widely outside Canada, but since the beginning of the twentieth century an effort has been made to have Canadian publications available abroad. This is done by selling the reprint and publishing rights to British and United States publishers, but has also recently taken the form of direct selling abroad of Canadian books by the Canadian publisher. The growth of bookshops in various parts of the world which specialize in Canadian books has been slow, but these are starting to appear in some parts of Europe and Asia as well as in the United States. For many reasons, it is still often too difficult for readers outside Canada to have quick access to Canadian publications even when they are aware that such publications exist. With the increasing demand for these works the situation is likely to improve.

Some Canadian organizations, notably the University of Toronto Press, the firm of McClelland & Stewart, Toronto, and non-commercial organizations such as the Toronto Public Library are now reprinting basic Canadian works which are no longer available. This initiative is of importance within Canada in order to supply the new schools and universities with reference collections of Canadian materials. Where out-of-print works are mentioned in the following chapters, it is with the hope that they may again soon be in print.

Efforts have been made to include in the main those books that have been published recently and are assumed to be in print. Out-of-print titles have been included where the information contained in them is not readily available elsewhere.

The selection of works has been based mainly on those in English, with a few in French for which no English edition has appeared. Where a work exists in French as well as in English, this has been noted in the Index (see pp. 219 ff.). A separate guide in French could be written to sources of Canadian information, and it would include many hundreds of titles not listed here, so great is the difference in coverage of Canadian materials by the two languages of Canada.

Chapters 1, 13, 14, and 15 have been prepared by Mr. David Skene Melvin, head of the Technical Services Division of the

Toronto Public Libraries. Chapters 10 and 11 have been prepared by Mr. Alan Suddon, head of the Fine Art section of the Toronto Public Libraries, Central Library, assisted by staff members of the section.

The annotations for titles included have been prepared in part by the following staff members of the Toronto Public Libraries: Miss Diane Brittain, Miss Barbara Byers, Miss Margaret Calder, Mrs. Patricia Fleming, Mr. Robert Foster, Mr. John George, Miss Marjorie Hair, Mrs. Nancy Hall, Mr. Cameron Hollyer, Mrs. Clara Kingston, Miss Anne Mack, Miss Heather McCallum, Mrs. Marjorie McLeod, Miss Mary McMahon, Mrs. Ogreta McNeill, Miss Gail Randall, Mr. Gregory Rickerby, Mr. Abdus Salam, Miss Beverly Sandover-Sly, Mr. Albert Spratt, Mr. Donald Watt, and Mr. Leonard Wertheimer. Other staff members have assisted in many ways.

Help in making the choice of titles was received from Mr. Robert Hamilton and the students at the School of Library Science of the University of British Columbia who have compiled a basic list, as yet unpublished, of Canadian reference works.

Mr. Jacques Sansfaçon of the École de bibliothéconomie, University of Montreal, aided in the selection and description of some of the titles in French.

The work would not have appeared without the devoted help of Miss Raye Howard of the Toronto Public Libraries who painstakingly made sure that all material was included in the right place. The assistance of Mrs. Elisabeth Randall in typing the manuscript is gratefully acknowledged.

H. C. CAMPBELL,
Chief Librarian, Toronto Public Libraries

CHAPTER I

General Guides to Canadian Achievement

Bibliographies and Catalogues

One of the most direct ways to find out about Canadian publications is to look in bibliographies and lists of books in order to secure titles of periodicals, pamphlets, and articles. There are many such lists of Canadian books, some covering the country as a whole, others dealing with specific periods, still others concerned only with certain regions. Some are lists of books published in a certain part of Canada or books published during a certain period. Some are lists of old books giving their value, while others are lists of books in print and available for purchase.

An important "books in print" for Canadian items published in French is the *Catalogue de l'édition au Canada français*, produced by the Association des Éditeurs Canadiens and published in Montreal with the assistance of the Quebec Department of Cultural Affairs. The latest edition is the fourth, published in 1967. The *Catalogue* is not limited to books printed in the French language but includes publications of all publishers situated within the Province of Quebec and those located elsewhere in Canada who publish material either in French or related to French Canada. It is arranged by broad subject classes following the Dewey Classification, with both an author and a title index as well as a directory of publishers. Each entry gives author, title, type of binding, pagination, publisher, place, date, and price.

A similar work for Canadian books in print in English is sponsored by the Canadian Booksellers Association, the Canadian Library Association, and the Canadian Book Publishers Council entitled *Canadian Books in Print*: *Catalogue des livres canadiens en librairie*, Toronto, 1967. The work has two main sections, a listing arranged alphabetically by authors and including cross-references from co-authors, editors, translators, and a listing arranged alphabetically by title and including additional entries under series where applicable. There is a list of Canadian publishers and their addresses. A book is included if it is written by a Canadian citizen, resident, or expatriate in any language and published in Canada, or written by a Canadian and published abroad but distributed in Canada by a Canadian agent. Maps, sheet music, government documents, newspapers, and pamphlets of an ephemeral nature are excluded. Each main entry will give information on author, title, publisher, year of copyright, price, series, and such other notations as edition, volume, etc., where applicable.

Canadian Book Prices Current, compiled originally by Robert Hamilton and latterly by Rita Butterfield, was published in 3 volumes by McClelland & Stewart, Toronto. Volume 1, including old and rare books sold at auctions or listed in rare and second-hand book dealers' catalogues between 1950 and 1955, was published in 1957. Volume 2 covers the period 1956–8 and volume 3 the years 1959–62. These volumes list out-of-print books published in or published elsewhere and relating to Canada in an alphabetical-by-author arrangement. Each entry gives author, title, place, date of publication (but unfortunately not the publisher), edition, the number of pages where it is significant, the name of the dealer offering the book, price, and its condition at time of sale. Since the same book may appear in all 3 volumes, one can chart its rise or fall in popularity with collectors or its increasing rarity. Volume 1 includes only books published before 1940 and worth more than $2.50; volume 2, books published up to 1945 and worth more than $2.50; and volume 3, books published before 1956 and worth over $3.50. The volumes also provide a partial directory of dealers in old and rare Canadiana.

Articles in Canadian periodicals and magazines have been listed in the Canadian Library Association's *Canadian Index to Periodicals*

ONTARIO chamber of commerce
McGibbon heads 50,000 businessmen in Ontario. port. Fin Post 58:39 My 16 '64
Ontario, Quebec set up controversial agenda. Fin Post 58:11 Mr 28 '64
Quebec and Ontario businessmen try their own unofficial 'entente'. D. Crane. Fin Post 58:1,3 Ja 18 '64

ONTARIO conference on automation. See Conference on automation and social change

ONTARIO curriculum institute
How not to reform the curriculum. A. Wittenberg. Can Forum 43:270-2 Mr '64

ONTARIO federation of anglers and hunters, incorporated
OFAH news notes. See monthly issues of Rod and Gun to Je '64

ONTARIO federation of labour. See Canadian labour congress - Ontario federation of labour

ONTARIO historical society
Financial statement. Ont Hist 56:143-4 Je '64
Membership. Ont Hist 56:145 Je '64
Report of the Museums section of the Ontario historical society, 1961-1963. G. Metcalfe. tab Ont Hist 56:150-1 Je '64

ONTARIO housing corporation
Ladyman to Ontario housing corp. Can Lab 9:27 O '64
Ontario's new housing chiefs. Fin Post 58:39 Ag 22 '64

ONTARIO institute of chartered accountants scholarships. See Scholarships and fellowships

ONTARIO library association
..Executive 1964-1965. Ont Lib R 48:162-3 Ag '64
Circulation services section
..Annual meeting, May 1964. M. Kannins. Ont Lib R 48:164 Ag '64

ONTARIO research foundation
Barrington ORF chairman. Fin Post 58:21 My 2 '64
ORF next to start building as 'research village' grows. Fin Post 58:36 F 29 '64

ONTARIO safety league
Bell heads Safety league. port Fin Post 58:26 Mr 21 '64

ONTARIO souvenir industry exhibition
Ontario souvenir industry exhibition seeks to recover $33 million spent every year on imported items. il Ind Can 64:16 Ap '64

ONTARIO urban renewal conference, 1957
[From some of our honorary members, CPAC] W.A. Dempsey. bibliog f Com Plan R 14:30-1 [summer '64]

ONTARIO water resources commission. See Ontario - Water resources commission

ONTARIO welfare council
Ont. welfare council approved medicare. Can Lab 9:38 Jl-Ag '64

ONTOLOGIE. Voir Ontology

ONTOLOGY
Essai sur le caractère ontique du droit. J. Kalinowski. bibliog f R de l'Univ d'Ottawa 34:81*-99* av-jn '64

OOKPIK. See Eskimos - Art

OPALOV, Leonard
Epistle; poem. Fiddlehead no 60:19 spring '64

OPEMISKA copper mines limited
Un village déchiré: Chapais. J. Bamber. il ports Mag Macl 4:30-2,62+ o '64

OPEN-end investment funds. See Investment trusts

OPEN-mindedness. See Toleration

FIG. 1. *Canadian Periodical Index,* 1964.

and Documentary Films: an author and subject index, dating from 1948, Canadian Library Association and National Library of Canada, Ottawa. Prior to this date there are 10 cumulated annual volumes for the years 1938–47, which were issued by the Public Libraries Branch of the Ontario Department of Education, Toronto and reprinted in 3 volumes in 1966. The periodicals which are indexed are always under review, and titles are added and dropped year to year depending on the value of their articles. In May 1966, 85 periodicals, 17 of them in French, were being indexed. Since 1964 the National Library, Ottawa, has been responsible for indexing documentary films and these are now included in *Canadiana*, the official national bibliography.

The present title of the Library Association index is the *Canadian Periodical Index*: *Index des périodiques canadiens* (Fig. 1). It provides cumulated volumes covering 1938–59, annual volumes from 1960, and monthly issues from the most recent annual cumulation to date. All articles are listed under both author and subject in one alphabetical arrangement. Each entry gives the title of the article, whether illustrated, the magazine in which it is to be found, volume number, inclusive paging, and date. Subject headings are in English with *see references* in French. Book reviews are included under that overall heading, and reproductions of paintings and sculpture are listed under the artist's name.

Older books published in or about Canada are listed in several sources. One of these is the *Canadian Catalogue of Books published in Canada, Books about Canada, as well as those written by Canadians, with Imprint, 1921–1949*, published by the Toronto Public Library, Toronto. This is a record of books and pamphlets of Canadian interest published in Canada or abroad, and books written by Canadians regardless of whether or not they concern Canada or where they were published. It also includes a very small selection of federal and provincial government publications of general interest. To a limited extent the *Canadian Catalogue* is also a guide to the holdings of Canadiana of the Toronto Public Library. It was originally published yearly from 1921–2 to 1949, and in 1950 was succeeded by the National Library's *Canadiana*

Publications du Gouvernement du Canada

Un index des noms d'auteurs individuels et des titres distinctifs de la 2e partie, intercalés avec ceux de la 3e partie, se trouve à la fin du volume et comprend le groupe de pages numérotées B 1 etc.

Abréviations: *Agr.* Division de l'information, Ministère de l'agriculture, Ottawa; *BFS.* Bureau fédéral de la statistique, Ottawa; *CNR.* Conseil national de recherches, Ottawa; *IR.* L'Imprimeur de la Reine, Ottawa; *Min.* Ministère, bureau, office, etc. nommé comme auteur de la publication.

Annuaire téléphonique, Gouvernement du Canada, Ottawa. Janv. 1966. ɾOttawa, Imprimeur de la Reine, 1966.ɹ

140 p. 28 cm.

Titre de la couverture.
Éd. antérieure juin 1964.
Préparé par le Bureau du service téléphonique, Ministère des finances.
$1.30 IR

CG66-889

Canada. *Bureau de la statistique. Division de l'agriculture.*

Canada. *Bureau de la statistique. Division de l'industrie.*

La Division de l'industrie et du commerce est devenue la Division de l'industrie et la Division du commerce et de services le 1er juil. 1963.

—— Diverses transformations du papier; recensement annuel des manufactures. 1963. Ottawa, Imprimeur de la Reine, 1966.

21 p. ill. 28 cm.

Titre de la couverture.
Texte bilingue, anglais et français.
Le titre varie: -1959, L'industrie des articles divers en papier.
50c. QP

FIG. 2. *Canadiana*, 1966.

(Fig. 2). In 1959 the English sections of the *Canadian Catalogue*
for 1921 through 1949 were reprinted in 2 volumes with a cumulated author index for each volume, volume 1 covering 1921–39
and volume 2 covering 1940–9.

*Canadiana: publications of Canadian interest noted by the
National Library*, Queen's Printer, Ottawa, is the current official
Canadian national bibliography which began publication in 1950,
taking over the listing previously done by the Toronto Public
Library in the *Canadian Catalogue*. It attempts to list all current
items classifiable as Canadiana. It has a four-part arrangement:
Part I is a subject arrangement in Dewey Decimal Classification,
with Fiction arranged alphabetically by author at the end of the
Literature class, and Juveniles listed at the end of the regular
Dewey order; Parts II and III list the publications of the Government of Canada and the provincial governments respectively,
each arranged alphabetically by name of issuing department;
Part IV is a title arrangement of films and filmstrips produced in
Canada. Part I and Parts II and III have separate author–title
indexes. *Canadiana* appears monthly with yearly cumulations;
there is also a retrospective index covering 1950–62.

In addition to *Canadiana* the National Library in Ottawa also
publishes *Canadian Theses*: *Thèses canadiennes*, which began in
1953 and has been appearing on a regular basis since that date.
This lists theses accepted by Canadian universities for postgraduate work and arranges them in Dewey Decimal Classification order with an author index.

Canadian Government Publications: a manual for librarians, was
compiled by Marion V. Higgins and published by the American
Library Association in Chicago in 1935. It provides a guide to the
publications of the Canadian Federal Government from 1840 on-
ward, department by department, agency by agency, listing them
with a preface which gives a history of the issuing body.

The story of Canadian government publishing is a complicated
one. After Great Britain gained Canada from France in the
eighteenth century, part of the territory governed as a colony was
known as Quebec. In 1791 this territory was divided into two

colonies, named Upper Canada and Lower Canada, the latter being the original area of settlement of the French. In 1840 these two colonies were rejoined under the name of Canada. When most of the colonies of British North America confederated in 1867, what was then Canada was redivided. What had been Upper Canada became Ontario, and Lower Canada reverted to the name of Quebec. The name Canada was adopted for the new nation as a whole. Olga B. Bishop's *Publications of the Government of the Province of Canada, 1841–1867*, National Library of Canada, Ottawa, 1963, is concerned with the official government publications of that British colony known as Canada, comprising Upper and Lower Canada, during the period from 1841 to Confederation. This bibliography serves to bring to light the extent and variety of information to be found in these official publications. Printed laws, journals, proceedings of committees, departmental reports, returns, and other papers, ordered printed by the Governor-General, Legislative Council, or Legislative Assembly, have been listed.

Canadian Government Publications, Catalogue, Queen's Printer, Ottawa, dealing with current publications only, is issued in English and French on a monthly and an annual basis and records the publications offered for sale by the Queen's Printer.

The *Publications of the Government of Ontario, 1901–1955: a checklist*, compiled by Hazel I. MacTaggart and printed and distributed by the University of Toronto Press for the Queen's Printer in 1964, provides a much-needed guide to the publications issued by the Province of Ontario during the first half of the twentieth century. It furnishes an important historical record of the activities of the Government of Ontario for those years.

Other sources for government publications are: *Publications of the Government of Nova Scotia, Prince Edward Island, New Brunswick, 1758–1952*, compiled by Olga B. Bishop, Queen's Printer, Ottawa, 1958; *Publications of the Government of British Columbia, 1871–1947*, compiled by Marjorie C. Holmes, King's Printer, Victoria, 1950; *Publications of the Government of the North-West*

Territories, 1876–1905, and of the Province of Saskatchewan, 1905–1952, compiled by Christine MacDonald, Legislative Library, Regina, 1953.

Henry J. Morgan's *Bibliotheca canadensis: or, a manual of Canadian literature* was published in 1867 by G. E. Desbarats of Ottawa. This is the classic bibliography of English-language Canadiana for the period 1760–1867. Another important bibliography of Canadiana is Marie Tremaine's *A Bibliography of Canadian Imprints, 1751–1800,* published by the University of Toronto Press in 1952. This work includes books, pamphlets, leaflets, broadsides, handbills, and some pictorial publications, recorded year by year, with the addition of newspapers and magazines produced in those colonies of British North America now comprising provinces of Canada, from 1751 through 1800. It includes works known to have been produced whether they are known to have survived or not. The items are arranged chronologically by date of imprint regardless of place of publication. Full bibliographical information and explanatory notes are given for each entry. The section on newspapers gives a history of each, and there is a list of printing offices in Canada during the period covered, with biographical notes on each of the printers concerned. The *Bibliography of Canadian Imprints* has the great advantage over others of its kind by having an excellent author–title–subject index.

Published in 1934 by the Toronto Public Library, *A Bibliography of Canadiana: being items in the Public Library of Toronto, Canada, relating to the early history and development of Canada* (Fig. 3), edited by F. M. Staton and Marie Tremaine, is a record of the significant items held in the Toronto Public Library concerning events in connection with Canada from the voyage of Jacques Cartier in 1534 to the Confederation of the Provinces and the emergence of Canada as a nation in 1867. The books and pamphlets included were chosen to form a chronological record of the history of Canada from its discovery to 1867. The items are arranged regardless of place or date of publication to set forth the social, political, and economic activities in Canada from year to

16 p.   21.2 x 13 cm. Caption title: Sermon.   For after that in the wisdom of God. . .it
pleased God by the foolishness of preaching to save them that believe.—I. Corinthians i, xxi.
   The Author came from Ireland as a boy.   He was ordained a minister of the Methodist
Church in 1825.   From 1836 to 1839 he was Principal of Upper Canada Academy in Cobourg.
Later he held charges in Toronto, Kingston, Montreal and the Maritimes.

4908. SHERWOOD, G.

HYMN,/ For the commencement of the Year 1827./ (Spoken by Master
G. Sherwood, at the Royal Grammar/ School, on the 19th of January.)/ . . .
TO THE LADIES./ (Spoken by Master John Boulton, immediately/ after he
had repeated the original Greek Ode.)/ [York] 1827.

Broadside, 4 lines, 2 col. of 32 lines each. 33.3 x 20.8 cm.

4909. STEWART, ALEXANDER, d. 1840

Two Essays: the first, on the Gospel; the second, on the kingdom of
Christ; and A Sermon on baptism: with an appendix, containing remarks on
late publications: by Alexander Stewart Minister of the Gospel York, Upper
Canada.   Moreover, brethren, I declare unto you the gospel. . .and that he
rose again the third day, according to the scriptures. 1 Cor.15.1, 2, 3, 4.   Jesus
answered, my kingdom is not of this world. John 18.36.   One Lord, one faith,
one baptism. . .Eph.4.5.   *York: Printed at the Office of the Colonial Advocate,
by William Lyon Mackenzie, Printer to the House of Assembly, and sold by
E. Lesslie and Sons—York, Kingston, and Dundas: and by all others entrusted
with subscription papers. [pref. 1827]*

96 p. 19.4 x 11.9 cm. Corrigenda, p.96. Foxed.

Wallace, 2d ed.

4910. UNITED EMPIRE LOYALISTS' ASSOCIATION OF ONTARIO

Transactions, Hamilton Branch, March 10, 1903. [*The Griffin & Kidner
Co., Ltd. Printers Hamilton, Canada 1903*]

12 p.   24.3 x 15.2 cm. Cover title.   Imprint taken from p.[2]   Includes A Register of
Marriages and Baptisms in the Gore and London Districts, by the Rev. Ralph Leeming, from
1816 to 1827 (p.5–12)
   This Clergyman, after ordination, was sent as a missionary to Canada by the Society for
the Propagation of the Gospel in Foreign Parts. He became the first rector at Ancaster in 1816,
a charge he seems to have held till 1827 only, though no successor took his place till John Miller
arrived from Ireland in 1830.

Can. Arch. (vide Register)

1828

4911. BRIEF REMARKS ON A PAMPHLET

Brief Remarks on a Pamphlet, entitled "Arguments to prove the Policy
and Necessity of granting to Newfoundland a Constitutional Government."
"By P Morris, an inhabitant of the Colony of Newfoundland."   By the Author
of "A View of the Rise, Progress, and Present State of the Newfoundland
Fishery."   "Rien n'est si dangereux qu'un indiscret ami; Mieux vaudroit un
sage ennemi." La Fontaine.   *Poole: Printed and sold by Moore and Sydenham:
Sold also by G. B. Whittaker, Ave-Maria Lane, London. 1828.*

2 p.l., 35 p. 21.4 x 13.2 cm.

Vide no.4917

4912. CANADA. PUBLIC ARCHIVES

. . .Documents relating to the Constitutional History of Canada. . .   *Ottawa J. O. Patenaude. Printer to the King's Most Excellent Majesty, 1907–35*

3 v. [v.3]: xi, 538 p. 23.9 x 15.8 cm. At head of title: Public Archives—Appendix.   Contents: [v.3], 1819–1828, selected and edited with notes by Arthur G. Doughty and Norah Story.
Issued as an appendix to the Report for 1934.

Vide no.1134
B.M., L.C.

FIG. 3. *Bibliography of Canadiana*, 1934.

year. In 1959 the Toronto Public Library published a *Supplement*, arranged on the same pattern as the main volume.

A Check List of Canadian Imprints, 1900–1925, compiled by Dorothea D. Tod and Audrey Cordingley, and published by the King's Printer, Ottawa, 1950, attempts to supply a comprehensive and co-ordinated list of Canadian publications for the first quarter of the twentieth century, excluding government documents. Only a mimeographed preliminary edition, known to be incomplete, was produced. A final edition clearly including the vast majority of publications which appeared between 1900 and 1925 is planned but has yet to appear. The arrangement is alphabetical by name of author, with each entry giving author's name, dates if known, title, pagination, place of publication, publisher, and date of publication. Once again, as with the majority of bibliographies of Canadiana, its efficiency is hampered by the lack of a title index, but it is still, despite its incompleteness and shortcomings, a very useful reference tool.

The foregoing are primarily though not entirely concerned only with publications in the English language. Information regarding publications in the French language may be obtained through two basic sources, the first of which is Narcisse Eutrope Dionne's *Inventaire chronologique . . .*, published in Quebec by the Royal Society of Canada in 4 volumes with supplements between 1905 and 1912 and now unfortunately out of print. It was also issued in the Royal Society of Canada's *Proceedings and Transactions*, 3rd ser., **10–12**, 14 (1904–6, 1908); 3rd ser., **5** (1911). Volume 1, Part I, is a chronological inventory of books, brochures, newspapers, and periodicals published in the French language in the province of Quebec since the establishment of printing in Canada in 1764 until 1905. Volume 1, Part II, gives tables of contents and names with a chronological inventory of books, etc., published in the French language in the province of Quebec from 1764 to 1906. Volume 2 is a bibliography for Quebec and New France giving a chronological inventory of works published in diverse foreign languages covering 1534 through 1906. Volume 3 is a chronological inventory of books, brochures, newspapers, and periodicals published in the English language in the province of Quebec during the period 1764–1906. Volume 4 is a chronological inventory of charts, maps, and atlases relative to New France and the province of Quebec produced between 1508 and 1908. The Supplements cover 1904–12.

The second basic source for French-language publications is the *Bulletin bibliographique de la société des écrivains canadiens* published annually in Montreal by the Society between 1937 and 1959. It is complete in the sense that it includes all publications which were sent by the writer or publisher to the Society, or which came to the attention of the compilers. It is of principal value on account of the literary items that are included. The arrangement is alphabetical by author and there is an annual index by author, joint author, translator, and title. A list of members of the Society is given in each volume.

Two bibliographies are available which list Canadian cultural periodicals. The first is *Canadian Cultural Publications: Publications culturelles canadiennes* which has appeared annually since 1952. Formerly issued by the Canada Foundation, Ottawa, it is now published by the Canadian Cultural Information Centre under the joint sponsorship of the Canada Foundation and the Canada Council, Ottawa. Referring mainly to the arts, this publication supplies an alphabetical title listing of Canadian periodicals with publisher, price, and very brief annotations in both English and French. Part I: Cultural publications; Part II: Additional publications which frequently carry cultural materials; Part III: Bulletins and catalogues containing cultural materials related to art, ballet, film, music, poetry, theatre, etc.

The other item dealing with cultural periodicals is *A Bibliography of Canadian Cultural Periodicals* (*English and French from Colonial Times to 1950*) *in Canadian Libraries*, edited by Emilio Goggio and published by the Department of Italian, Spanish, and Portuguese of the University of Toronto in 1955. Whereas the *Canadian Cultural Publications* lists only those periodicals being currently published, the *Bibliography of Canadian Cultural Periodicals* is a joint catalogue or union list of those Canadian periodicals published any time up to 1950, whether still extant or not, which could be considered cultural or literary. It includes literary, historical, and fine arts periodicals, but omits religious and political ones. Arrangement is alphabetical by title of periodical and gives place of publication. The Canadian libraries holding particular periodicals are listed by the length of the run each has. No indication is given as to when any periodical commenced or ceased publication.

One of the foremost and most outstanding regional bibliographies for any area of Canada is Bruce Braden Peel's *A Bibliography of the Prairie Provinces to 1953*, published in co-operation with the Saskatchewan Golden Jubilee Committee and the University of Saskatchewan by the University of Toronto Press. The first volume was published in 1956 and there is a *Supplement*, 1963. Items included are listed chronologically by imprint date. There are separate subject, title, and author indexes. In the subject index, the subjects are arranged in broad groups and the authors arranged chronologically under each subject. This chronological arrangement enables the user to see the development of the literature in that field.

The *Bibliography of Canadian Bibliographies* (Fig. 4), compiled by Raymond Tanghe, was published in association with the Bibliographical Society of Canada by the University of Toronto Press. The main volume appeared in 1960. Since then, the Bibliographical Society of Canada has produced *Supplement, 1960 and 1961*; *Supplement, 1962 and 1963*; and *Supplement 1964 and 1965*, compiled by Madeleine Pellerin. It lists bibliographies, defined as a list of books, brochures, newspapers, periodicals, or maps, with information for their identification, usually author, title, place, publisher, and date, whose subject is wholly or principally Canadian, be they about persons, events, or places. It does not include bibliographies included in books or in periodical articles, but rather bibliographies that have been published separately. The bibliographies are arranged according to their main subject and cover such topics as newspapers, temperance, religion, folklore, politics, law, education, commerce, anthropology, biology,

92 ROUILLARD, Eugène
Les premiers almanachs canadiens. *Lévis, Roy, 1898.* 80 p.
17 cm. (Bibliothèque canadienne)

93 ROYAL COLONIAL INSTITUTE, London. Library
Catalogue of the library of the Royal Colonial Institute, to
October 1881. ₍Chilworth and London, Unwin, 1881₎ 29 p.
22 cm.

——Catalogue of the library of the Royal Colonial Institute, 1886.
London, Spottiswoode, 1886. 3 p. *l.*, ₍v₎-1, 179 p. 28 cm.
Introduction signed: C. Washington Eves.
——Catalogue of the library of the Royal Colonial Institute. (Founded
1868. Incorporated by royal charter, 1882) *London, The Institute, 1895.*
clv, 543 p. 28 cm.
By James R. Boosé, librarian.
——First supplementary catalogue of the library of the Royal Colonial
Institute. Compiled by James R. Boosé. *London, The Institute, 1901.*
cclxxviii, 793 p. 28 cm.

94 ROYAL EMPIRE SOCIETY, London. Library ·
Subject catalogue of the library of the Royal Empire Society,
formerly Royal Colonial Institute, by Evans Lewin. v. 3. The
Dominion of Canada and its provinces, the Dominion of New-
foundland, the West Indies and colonial America. ₍London, The
Society₎ 1932. ·xvii, 822 p. 29 cm.

Formerly Royal Colonial Institute, now Royal Commonwealth Society.

95 SABIN, Joseph
Bibliotheca americana. A dictionary of books relating to Ameri-
ca, from its discovery to the present time. Begun by Joseph
Sabin, continued by Wilberforce Eames and completed by
R. W. G. Vail, for the Bibliographical Society of America. *New
York, 1868–1936.* 29 v. 23–25 cm.

Imprint varies.
Issued in 172 parts.

96 SAMUEL, Sigmund
A catalogue of the Sigmund Samuel collection, Canadiana and
Americana. Comp. and annotated by Charles W. Jefferys.
Toronto, Ryerson, 1948. xxxii, 180 p.· 24 cm.

FIG. 4. *Bibliography of Canadian Bibliographies*, 1960.

botany, zoology, agriculture, music, literature, geography, and history. There are very complete bilingual indexes to subjects, compilers, and authors.

Encyclopedic Works

The *Canada Year Book* (Fig. 5), Queen's Printer, Ottawa, is an official descriptive annual publication of the resources, history, and social conditions of Canada, giving factual information on almost every phase of Canada's development. The Bureau of Statistics, Ottawa, summarizes each year a great mass of detailed statistical, legislative, and other pertinent information for inclusion in the *Year Book*. Among subjects covered are physical description, history, constitution and government, institutions, population, production, industry, trade, transportation, finance, labour, education, resources, and communication of Canada. Special feature articles are presented and there is an index of special material appearing in former issues. Typical of those found in the recent editions are: Federal Government Surveying and Mapping; Astronomy in Canada; Use of English and French Languages in Canada; Agriculture in the Canadian Economy; Canadian Forest Products and Changing World Markets; Operational and Technological Changes in Rail Transport. The inclusion of a list of books about Canada compiled by the National Library, a directory of sources of official information, a register of official appointments, federal legislation and a Canadian chronology serves to increase the coverage of the *Year Book*. Much of the statistical data presented can be updated by using the various publications of the Bureau of Statistics, Ottawa, in different subject areas. Each issue of the *Year Book* usually runs in size to over 1000 pages.

In addition to the *Year Book*, the Bureau of Statistics annually issues in English and French a smaller handbook, *Canada, the Official Handbook of Present Conditions and Recent Progress*, Queen's Printer, Ottawa. The information in this work of approximately 300 pages is drawn from the official sources of the Bureau

CHAPTER XXI.—PUBLIC FINANCE*

CONSPECTUS

The interpretation of the symbols used in the tables throughout the Year Book will be found facing p. 1 of this volume.

Combined statistics of public finance for all governments in Canada—federal, provincial and municipal—are presented in Section 1 of this Chapter and Section 2 covers the incidence of taxation at the three levels. More detailed information for each level of government is given in Sections 3, 4 and 5.

A report on the financial statistics of Federal Government business enterprises was issued for the first time in October 1962; analyses of their assets, liabilities, revenues and expenditures are shown in Section 3, pp. 995–996. The first report on the financial statistics of provincial government enterprises, released in the autumn of 1963, is summarized

Fig. 5. *Canada Year Book*, 1965.

of Statistics. Its avowed purpose is "to portray the economic, social, and cultural developments of the Canadian nation" in a convenient pocket size format. Illustrated with numerous colour plates, the text is arranged by major topics, further illustrated with detailed statistical tables. Although each annual issue has its own special feature, there is a standard arrangement of material within each volume. Canada is discussed topically under landscape, climate, history, population, and government. Further, her natural resources in farming, fishing, mining, forestry, and electric power are analysed descriptively and analytically in terms of the production in the past years. Following this are the current trends in business, industry, and manufacturing. The finances of the Federal Government, revenue, and expenditures are included as well as figures for domestic and foreign trade. General articles giving short résumés and current analyses in the fields of labour, health and welfare, education, research, the arts, and recreation conclude the book. Other useful inclusions are the chronological tables of events from the previous year and a folding map inside the back cover. An inexpensive and attractive paperback, *Canada, The Official Handbook* . . ., is a convenient and topical guide.

An important source of general information on Canada consists of the published *Official Report* of the *House of Commons Debates* and *Debates of the Senate*, Queen's Printer, Ottawa. It is usually called *Hansard* because of its prototype, the reports of the British House of Commons. From 1875 to 1879 the contract for reporting the Canadian House of Commons debates was awarded to private reporters, but from 1880 on an official staff was appointed in order to secure permanency and uniformity. An official reporter for the Senate was appointed in 1917. There are several volumes for each session which record the debates of the Houses day by day, messages of the Governor-General, and varying information such as lists of members, committees, the Ministry, etc. Such lists are sometimes omitted, sometimes included.

A daily edition is issued on the morning following each day's sitting, the speeches being reported in the language in which they are delivered. Speeches in French are translated into English and appear in that form as an appendix to the daily issue. Speeches in English are translated and appear in the French edition on the day following their delivery. Names of members and their political affiliations are given. An index by subject and by names of members who spoke, and covering each session, is published in a separate volume. The index volume for the Commons contains lists of members of the Government, parliamentary assistants, officers, an alphabetical list of members, and an alphabetical list of the constituencies. An index of the debates of the Senate is also published at the end of each session.

The Canadian Almanac and Directory, Copp Clark, Toronto, published since 1847, is an annual publication containing over 50,000 listings of federal and provincial officials; post offices and transportation directory, judges and court officials; salutations and forms of address; barristers and solicitors; chartered banks and their branches; trust and loan companies; registrars in bankruptcy; newspapers and periodicals; associations and societies; educational institutions, boards of education, and school inspectors; religious organizations; diplomatic representatives and foreign consuls in Canada; city managers, boards of trade, and chambers of commerce; radio and television listings; insurance companies, principal libraries, book publishers, art galleries, and museums in Canada; and centennial committees. Additional features include commentary on principal federal legislation, population, trade and vital statistics, weight and measures, anniversaries and holidays, abbreviations, astronomical calculations, climatic data, and customs information. It is very useful in the school, library, and office for checking addresses, spellings, precise titles of government departments and officials, associations, and their executives. *The McGraw-Hill Directory and Almanac of Canada*, Toronto, 1966, is a new annual listing of similar material, from original sources.

The *Encyclopedia Canadiana*, the Canadiana Company, Ottawa, 1958, was prepared by a subsidiary of the well-known Grolier Company of New York. Canadian life in all its aspects is the subject of this comprehensive encyclopedia. It provides, in 10 volumes, authoritative current and historical information on people, places, things, events, and ideas in Canada. The contributors are recognized authorities in their fields from all parts of the country, including writers, professors, government officials, and leaders in the arts and sciences. There are biographical articles on Canadian citizens from all walks of life and on citizens of other countries who have made notable contributions to the development of Canada. The work is lavishly illustrated with photographs, diagrams, maps, charts, graphs, drawings, and art reproductions. There are elaborate colour sections preceding important articles, such as the ones on the provinces, which include coats of arms, flags, floral emblems, etc. There are hundreds of articles which deal with localities and geographical features, some even for small villages. There are many maps, from the small sketches locating individual towns to the full-page plans for major cities. There is a full-colour atlas at the end of Volume 10. Many of the articles include brief bibliographies. These are, for the most part, selected lists of published books and magazine articles. There are many long, signed articles on historical subjects such as "Constitutional History", "Population Growth", "Indians of Canada", "Political History", "Immigration", etc., as well as shorter articles on specific events such as the "Quebec Act" and the "Fenian Raids". There are long articles on important industries and products such as "Aluminium", "Pulp and Paper Industry", and "Hydro-electric Power". Since the arrangement is alphabetical and numerous cross-references appear in the text, there is no separate index. A frequently found symbol is the asterisk (*) referring to the article that appears under the word so marked. The *Encyclopedia Canadiana*, although in need of basic revision, is, as the publishers claim, the largest and most comprehensive work of reference on Canada that has appeared.

Revived after a lapse of 26 years, the *Canadian Annual Review*, University of Toronto Press, edited by John T. Saywell, has surveyed, analysed, and evaluated yearly many aspects of Canadian life since 1960. It has included politics, foreign affairs, defence, economics, education, religion, theatre, art, music, and sport. The

25–30 contributors to each volume have provided well-researched and readable articles. Each has attempted objective presentation and treatment of his subject, but occasionally personal comments and points of view are found. Some critical and probing analyses are included. Some articles are of permanent historical value. A few articles that are concerned with questions relating to Quebec are written in French. All the others are in English. The fields of government and public affairs are the most thoroughly covered. The broad headings Parliament and Politics, External Affairs and Defence, and The National Economy take up about two-thirds of each volume. The remaining part, Life and Leisure, covers education, the arts, and sport. In the 1960–3 volumes, there are articles on French- and English-Canadian literature, but these were dropped in 1964 because of the coverage of these topics in other publications such as the Letters in Canada section of the *University of Toronto Quarterly*, July issue, and *Canadian Literature*. Each volume of the *Review* opens with Canadian Calendar, a day-by-day chronology of the year's most significant events. Brief obituaries of important people who have died during the year are included at the end of each volume. The work is thoroughly indexed. These annual indexes provide a valuable quick reference source to contemporary history.

Jean-Jacques Lefebvre's *Le Canada, l'Amérique—géographie, historique, bibliographique, littéraire: supplément du Larousse canadien complet*, was published in Montreal, Beauchemin, 1954. This encyclopedic dictionary comprises nearly 10,000 brief articles, concerned for the most part with history and geography. The biographical section covers persons in all parts of the country, with considerable emphasis on Canadian writers, both English and French, and giving lists of their work.

The *Dictionnaire général de biographie, histoire, littérature, agriculture, commerce, industrie et des arts, sciences, coutumes, institutions politiques et religieuses du Canada*, University of Ottawa, Ottawa, 1931 was compiled by Prof. L. M. LeJeune, OMI, in 2 volumes. This work is an encyclopedic dictionary of which the biographical part is the most extensive. In general the articles are

c

short, though there are some rather long ones—for instance, 10 pages are given to England. The arrangement is alphabetical. There are selective bibliographies at the end of each chapter.

J. M. S. Careless and Craig Brown have prepared *The Canadians, 1867–1967: a record of achievement*, Macmillan, Toronto, 1967. This is a 1-volume compilation of over 1000 pages giving a chronological listing of each decade since the Confederation of Canada, and then a topical analysis of the past 100 years in fields such as Canadian education, transportation, cultural affairs, etc. The work is complete with an extensive index. It is the best 1-volume source-book on the general progress and development of this period of Canadian history. *The Canadian Centennial Library*, published by the Canadian Centennial Publishing Co., Toronto, 1966, is a multi-volume anthology series heavily documented with black and white and colour illustrations, prepared under the editorship of Pierre Berton, with Ken Lefolii as managing editor and Frank Newfeld as art director. The separate volumes deal with Canadian history, achievements, photography, biography, writing, painting, food, and sports. Each is compiled in a popular manner and each contains an extensive amount of material not easily located elsewhere. The work was published in an edition of over 100,000 copies. There are useful indexes to the Canadian authors and sources quoted and to the primary information used, and other reading that complements each anthology. The work serves as a useful popular secondary guide to Canadian achievements over the past century.

Museums, Libraries, and Archives

The *Museum Directory of the United States and Canada*, 2nd edn., American Association of Museums, Washington, D.C., and the Smithsonian Institution, 1965, provides separate listings for over 350 Canadian museums and art galleries, archives, parks, and zoos under province, name, chief officers, and types of institution. Full details of the museum, date established, address, collections, hours, publications, and special activities are provided in the first listing. The National Museum of Canada, Ottawa, is divided into a natural history and a human history branch, and also maintains a Canadian War Museum, Ottawa, and a National Aeronautical Museum at Uplands, Ontario. The Canadian Museums Association, Toronto, has published a *Bulletin* since 1948 and a *Directory* beginning in 1956.

The National Library of Canada was established in 1950 and the National Library building will open in Ottawa in June 1967. It was formed to act as a research centre and to house collections of materials pertaining to Canada. It shares this task with other government libraries in Ottawa such as the National Science Library at the National Research Council, the Library of Parliament and the Supreme Court Library. In addition to providing various national bibliographical guides and publications, the National Library acts as the headquarters for the National Union Catalogue which maintains a record of the book holdings of all of the principal libraries of Canada.

In its work the National Library is joined by the Public Archives, Ottawa, which for many years was the principal national source of information on official Canadian publications and records. The Manuscript Division of the Public Archives has published many *Preliminary Inventories* and *Inventories* to its manuscript and other record groups. One of its early publications was the *Catalogue des cartes, plans et cartes marines*, Imprimerie Nationale, Ottawa, 1912. This lists world maps, boundary maps of North America, New France, Ontario, and the other provinces, and foreign maps and atlases which are held by the Archives, and describes them in detail. The Archives has also published *Sixteenth Century Maps relating to Canada, a Check List and Bibliography*, Queen's Printer, Ottawa, 1957, a valuable guide to the literature and publications in this field, listing in systematic order the sources for both originals and reproductions. The various *Annual Reports* of the Public Archives, Ottawa, issued since 1867, contain much published material. For a list of them, reference should be made to "Guides to calendars of series and collections in the Public

Archives", Public Archives of Canada, *Annual Report*, Ottawa, 1949.

The Archives of the Province of Quebec do not include administrative records before 1759, since this material was returned to Paris by the Government of France. However, much has been copied from the archives of Paris, and much can also be found in the archives of the Roman Catholic establishments throughout Quebec. Two valuable guides to such material are J.-E. Roy, *Rapport sur les archives de France relatives à l'histoire du Canada*, Public Archives of Canada, Ottawa, 1911, and H. P. Beers, *The French in North America: a bibliographical guide to French archives, reproductions and research missions*, Baton Rouge, Louisiana, 1957.

The provincial archives in all provinces maintain guides and indexes to their contents but not all of these have been published. Valuable holdings of information about Canada are contained in the Archivum Romanum Societatis Jesu, Rome; the Public Record Office, London; the Hudson's Bay Company Archives, London; and the public and private archives in Massachusetts, New York, Pennsylvania, and other American states, as well as in many private and commercial collections in Europe and North America.

Many Canadian institutions have prepared guides to their manuscript holdings. Among these is the *Guide to the Manuscript Collection* of the Toronto Public Library, Toronto, 1954. This records family papers, business records, and official and semi-official correspondence from the early part of the eighteenth century that has to do with Upper Canada. Gaston Carrière, in the Report of the Canadian Catholic Historical Association, Montreal, 1963, presents a survey of the holdings of diocesan archives in Canada.

The Canadian Library Association, 63 Sparks Street, Ottawa, issues a *Canadian Library Directory: Répertoire des bibliothèques canadiennes*, published annually in January as Part II of *Canadian Library*, the regular periodical publication of the Association. This directory includes only members of the Association, and does not list all Canadian libraries.

R. R. Bowker's *American Library Directory*, New York, 1966, published triennially, is a classified list of all types and classes of libraries, and includes those of Canada. Information is presented by provinces, with each library listed under the name of the town or city in which it is located. The names of the librarians and some statistical data on library holdings are included.

Newspapers and General Periodicals

N. W. Ayer & Son, Philadelphia, has published its *Directory of Newspapers and Periodicals* annually since 1868. This includes most of the periodicals and newspapers published in Canada. The arrangement is geographical—first the states of the United States and then the provinces of Canada, in alphabetical order. Within each province the places where each newspaper is published are listed in alphabetical order. Under the name of any locality, the newspapers and periodicals currently published are arranged alphabetically by title. This information is brought together in a single title index. Each entry gives the name of the editor, the publisher and address, date of origin, size, circulation, and subscription price. There is a subject index.

A representative sample of the main Canadian daily newspapers now published currently, showing date of founding, is as follows: *Calgary Herald*, 1885; *Guardian*, Charlottetown, 1891; *Edmonton Journal*, 1903; *Globe and Mail*, Toronto, 1844; *Chronicle-Herald*, Halifax, 1844; *Hamilton Spectator*, 1846; *London Free Press*, 1849; *Gazette*, Montreal, 1778; *La Presse*, Montreal, 1884; *Ottawa Citizen*, 1844; *Leader-Post*, Regina, 1883; *Telegraph-Journal*, Saint John (NB), 1868; *Evening Telegram*, St. John's (Nfld.), 1879; *The Telegram*, Toronto, 1876; *Toronto Daily Star*, 1892; *The Province*, Vancouver, 1898; *Winnipeg Free Press*, 1874.

Among guides to early periodical publications, *Early Toronto Newspapers*, Baxter Publishing Co., Toronto, 1961, is a unique example. It is an illustrated catalogue of 82 newspapers which appeared in Toronto before 1867. It was compiled by Edith Firth and gives details of the operations and politics of the papers, along with illustrations showing their format.

It is not possible to mention all of the general periodicals, both scholarly and popular, which contain essential information on Canadian life and achievements. The best list of current Canadian periodicals and newspapers is that found in *Canadian Advertising* (see p. 88). Mention has been made previously of the *University of Toronto Quarterly*. A companion French-language journal of comparable stature is the quarterly *Revue de l'Université Laval*. It began publication in 1946, succeeding *Le Canada français*, which was founded in 1888. Other important scholarly journals are published by Dalhousie University, Halifax; Queen's University, Kingston; the University of Montreal; and Trent University, Peterborough, Ontario, whose *Journal of Canadian Studies: Revue d'études canadiennes* began to appear in 1966.

CHAPTER 2

Canadian Thinkers and Religious Writers

Philosophy

The University of Toronto and Laval University in Quebec have been centres for philosophical study in Canada for many years. They are now being joined by many other centres across the nation. *Philosophy in Canada: a symposium*, edited by J. A. Irving, was published by the University of Toronto Press, 1952. The symposium took the form of two papers delivered by Professors J. A. Irving and C. W. Hendel, followed by a short commentary on each paper. Professor Irving's paper, "One hundred years of Canadian philosophy", traces the evolution of Canadian philosophical conscience since 1850 through several stages as exemplified in the work of Thomas Reid, Dugald Stewart, John Watson, G. S. Brett, and R. C. Lodge. He also includes a survey of contemporary philosophy teaching in Canadian universities. Professor Hendel's paper, entitled "The character of philosophy in Canada", establishes that in respect to philosophy there is a certain ground of community between French and British Canada. He also draws attention to the teaching and work of G. S. Brett of Toronto.

Starting in 1962 the Canadian Philosophical Association sponsored the publication of a quarterly review, *Dialogue*, Queen's University, Kingston. It contains articles by Canadian scholars, discussions, critical notes, book reviews, and announcements. Editorial consultants are maintained in major centres for philosophical studies throughout the world. The quarterly is bilingual English and French, with articles in either language appearing without translation.

The Canadian Philosophical Association has been the host of several international gatherings, including the Seventh Inter-American Congress of Philosophy held at the University of Laval, and the Fourth Congress of the Société internationale pour l'étude de la philosophie médiévale at the University of Montreal in 1967.

Many distinguished philosophers have contributed to Canadian philosophical teaching. Among those whose writings have attracted international attention are Etienne Gilson, *Being and Some Philosophers*, Pontifical Institute of Mediaeval Studies, Toronto, 1949, and Charles De Koninck, whose *Tout homme est mon prochain* appeared in 1964 from the Presses de l'Université Laval, Quebec.

Religion

In contrast to many European countries from which religious faiths were brought to Canada in the eighteenth and nineteenth centuries, religion occupies a decisive role in Canadian public life. It is difficult to say whether this is because learning and teaching in Canada for nearly 300 years were the prerogative of religious orders, or whether Canada has always provided a fresh field for religious proselytizing, or whether the personal freedom available in Canada gave rise to many more heterodox personal religious beliefs. In any case, many religious faiths have found fresh soil and have flourished, and many hundreds of sects and groups of special believers exist at the present time in all parts of Canada.

There have been few attempts made to describe comprehensively the religious development of the nation from its beginnings to the present, encompassing all major denominations and their intimate relationship to political and economic life. One such work is H. H. Walsh's *The Christian Church in Canada*, Ryerson, Toronto, 1956. Professor Walsh has used original source material to describe the interaction of the two great cultural groups of Canada, the tensions between the central denominations and grass-roots sects, the traditional political inclinations of churches in society, and the gradual transformation of strong European backgrounds into a characteristic Canadian outlook.

The religious faiths are by no means confined to those from European countries. Moslems, Hindus, Buddhists, and others of the religions of Asia and the Middle East have been transplanted to Canada. The largest and strongest of the various religious groups are the three that form part of the Jewish–Christian tradition. The Roman Catholic, Protestant, and Jewish faiths numbered 8,342,826, 8,678,347, and 254,368 adherents in 1961 respectively. Nearly a million persons are members of other faiths.

The Roman Catholic Church was the first to be established at Quebec in 1608. Dominique de Saint-Denis, OFM, has written *L'Église catholique au Canada*: *The Catholic Church in Canada*, Thau, Montreal, 1956, which is a concise and detailed history not only of the Catholic Church, but also of Canada in relation to its Catholic population, back to the arrival of the first missionaries. The fifth edition (1944) of this work is in French only, while the sixth (1956) is also in English. In the introduction, the growth of the Catholic Church is described for each part of Canada. In the first chapter the general history of the Church is related, while subsequent chapters deal with Newfoundland, the other three maritime provinces, the central provinces of Quebec and Ontario, and the four western provinces with the North-west Territories. Information is given on total population, Catholics, other religions, racial origins of population, Indians, schools, divorce, clergy, and missions. Statistics are taken from the Canadian Census, but presented and interpreted to support the author's view on the duty of Catholics to take their rightful place in Canadian life. The historical part contains a description of the Capuchins' hardships under English and French rule, while the remainder is a handbook useful to anyone concerned in education, commerce, and public administration. The 1956 edition has precise data on every diocese in Canada and also a final section on the activities of the Catholic Church of Canada abroad, with an account of its missionaries throughout the world. Each chapter has a bibliography.

Le Canada ecclésiastique, Beauchemin, Montreal, published each year since 1887, is the most complete annual Canadian

c*

directory of the Roman Catholic Church. A large directory of over 1400 pages, it is in French, but because of the nature of the arrangement (i.e. there are coloured tabs indicating the particular sections and the headings used are easily recognized names), it is as accessible to the English-speaking reader. It contains a list of the popes and of present members of the College of Cardinals, followed by a directory of early Canadian Catholic conferences. The main section of the book consists of detailed statistics on each diocese including lists of all parishes, clergy, religious communities, and institutions. The excellent indexing continues in further alphabetical lists of communities of priests, brothers, and sisters, and then of all Canadian clergy with not only the present parish listed but also the date of ordination, and, lastly, an index of parishes. The book contains in addition a *guide d'achat* (buyer's guide) to equipment in many fields.

The only comparable English list is the *Official Catholic Directory*, published annually by P. J. Kennedy & Sons in New York, which includes a separate section of some 180 pages on the "Catholic Church in Canada". The *Ontario Catholic Directory*, Newman Foundation of Toronto, is an annual guide to events and persons prominent in Catholic affairs in Ontario.

Abbé Lionel Groulx has written *Le Canada français missionaire*, Fides, Montreal, 1962. This is an account of the missionary activities of French-Canadian Catholics since the early days of Canada. It includes a history of work done both within Canada and abroad. There is a very complete bibliographical section which documents the activities described in the text. There are indexes by names of persons cited, by place and by subject.

The *Histoire documentaire de la Congrégation des Missionnaires Oblats de Marie-Immaculée dans l'Est du Canada*, by Gaston Carrière, Éditions de l'Université d'Ottawa, Ottawa, 1957–63, has appeared in 5 volumes. The work is not yet completed, but when finished will trace in detail the activities of this Order from its beginnings in Canada in 1841.

L.-E. Hamelin and C. Hamelin have prepared *Quelques matériaux de sociologie religieuse canadienne*, Édition du Lévrier,

Montreal, 1956. Nearly 300 books and periodical articles in the French language which deal with the social role of religion in the Province of Quebec are listed in this annotated and critical bibliography. A large part of the work deals with religion in the Three-Rivers diocese. The arrangement is by subject. The list of periodicals and bibliographies which have been drawn on to make up this work is included. There is no index to the names of authors cited.

Albert Rose has compiled *A People and its Faith*, University of Toronto Press, 1959. This is a collection of essays placing the Jewish community in perspective in Canadian life, and showing the relation of the non-Jewish community to Jewish life in one part of Canada. An essay of special importance is: "Essence of Jewish existence, the faith and worship of reformed Judaism and its direction in coming years." The Canadian Jewish Congress, Bureau of Social and Economic Research, has prepared *Canadian Jewish Population Studies*, the Congress, Montreal, 1946–65. The Congress, in a series of studies based upon the statistical information supplied by the Canadian Census, surveys the history, growth, characteristics, and distribution of Jewish population in Canadian cities, towns, and villages from (in some cases) 1851 to the present time. This series deals with such subjects as age, sex, distribution, immigration, intermarriage, occupational distribution, mother tongue, etc., among the Canadian Jewish community.

In recent years several steps have been taken to establish better relations between the various religious bodies in Canada. *The Principles of Union between the Anglican Church of Canada and the United Church of Canada*, a 4000-word document proclaiming a "full and unanimous agreement" on matters of faith and laying down the main principles of union for the two churches, was published by the Anglican and United Churches, Toronto, in 1965. A new Lutheran Council of Canada, to replace the former Canadian Lutheran Council, was established in 1967 and brought together the three major Lutheran churches in Canada: the American Lutheran Church, the Lutheran Church in America, and the Lutheran Church, Missouri Synod.

Following the promulgation of the decree *On Ecumenism*, the Roman Catholic Church, in December 1965, announced the establishment of a commission on ecumenism in Canada.

The Changing Church in Canada: beliefs and social attitudes of United Church people was prepared by the Rev. Stewart Crysdale, Ryerson, Toronto, 1965. It describes the impact of urbanization on the beliefs of individuals, and shows the extent to which religious beliefs once held strongly are now not so held in Canadian communities.

Church and Sect in Canada by S. D. Clark, University of Toronto Press, 1948, is a good introduction to the rise of various sects in the Protestant Church in Canada in the period up to 1900. The social and political development of Canada has been characterized by a succession of such movements. In 1922 William Aberhart emerged as a prophet in southern Alberta to launch a religious movement which in 1934 brought the Social Credit Party to power in that province, a victory which they have maintained to the present. In contrast to these sects are the established Protestant churches having the support of powerful economic and social interests. It is the conflict between these two phenomena, the church representing the forces of order and the sect representing the forces of separation, with which the author is concerned. Professor Clark seeks to offer an explanation of religious changes in terms of underlying changes in social conditions, the church growing out of the conditions of a mature society and the sect more the product of what might be called the frontier conditions of social life. The study is confined to the period 1760–1900 and serves to provide a background view of the religious organizations in Canada today.

Archbishop Philip Carrington has written *The Anglican Church in Canada: a history*, Collins, Toronto, 1963. The Anglican Church of Canada is an autonomous religious denomination comprising part of the worldwide Anglican Communion. The first church in Canada was built in 1701 in Newfoundland, and since that time it has established itself in all ten provinces with a membership of about 2 million in its twenty-eight dioceses. In relation to the

Anglican Community at large, it presents an example of the democratization of the old catholic and episcopal order which was first worked out in the Episcopal Church of the United States; but it has preserved a fuller degree of local autonomy and freedom in the dioceses and provinces. Archbishop Carrington has tried to do justice to these various local adventures and achievements, beginning with the first missionaries and pioneers. The book is a useful book of reference, complete with index, maps, illustrations, and bibliography.

The Anglican Year Book is published yearly by the General Synod of the Anglican Church, Toronto, and reports on the work of the Church. It includes plans for the coming years and gives information of current interest. Under headings such as General Synod, Financial Summaries, Anglican Foundation, Woman's Auxiliaries, Universities, and Schools, information is listed on officers, members, meetings held, departments, and committees. The various dioceses in Canada are given with general information and each lists the names of bishops, deans, and other dignitaries, the parishes of the dioceses, and the clergy. At the end of the volume are alphabetical lists of communities served by the Church and clergy with their addresses.

The United Church of Canada was formed by a union of the Congregationalists, Methodists, and Presbyterian churches in 1924. Prior to this time the various divisions within these churches had been drawing together, but the churches themselves went their separate ways, continuing the differences of their parent church bodies in England, Scotland, and the United States. With the passing of time these differences no longer seemed valid and unification became possible. However, about one-third of the Presbyterians felt so strongly about the mechanics of the union, they chose not to join and have continued as the Presbyterian Church of Canada. Dr. Pidgeon, as the last Moderator of the Presbyterian Church of Canada and the first Moderator of the United Church, is well qualified to tell the story of this union in *The United Church of Canada*, Thorn Press, Toronto, 1950. An appendix contains the legislative history of the United Church of Canada Act through the federal and provincial parliaments, as well as a discussion by various authorities on the right of churches to unite.

The Canadian Society of Church History was founded in 1959 in order to keep Canadian church historians closely in touch with each other's projects. The Society is concerned mainly with the histories of the Protestant churches. In collaboration with Victoria University, Toronto, the Committee on Archives of the United Church publishes an annual *Bulletin*, first issued in 1948 by the United Church Publishing House, Toronto. The *Bulletin* contains studies and reports of various aspects of church history.

J. E. Sanderson wrote *The First Century of Methodism in Canada*, vol. 1, *1775–1839*, William Briggs, Toronto, 1908. This important work documents the Methodist movement which began in Canada at the end of the eighteenth century.

A short account of the history and antecedents of the Presbyterian Church of Canada was written as a handbook for members of the Church by Stuart C. Parker, entitled *Yet not Consumed*, Thorn Press, Toronto, 1947. The larger part of the book describes the early history of Christianity and the Church in Scotland. The remaining third describes the history of the Presbyterian Church in Canada, which had its beginnings in Halifax in the late 1700's, moved westward to Upper and Lower Canada (present-day Ontario and Quebec), and was augmented by the arrival of immigrants from the American colonies. As the number of churches increased, colleges were founded for the training of new ministers. Great disruption and much argument took place before the eventual union of the Presbyterian and Methodist Churches in 1924. This history is taken up to the year 1946. Other longer and earlier works on the Presbyterian Church are the following: William Gregg, *History of the Presbyterian Church in the Dominion of Canada: from the earliest times to 1834*, Presbyterian Printing and Publishing Co., Toronto, 1885; and John T. McNeill, *The Presbyterian Church in Canada, 1875–1925*, General Board, Presbyterian Church in Canada, Toronto, 1925.

The Baptists in Upper and Lower Canada before 1820 was prepared by E. H. S. Ivison and F. T. Rosser, University of Toronto

Press, 1956. The Baptist Church in Canada had its beginning largely as a result of the efforts of Baptist missionary organizations in the United States. By the opening of the nineteenth century, there were at least six of these organizations evangelizing in the pioneer settlements of Ontario. In 1859 the Baptists in Upper and Lower Canada began collecting the materials that now form the Baptist Historical Collection at McMaster University, Hamilton. From these records the author has been able to document how the earliest Baptist churches arose, their location and who founded them. By 1820 most Canadian Baptist churches had severed their ties with American associations and had set up organizations of their own in Canada. The scope of this work, therefore, has been deliberately limited to the period between the American Revolution and the year 1920.

Humanities

The Humanities Research Council was established in Ottawa in 1943 on the initiative of the Royal Society of Canada and the Canadian Social Science Research Council to promote the cause of research in the humanities in Canada. The Council consists of scholars in the classics, oriental, English, French, and other modern languages, philosophy, and history. The Humanities Association of Canada was organized in 1950 and meets regularly with the other Canadian learned societies.

The Humanities in Canada by F. E. L. Priestley, University of Toronto Press, 1964, is a survey of university teaching and research since 1947, outlining existing conditions, as well as potential for expansion and development. Within the terms of reference of the humanities, Professor Priestley discusses the curricula of the various colleges in general and honours courses and in graduate studies. Special attention is given to library facilities, aids for research, and some of the problems and opportunities involving faculty personnel. The second part of the book, extending for 150 pages and devoted to a comprehensive bibliography of publications (mainly since 1950), is a valuable contribution to research.

R. M. Wiles prepared *The Humanities in Canada: supplement*, University of Toronto Press, 1966. This contains a record of books, articles, reviews, and works in progress by Canadian scholars in the humanities which did not appear in the volume prepared by Prof. Priestley. The primary aim is to list all published books, pamphlets, articles, and essays that may properly be regarded as scholarly contributions to knowledge in the humanities; this work brings the record up to date to the end of 1964. An index covering both *The Humanities in Canada* and this *Supplement* simplifies the process of finding out what has been published by individual authors.

A retrospective bibliography, *Canadian Graduate Theses in the Humanities and Social Sciences, 1921–1946*, was prepared by the Humanities Research Council and published by the King's Printer, Ottawa, 1951.

Psychology

Psychology and related studies are taught in all of the universities and colleges, and the Canadian Psychological Association has been in existence since before 1940. From 1940 to 1946 it published a quarterly *Bulletin*, and since then the quarterly *Canadian Journal of Psychology*, Toronto. Canadian psychologists are engaged in many aspects of experimental investigation—comparative studies, neuro-physiological problems, social psychology, etc. In 1955 the Social Science Research Council of Canada, Ottawa, published *Psychology in Canadian Universities and Colleges* by R. B. MacLeod, which set out the extent of Canadian work at that time.

The Canadian Mental Health Association, Toronto, with branches across Canada, publishes occasional pamphlets and reports on mental hygiene.

CHAPTER 3

Canadian Social and Political Structure

Social Sciences

The establishment of the Social Science Research Council of Canada in Ottawa in 1940 brought together many specialists concerned with the investigation of Canadian social conditions. Since that date, the Council, at its meetings with the other learned societies of Canada, has established a systematic programme for the furtherance of economic, sociological, political, and other studies. It has aided the Canadian Political Science Association, the Canadian Association for Sociology and Anthropology, the Canadian Economic Association, and individual social scientists to carry out their research and to publish many items of value.

Many studies in the social and political fields are carried on by governments, industry, labour unions, co-operatives, and the various Canadian political parties. Publications from these sources are issued regularly, and this steady flow of documents provides a complex literature of statistics and analysis. Most of the basic studies are noted, along with criticism and reviews, in the quarterly *Canadian Journal of Economics and Political Science*, University of Toronto Press, and other Canadian social science periodicals. Only a selection of the important sources can be considered below.

Does Canadian culture have a character of its own? To what extent is it derived from French, British, and American sources? These are the questions that twelve writers in the mid 1950's attempted to answer. Julian Park has edited their responses in *The Culture of Contemporary Canada*, Cornell University Press, 1957. The writers concluded that Canada's culture *is* distinctive, but they stressed its immaturity and the limiting effect on it of climate, geography, and the great confrontation of minority with majority: French with English; Canadian with American. The contributors, who include such authors as Roy Daniells, Mason Wade, and Wilfrid Eggleston, strive for fairness and objectivity. The editor, an American, hopes the book will stimulate an interest in Canada among Americans. The work was brought to publication with the assistance of a grant from the Ford Foundation.

French Canada in Transition by Everett C. Hughes, Phoenix edn., University of Chicago Press, 1963, was first published in 1943, and is one of the classics of Canadian sociological investigation. It traces the origins in the economic and industrial changes which have brought about political change in this part of Canada. Another examination of social change is *Crestwood Heights* by J. R. Seeley, R. A. Sim, and E. W. Loosley, University of Toronto Press, 1956. This is the study of Forest Hill, a former independent suburban village, but since 1967 incorporated as part of the City of Toronto. The study pays particular attention to the impact which North American elementary and secondary school education has had on Canadian urban families, and indicates the dilemmas and uncertainties which have arisen in the lives of both parents and children. The work is of particular value in showing how little the Canadian pattern of middle-class urban living differs from that in the United States.

Professor John A. Porter has produced *The Vertical Mosaic: an analysis of social class and power in Canada*, University of Toronto Press, 1965. A detailed view of the Canadian power and class structure emerges from this expertly documented study. Professor Porter first considers the fabric of social class in Canada and then proceeds to a definition of political and economic power and the means by which it is consolidated and exercised by interrelated self-perpetuating élites. This concentration of authority in the hands of a relatively few individuals results in a vertical stratification of the social order which becomes rigid and restricted in opportunity. This is a stimulating and basic work on Canadian social conditions that identifies some of the important determinants in Canada's national life.

Marcel Rioux and Yves Martin have collaborated to produce *French Canadian Society*, McClelland and Stewart, Toronto, 1964. Volume 1 consists of selected extracts from various recent periodicals and monographs and provides a basic source of readings on French-Canadian society. It is divided into two main sections, "The sociology of French Canada in historical perspective" and "The social structure of contemporary French Canada". The nineteen contributors are all acknowledged experts on French Canada, and include Nathan Keyfitz, Chicago, Pierre Desfontaines, Barcelona, Norman W. Taylor, Pennsylvania, as well as specialist from Canadian universities. The work is No. 18 in the Carleton Library, prepared under the editorial supervision of Robert L. McDougall at the Institute of Canadian Studies at Carleton University, Ottawa. Volumes of the Carleton series of reprints and collections of sources contain material in the fields of history, commerce, and transportation, as well as political and social affairs. The works reprinted are generally not readily available in their original state. Some of the titles published since 1956 are: *The Confederation Debates in the Province of Canada, 1865*, edited and with an introduction by P. B. Waite; *The Rowell/Sirois Report*, Book I, edited and with an introduction by Donald V. Smiley; *The Unreformed Senate of Canada* by Robert A. MacKay, revised and with an introduction by the author; *The Reciprocity Treaty of 1854* by Donald C. Masters, with a new introduction by the author; *Political Unrest in Upper Canada, 1815–1836* by Aileen Dunham, with an introduction by A. L. Burt; *The Economic Background of Dominion–Provincial Relations* by W. A. Mackintosh, with an introduction by J. H. Dales; *The Canadian Commercial Revolution, 1845–1851* by Gilbert N. Tucker, edited and with an introduction by Hugh G. J. Aitken; *Leading Constitutional Decisions*, compiled and with an introduction by Peter H. Russell; *Indians of the North Pacific Coast*, compiled and with an introduction by Tom McFeat; *The Race Question in Canada* by Andre Siegfried, edited and with an introduction by Frank H. Underhill; and *North Atlantic Triangle* by J. B. Brebner, with an introduction by D. G. Creighton.

Sponsored by the Social Sciences Research Council of Canada and edited by Mason Wade of Rochester University, New York, *Canadian Dualism, Studies of French–English Relations*, University of Toronto Press, Presses Universitaires Laval, 1960, is a collection of papers from outstanding Canadian scholars who attempt to analyse and interpret the bicultural condition of Canada in 1960, in philosophy, law, economics, politics, and labour, and the levels of friction and disagreement between the two founding groups. Each topic is discussed by an English Canadian and a French Canadian; and the papers are summed up and concluded by Professor Wade, who suggests further lines of research.

The epoch-making *Report of the Royal Commission on National Development in the Arts, Letters and Sciences*, King's Printer, Ottawa, was published in 1951. Based on months of careful study and on numerous reports submitted by organizations and private individuals, the Commission included author and Professor of History Miss Hilda Neatby; the Most Reverend Georges-Henri Lévesque, then Dean of the Faculty of Social Sciences, Laval University, Quebec; Arthur Surveyer, a civil engineer from Montreal; Norman A. M. MacKenzie, now President Emeritus, Honorary Professor of International Law, University of British Columbia, Vancouver, and was headed by the former Governor-General of Canada, the Right Honourable Vincent Massey.

The larger part of the report was devoted to an examination of the cultural institutions of Canada with particular attention being given to the Canadian Broadcasting Corporation, the National Film Board of Canada, and such bodies as art galleries, museums, public and university libraries, and musical, dramatic, and art societies that flourished in the country at the time of survey. This was the first such comprehensive review of arts and science in Canada.

In the latter part of the book the Commission lists its recommendations and explains the basis on which the decisions were made. This report led to the establishment of the Canada Council in 1957 which since then has vigorously supported the arts, letters, and social sciences in Canada. As well, an expanded programme of financial aid by the Federal Government for study and research in the social sciences and humanities has been implemented by succeeding parliaments. The Canada Council is also responsible for acting as the Canadian National Commission for UNESCO. Since 1958 it has financed the work of this Commission, and has stimulated Canadian participation in the work of that Organization.

Many social surveys are produced in Canada dealing with various aspects of the industrialization of the country and the rapid economic and political changes which are taking place. These reports are published by local provincial and federal authorities.

Michael Oliver has edited *Social Purpose for Canada*, University of Toronto Press, 1961, as a sequel to the earlier *Social Planning for Canada*, published by the University of Toronto Press in 1935. These works provide a base for criticism of the Canadian scene, and have had considerable impact on Canadian political thinking. *Social Purpose for Canada* is a collection of essays by seventeen Canadians. Each essay levels detailed criticism at the purposelessness, mediocrity, and inequity to be found in various areas of Canadian life. "The mass media" are discussed by Neil Compton, G. Rosenbluth deals with "Concentration and monopoly in the Canadian economy", and F. R. Scott discusses "Social planning and Canadian federalism". The essays are thoughtful and sincere, and the criticisms which they make are not ones that can be easily discounted.

Professor S. D. Clark, in *Urbanism and the Changing Canadian Society*, University of Toronto Press, 1961, has brought together a representative picture of the effect of rapid growth on one Canadian city. Sociologists from the University of Toronto describe six facets of the City of Toronto's life, population, suburbanism, slums, moral standards, the professions, and radical politics. Developing each from the past, they produce a valuable analysis of English-Canadian urban society.

Toronto's much-discussed moral standards originated when conservatively religious businessmen replaced the former British aristocratic ruling class. Their decline came when the new leaders took on the characteristics of the class they had replaced, and also when the population changed from basically Anglo-Saxon to polyglot. The effect of church, school, police, crime, beer parlour, and friendship group upon the population spectrum—from the suburban élite of Don Mills to the central slum in the "Lower Ward"—are noted. Depicted also is the action and interaction of these population groups on the various professions and political machines, old and new.

W. D. Wood and R. S. Thomas have edited *Areas of Economic Stress in Canada*, Industrial Relations Centre, Queen's University, Kingston, Ontario, 1965. In view of the differences in the economic conditions of different parts of Canada, a good deal of attention has been given to the study of various Canadian regions. Of central concern for the future is the interrelation of regional problems and national policies. A conference on Areas of Economic Stress in Canada was held in Kingston in January 1965, and this volume contains a detailed account of the topics presented and a summary of the discussion. Declining regions in Canada are identified, and treatment for them is suggested.

Discussion was not limited to the Canadian scene. Policies of the United States and Great Britain in the treatment of areas of economic stress were considered with a view to determining what might usefully be adapted for the Canadian situation.

Statistics

Canada One Hundred 1867–1967, Queen's Printer, Ottawa, is a centennial reference work containing statistical information on Canadian economic, social and cultural progress over the past 100 years, which constitutes a valuable one-volume guide to Canada's growth.

Basic to all work in the social sciences in Canada is the role of the Dominion Bureau of Statistics of the Federal Government in Ottawa. Available reports and studies of the Bureau are listed in *Publications of the Dominion Bureau of Statistics*, Queen's Printer, Ottawa, 1965. Many hundreds of such documents are issued by the Bureau, including a *Daily Bulletin*, as well as others on a weekly or monthly basis in English and French, but none of more basic importance than the recurring *Census of Canada*, Queen's Printer, Ottawa. Every decade since 1871 this census has provided detailed information on the composition of the Canadian population. (Canada's census, unlike that of the United States, is based on the first year of the decade.) The census is a prime source of information for students of Canadian affairs. The first volume of the *Census of Canada, 1961* (Fig. 6), provides basic data on the population—age groups, sex, marital status, religious affiliations, national origins, official language, and population figures for provinces, counties, and incorporated cities, towns, and villages. Other volumes are concerned with the economic and social characteristics of the population. Facts relating to housing, the labour force, agriculture, and commerce are given in separate volumes. Further volumes contain separate studies of important urban and rural areas. The final volume furnishes an excellent review of the census and makes historical comparisons.

A further important source of information is the monthly *Canadian Statistical Review*, Queen's Printer, Ottawa. This *Review*, which has weekly and annual supplements, is a summary of current economic indicators in Canada, showing the monthly or quarterly figures as well as the annual totals for a period of at least 2 years. Included are vital statistics, immigration by countries, income, expenditure, gross national product, wages, employment, prices, manufacturing, energy output and consumption, construction, domestic and foreign trade, transportation, and finance. It contains a large number of tables of basic statistics, and a special section of seasonally adjusted major indicators and charts of significant data.

Various provinces issue statistical information to supplement that provided by the Dominion Bureau of Statistics. *The Atlantic Year Book*, edited by D. Kermode, Fredericton, Brunswick Press, is published annually. Also of value is the *Annuaire du Québec*: *Quebec Yearbook*, Queen's Printer, Quebec. This yearly bilingual volume, which has been published since 1914, provides a statistical review of the economic and social conditions in the Province of Quebec. It contains special articles on the economic development

A brochure is available listing the individual reports for other Volume Series of the 1961 Census, as well as special reports, etc. For a copy of this brochure, or for further information on census publications, address your inquiry to the Information and Public Relations Division, Dominion Bureau of Statistics.

Volume I (Part 1) — Population: Geographical Distributions

92-530 Electoral districts (1.1-1). — By counties and subdivisions, 1961 and 1956 (96 pp., $1.00)

92-531 Counties and subdivisions (1.1-2). — By sex, Nfld., P.E.I., N.S., and N.B., 1961 (8 pp., 25¢)

92-532 Counties and subdivisions (1.1-3). — By sex, Que., 1961 (20 pp., 50¢)

92-533 Counties and subdivisions (1.1-4). — By sex, Ont., 1961 (12 pp., 50¢)

92-534 Census divisions and subdivisions (1.1-5). — By sex, Man., Sask., Alta., B.C., Yukon and N.W.T., 1961 (16 pp., 50¢)

92-535 Incorporated cities, towns and villages (1.1-6). — With guide to locations, and including metropolitan and other major urban areas, 1961, 1956 and 1951 (32 p., 50¢)

92-536 Rural and urban distribution (1.1-7). — Rural farm, rural non-farm and urban population, by sex, for counties, 1961 and 1956 (20 pp., 50¢)

92-537 Census tracts (1.1-8). — Population totals for census tracts of major cities, including reference maps, 1961 (40 pp., 75¢)

On peut se procurer une brochure qui énumère les rapports des autres séries des volumes du recensement de 1961, ainsi que les rapports spéciaux, etc. Pour en obtenir un exemplaire et pour tout autre renseignement au sujet des publications du recensement, prière de s'adresser à la Division de l'information et des relations extérieures, Bureau fédéral de la statistique.

Volume I (Partie 1) — Population: Répartition géographique

92-530 Districts électoraux (1.1-1). — Comtés et subdivisions, 1961 et 1956 (96 p., $1.00)

92-531 Comtés et subdivisions (1.1-2). — Selon le sexe, T.-N., Î.-P.-É., N.-É. et N.-B., 1961 (8 p., 25c.)

92-532 Comtés et subdivisions (1.1-3). — Selon le sexe, Qué., 1961 (20 p., 50c.)

92-533 Comtés et subdivisions (1.1-4). — Selon le sexe, Ont., 1961 (12 p., 50c.)

92-534 Divisions et subdivisions du recensement (1.1-5). — Selon le sexe, Man., Sask., Alb., C.-B., Yukon et T.N.-O., 1961 (16 p., 50c.)

92-535 Cités, villes et villages constitués (1.1-6). — Avec guide des localités; zones métropolitaines et autres grandes agglomérations urbaines, 1961, 1956 et 1951 (32 p., 50c.)

92-536 Répartition rurale et urbaine (1.1-7). — Population rurale agricole, rurale non agricole, et urbaine, selon le sexe: comtés, 1961 et 1956 (20 p., 50c.)

92-537 Secteurs de recensement (1.1-8). — Population des secteurs de recensement des grandes villes, avec cartes de référence (40 p., 75c.)

FIG. 6. *Census of Canada, 1961.*

of the Province and more detail than is supplied from federal
government sources.

M. C. Urquhart (Editor), K. A. H. Buckley (Assistant Editor),
and many others have prepared *Historical Statistics of Canada:
earliest times to 1961*, Macmillan, 1965. This is a major reference
work sponsored jointly by the Canadian Political Science Association and the Social Science Research Council of Canada. Its
purpose is to bring together in one place the most important
economic, social, and political statistics from Confederation,
where possible, to 1960. The text describes the material in the
tables, and provides information on sources that are often very
hard to secure in any other publication. The contents include the
following: "Population and migration" by K. A. H. Buckley;
"Vital statistics, health, and welfare" by J. Henripin; "Wages and
working conditions" by D. G. Hartle; "National income and the
capital stock" by M. C. Urquhart; "Price indexes" by A. Asimak-
opulos; "Lands and forests" by G. K. Goudrey; "Electric power"
by J. Davis; "Manufacturers" by A. J. R. Smith.

Quick Canadian Facts, first published in 1945, Toronto, is an
annual pocket handbook of Canadian facts and statistics covering
history, geography, federal and provincial governments, trade and
industry, transportation, communication, finance, and taxes.

These Canadians, by N. K. Dhalla, published by McGraw-Hill
Canada, Toronto, 1966, is a statistical reference work containing
hundreds of pages of numerical charts. Most of the information
comes from the 1961 Census of Canada, with added data compiled
by the author. The book draws together information available in
a host of government reports about the Canadian population and
is designed for persons engaged in marketing and promotion.

Political Science

Party Politics in Canada, edited by Hugh G. Thorburn, Prentice-
Hall, Toronto, 1963, presents a selection of articles or excerpts
from monographs, biographies, etc., which provides a picture of
the background, organization, and policy of the four political

parties—Liberal, Progressive Conservative, New Democratic and Social Credit—dominating the national scene.

Most of the articles date from the mid fifties, so that it is necessary to consult the more current periodicals, books, etc., for the latest developments in the political arena.

The book opens with two selections devoted to the historical background of Canada's two oldest parties, the Liberals and the Conservatives. Both assume a good knowledge of Canadian history if one is to follow the survey with ease. The remainder of the selections, covering such topics as "Money in Canadian politics: the raising of party funds, their sources and the uses to which applied", "Democracy and political leadership in Canada", "The minor parties", and "Regional politics", provide a basic background for the trends of politics in Canada today.

Paul Fox has edited *Politics: Canada, recent readings*, McGraw-Hill, Toronto, 1966. Almost all of the selections in this work deal with the federal government. Material referring to the provincial or municipal governments is included only for the light it casts on the central government or because of its general applicability. The book fully examines public opinion, federalism, judicial interpretation, constitutional amendment, federal–provincial financial relations, Cabinet, civil service, judiciary, House of Commons, Senate, representation, and political parties. There is a valuable brief description and guide to the use of Canadian government publications which has been prepared by Brian Land, Director, School of Library Science, University of Toronto.

Jean-Charles Bonenfant has written *Les Institutions politiques canadiennes*, Presses Universitaires Laval, Quebec, 1954. This manual for students deals with the political institutions of Canada in brief outline. It is based on a series of twenty radio broadcasts, and each of its 20 chapters, of approximately 8–10 pages, gives an excellent and readable summary of Canadian political developments up to 1954. Although now in need of revision, it is a sound and useful guide to the basic political framework of Canada. Some references to other works are in each chapter.

A current work of reference on Quebec is *Le Bottin parle-*

mentaire du Québec by Paul E. Parent, Chez l'Auteur, Quebec. This is an account of the principal parliamentary events in that province since 1867, with detailed analysis of events of each year. It includes biographies of the ministers of the government and of the electoral members of both Chambers of the Legislature at the time. An *Essai sur la Constitution du Canada* by Judge Bernard Bissonnette is included in the 1962 volume and was later published separately by Éditions du Jour, Montreal, 1963.

International Affairs

Much of the internal political life of Canada is influenced by events on the international scene. This is particularly true with regard to the relations of Canada with Great Britain and the other members of the British Commonwealth and also with relation to the governments of the various Member States of the United Nations of which Canada has been a member since 1946. The Canadian Institute of International Affairs, 230 Bloor Street W, Toronto, has produced many books dealing with Canada's role in international affairs. The Institute is an unofficial and non-political organization founded in 1928. Its objective is to promote and encourage research and discussion in international affairs and to focus attention on Canada's position both as a member of the international community of nations and as a member of the Commonwealth of Nations. The Institute as such is precluded by its constitution from expressing an opinion on any aspect of international affairs: the views expressed in its publications are those of the writer. In addition to issuing a quarterly *International Journal* the Institute prepares a *Monthly Report on External Relations* and numerous research studies which are produced in book and pamphlet form. By far the most valuable publications are in the series Canada In World Affairs, published with the co-operation of Oxford University Press, Toronto. Each volume, by a different author, covers approximately 2 years and deals with the main themes in the topic indicated by the general title. Each is

supplied with footnotes drawing attention to virtually everything
published up to the time of writing. The references include government statements, parliamentary debates, various relevant documents and articles in the daily press, and periodicals. The authors
of the volumes are: for 1939–41, R. M. Dawson; for 1941–4,
C. C. Lingard and R. G. Trotter; for 1944–6, F. H. Soward; for
1946–9, R. A. Spencer; for 1949–50, W. E. C. Harrison; for
1951–3, B. S. Kierstead; for 1953–5, D. C. Masters; for 1955–6,
James Eayrs; for 1957–8, T. O. Lloyd; for 1959–61, R. A. Preston;
for 1962–3, Peyton Lyon; for 1963–5, Duncan Fraser. Several
volumes are in preparation.

The Federal Department of External Affairs, Ottawa, has regularly issued a monthly bulletin *External Affairs*, in both French
and English, since November 1948, containing speeches and
articles, and has regularly published *Canada and the United
Nations*, Queen's Printer, Ottawa, an annual review of Canada's
participation in that international organization.

Various authoritative background studies to Canada's position
in international affairs have been written. One such is Walter A.
Riddell's *Documents on Canadian Foreign Policy, 1917–1939*,
Oxford University Press, Toronto, 1962, which details the course
which Canada followed in dealing with other nations between the
wars. The volume consists of selections from documents arranged
in major groupings, such as the Empire Foreign Policy, the
Imperial and Washington Conferences of 1921, the Assertion of
an Independent Policy, The Statute of Westminster (1931), the
League of Nations, etc. Separate groups of documents deal with
Canada's relations with the USSR and the USA. There is an extensive bibliography of the sources of the documents cited.

A History of Canadian External Relations by G. P. de T. Glazebrook has been issued in 2 volumes as part of the Carleton Library,
McClelland and Stewart, Toronto, 1966. Chapters 1–11 of this
work were first published by the Oxford University Press in 1942
and the whole work was published by Oxford in 1950 in a series
sponsored by the Canadian Institute of International Affairs.
These volumes provide the most complete account yet available

of the growth of Canada's role in international affairs. Of particular value is a long bibliographical essay which cites all of the basic published statements and sources of information dealing with Canadian foreign relations.

Prof. James Eayrs has prepared *The Art of the Possible*, Macmillan, Toronto, 1964 which outlines some of the thorny problems which face the makers of Canada's foreign policy.

Other works of value in a study of Canada's participation in international affairs include Lester B. Pearson's *Diplomacy in the Nuclear Age*, Toronto, 1959. This series of essays by Canada's Prime Minister and former Minister of External Affairs reveal much of the thinking that has guided recent Canadian foreign policy. Hugh Keenleyside and six other Canadian international affairs specialists have prepared *The Growth of Canadian Policies in External Affairs*, Durham, North Carolina, 1960, published for the Duke University Commonwealth Studies Centre. This work summarizes the historical developments in Canadian foreign policy and shows Canada's role as part of the Commonwealth. Considerable attention is paid to the internal matters that have shaped Canadian foreign policy.

Marcel Cadieux, chief foreign officer for the Department of External Affairs, has published *Le Ministère des affaires extérieures*, Montreal, 1950, a brief account of the growth of the present-day practices in the Canadian foreign service. Canadian–US relations are usefully documented in H. L. Keenleyside and G. S. Brown, *Canada and the United States*, revised and enlarged edition, Knopf, New York, 1952. J. M. Callahan has written *American Foreign Policy in Canadian Relations*, Macmillan, New York, 1937, and Bruce Hutchison, *The Struggle for the Border*, Longmans, Toronto, 1955. The last work is popular in approach and records the development of US–Canadian relations.

Chief among the offices of the Canadian Federal Government concerned with international economic aid is the External Aid Office of the Department of External Affairs, Ottawa. This Office supervises the work done by Canada abroad in the fields of aid and economic and technical assistance in co-operation with various other government departments, industry, and private Canadian groups.

An organization concerned with developing international co-operation between voluntary Canadian groups and those abroad is the Overseas Institute of Canada, 56 Sparks Street, Ottawa. The Institute has published a *Directory of Canadian Agencies and Organizations in Overseas Aid*, Ottawa, May 1963, which gives particulars on sixty official and non-official Canadian bodies working in this field.

Law

The regular Acts of Parliament, more commonly known as the *Statutes of Canada*, are published in a single volume for each session of Parliament by the Queen's Printer, Ottawa. The volumes are divided into two sections—one covering public general acts and the other local private acts. Treaties, proclamations, orders-in-council, dispatches, appointments, and special regulations are included in a preliminary section. A table of contents and index for each session is included in each volume. *Revised Statutes of Canada* have been issued in 1887, 1906, 1927, and 1952. These revisions bring up to date the information included in earlier editions and are issued in both French and English with an index in the last volume arranged topically and alphabetically. Private acts are not included in the *Revised Statutes*.

The *Canada Gazette* (Fig. 7), published weekly, Queen's Printer, Ottawa, is the official gazette of Canada. Part I contains announcements of a general character, including proclamations, certain orders-in-council, regulations, notices (including divorce notices), and various other matters of official government business. Part II contains all orders, rules, etc., of an administrative nature having a general application or imposing a penalty under the laws and statutes of Canada.

The basic constitutional charter of Canada as a nation is contained in many works, including *British North America Acts and Selected Statutes, 1867–1962*. This has been compiled and

OTTAWA, THURSDAY, SEPTEMBER 22, 1966	OTTAWA, JEUDI 22 SEPTEMBRE 1966
PROCLAMATION	PROCLAMATION
GEORGES P VANIER [L.S.]	GEORGES P. VANIER [L.S.]
CANADA	CANADA
ELIZABETH THE SECOND, by the Grace of God of the United Kingdom, Canada and Her other Realms and Territories QUEEN, Head of the Commonwealth, Defender of the Faith.	ÉLISABETH DEUX, par la Grâce de Dieu, REINE du Royaume-Uni, du Canada et de ses autres royaumes et territoires, Chef du Commonwealth, Défenseur de la Foi.
To ALL To WHOM these Presents shall come or whom the same may in anywise concern, GREETING:	A TOUS CEUX À QUI les présentes parviendront ou qu'icelles pourront de quelque manière concerner,—SALUT:
A PROCLAMATION	PROCLAMATION
DONALD S. MAXWELL, Acting Deputy Attorney General, Canada. WHEREAS in and by section 46 of the Parliament of Canada, assented to on June 16, 1966, and entitled "An Act respecting the organization of the Government of Canada and matters related or incidental thereto", being chapter 25 of the	DONALD S. MAXWELL, Sous-procureur général suppléant, Canada. VU l'article quarante-six d'une loi du Parlement du Canada, sanctionnée le seizième jour de juin 1966 et intitulée Loi concernant l'organisation du gouvernement du Canada et les questions connexes ou accessoires, chapitre vingt-cinq des Statuts de 1966, lequel

FIG. 7. The Canada Gazette, 1966.

annotated by Maurice Ollivier and is published by the Queen's Printer, Ottawa, 1962.

As might be expected, the laws and statutes of the provinces are also issued at each session of the provincial legislatures, and are consolidated regularly. They are available on application to the various provincial legislative assembly buildings in each of the provincial capitals. For current provincial publications, Part III of *Canadiana*, Queen's Printer, Ottawa, provides an up-to-date list.

The Federal Minister of Justice has issued an *Office Consolidation of the Criminal Code, 1953–54, c. 51 as amended by 1960–61, cc. 21, 43, 44; and Selected Statutes*, Ottawa, Queen's Printer, 1963. This contains: (1) the table of contents of the Criminal Code; (2) the Criminal Code; (3) an index to the Criminal Code; (4) the table of contents to selected statutes; (5) selected statutes relating to the administration of the criminal law: Canada Evidence Act, Extradition Act, Food and Drugs (pt. 3) Act, Fugitive Offenders Act, Lord's Day Act, Narcotic Control Act, Parole Act, Penitentiary Act, and Prisons and Reformatories Act; and (6) an index to selected statutes. It incorporates all amendments to the end of 1962 and is issued for the convenience of lawyers and court officials.

An annotated edition in French of the Criminal Code has been prepared by Irénée Lagarde, *Droit pénal canadien*, Wilson & Lafleur, Montreal, 1962. Each section of the Code is quoted, followed by an explanation of the section and examples of judgements made under it. There is an index to the judgements cited as well as to the subjects covered by the Code.

A number of reference volumes provide an outline of the measures taken and judgements given under Canadian law. *Angers' Digest of Canadian Law*, 18th edn., Canada Law Book, Toronto, edited by F. R. Hume, has been published since 1903, and the *Annuaire de jurisprudence du Québec*, Wilson & Lafleur, Montreal, has appeared since 1955. This latter work includes reports of decisions arrived at in various courts of the Province of Quebec, and summaries and references to articles in periodicals

ntaining material on legal matters in the Province. It is arranged
subjects treated, but there are numerous cross-references.
ere is a list of the laws enacted during the year as well as an
dex to the decisions. This annual series follows the *Répertoire
néral de jurisprudence canadienne* for the years 1770–1955
eviously published.

*Canada Legal Directory: for the legal profession, containing the
mes of the judges, lawyers, court officials, etc., throughout
nada,* is published annually by Canada Legal Directory,
5 Lowther Ave., Toronto. It is a comprehensive directory that
als with all parts of Canada.

The *Canadian Bar Review*, Toronto, established 1923, is issued
times a year and carries news and information on legal
velopments across Canada. *La Revue du notariat*, Montreal,
tablished 1898, and *The Ontario Reports*, Toronto, founded in
00, provide a running account of decisions of interest to the
;al profession.

D. A. Schmeiser has prepared *Civil Liberties in Canada*, Oxford
niversity Press, Toronto, 1964. Professor Schmeiser has done a
eat deal of historical research, especially on the subject of denomi-
tional education. The background of the subject in Canada is
scussed both prior to and after Confederation. The work con-
ins valuable information on the development of civil rights
;islation in Canada.

Public Administration

The traditions of government and public administration in
nada have derived mainly from Great Britain, and there is a
od deal about Canadian government that resembles that of
gland. On the other hand, experiment and adaptation in Canada
ve gone forward and produced many unique constitutional and
vernmental arrangements. Professor Robert MacGregor Daw-
n's *The Government of Canada*, University of Toronto Press, 1963
the most comprehensive study of Canadian government written
date. The present edition has been revised by Professor Norman

Ward, a friend and former student of the author, who died in 1958. Professor Ward has amended and updated the text and provided numerous references to publications that have appeared since the last edition. Professor Dawson neglected French-Canadian politics to some extent. Professor Ward has made up for this lack by including many references to French Canada. The book begins with the constitutional development of Canada from colonial times to Confederation. It then deals in turn with the Monarchy and the Governor-General, the Cabinet, the public service, Parliament, the judiciary, and finally the various political parties. An Appendix provides the texts of the British North America Act, 1867, and the Statute of Westminster 1921. Provincial governments are not studied, but dominion–provincial relations and the division of power between the two jurisdictions are covered. The detailed workings of municipal governments are not covered. A select bibliography is included.

J. E. Hodgetts and D. C. Corbett have edited *Canadian Public Administration*, Macmillan, 1960. This is an outline in public administration for students and members of the public services. The editors, well-known scholars in political science in Canadian universities, have managed to organize the scattered writings and speeches of Canadian academics, civil servants, excerpts from government reports, debates of the House of Commons, and Royal Commission reports. Many valuable references to Canadian government practice are recorded here.

The Parliament of Canada by George Hambleton, Ryerson, 1961, has been prepared by a parliamentary journalist of many years' standing and latterly an adviser with Canada's Department of External Affairs, who sets out a lucid and well-informed explanation of Canada's Parliament, its beginnings, what it embodies, and how it works. Adroitly he carries us back through a description of some of its symbolic practices to its origin in Great Britain as the Witenagemot, the council from whom the Saxon kings sought wise advice. He tells how democratic government in North America had its start in Jamestown, Virginia, with the granting of right of assembly in the year 1619, and goes on to describe Canada's struggle to achieve representative and finally responsible government. The separate elements of Canada's parliamentary system are explored and made clearer through comparison with the functions of the President and Congress of the United States. The appendix includes the text of the Canadian Bill of Rights.

The official guide to the structure of Canadian government is *Organization of the Government of Canada*, published in loose-leaf form by the Department of the Secretary of State, Queen's Printer, Ottawa, 1965. All branches of the federal government are analysed and described, but the main emphasis is on the executive side. The bulk of the book deals in alphabetical order with the departments, public corporations, boards, and commissions which carry on Canada's business. For each of these bodies the table of organization, the minister responsible, and the higher civil servants in charge of its activities are shown. Some description of the functions of the department or organization is given as well. Thus this volume may be used both as a directory for names of officials and as a guide to the maze of government in Canada, which is, as elsewhere, a complicated business. Legislation authorizing and defining the powers and make-up of each body is cited. The structure and composition of Parliament and of the federal courts are shown, and a list of international organizations with which Canada is affiliated is appended. There are two indexes, one of personal names and the other names of government organizations. A table of organization showing the overall structure of the government, with each element in its proper place in the Canadian scheme, is included.

The Federal Government appointed a Royal Commission on Government Organization in September 1960, headed by J. Grant Glassco. The Report of the Commission was published in 5 volumes: vol. 1: *Management of the Public Service*, 1962; vols. 2 and 3: *Supporting Services for Government*, 1962; vol. 4: *Special Areas of Administration*, 1963; vol. 5: *The Organization of the Government of Canada*, 1963. This Report is a detailed appraisal of the policies and practices of all of the federal government departments, and points out many areas in which there is room for revision and updating of work methods.

The *Canadian Parliamentary Guide*, edited by Pierre G. Normandin, PO Box 513, Ottawa, has appeared regularly since 1912 and is the best source of information about all the legislative bodies of Canada. From it one may learn the present members of the Senate (an appointive body that changes slowly with the death or retirement of its members and the appointment of new ones); the names, party affiliations, and constituencies of members of the House of Commons and of the ten provincial legislatures (including the Province of Quebec's equivalent of the Senate); and the names and portfolios of federal and provincial cabinet ministers. Biographies are given for all members of these various legislatures as well as for higher court judges, privy councillors, and the representatives of the Queen—the Governor-General of Canada and the Lieutenant-Governors of the ten provinces. Historical tables show past governments of Canada and of the provinces, as well as dates of sessions of Parliament and legislatures. In addition, one may find here the names of the councillors and administrators of the Yukon and North-west Territories. Of historical value is the detailed district by district tabulation of election results for all federal elections since 1867 and for the most recent election in each province.

The organization of each provincial government is not as complex as for the federal government, but useful handbooks to their services are often available from each provincial legislature. A *1965 Directory and Guide to the Services of the Government of Ontario* has been produced by the Ontario Department of Tourism and Information, Queen's Printer, Toronto, 1965. These and other provincial government publications may occasionally be obtained outside of Canada. Some of the provincial governments, Ontario, British Columbia, and Saskatchewan, maintain overseas representatives in London, and the Province of Quebec maintains an overseas representation in Paris.

With the growth of towns and cities the question of municipal administration in Canada assumes larger proportions. One municipal annual budget, that of metropolitan Toronto, is the third largest government budget in Canada. Since municipalities are entirely organized by each provincial legislature, there are ten separate sets of municipal regulations for the ten provinces. These have been consolidated locally and are issued by the separate departments of municipal affairs in each province. Typical municipal regulations are those for the Province of Quebec, *Code Municipal de la Province de Québec: Municipal Code of the Province of Quebec*, Wilson and Lafleur, Montreal, 1960. The original edition of this work appeared in 1932. The present edition is based on that published in 1955 with the addition of the legislative amendments made under 4–5 Elizabeth II and 8–9 Elizabeth II. The work includes all laws governing municipalities, municipal councils, and corporations, including their powers and duties. There is a list of the financial standing of each municipality along with the names of the principal municipal officials. The volume is arranged by the chapters of each law, but there is a systematic index to the contents.

The Ontario Department of Municipal Affairs publishes the *Municipal Directory*, Queen's Printer, Toronto, annually. This is the best single source for quick, current information on municipal Ontario. Chief officials, annual assessment, taxable and exempt, and current assessed population are given for each urban centre. Provincial population and assessment trends are given in tabular form and all changes in municipal status are recorded and analysed graphically.

Current information and news of municipal government affairs is contained in *Civic Administration*, established 1949, a monthly publication, Maclean-Hunter, Toronto. The same firm has also published since 1956 an annual *Municipal Reference Manual and Purchasing Guide*, which gives information about and for local municipal services. *Municipal World*, established 1891, is a dependable monthly source of news and information on the changes taking place in Canadian local administration in all provinces.

Armed Forces

The Royal Canadian Navy, the Canadian Army, the Royal
Canadian Air Force, and other military establishments were inte-
grated into a single administration known as the Canadian Forces
in 1966. The previous separate organizations had existed for many
years, the Canadian Army especially, it having regiments which
can trace their antecedents back to the days of the French régime
and the British Empire.

C. E. Dornbusch has prepared the *Canadian Army, 1855–1958*,
Hope Farm Press, Cornwallville, NY, 1959. This is a listing of
regiments and other units of the Canadian Army with tabulated
information on organizational and name modifications since their
formation. Many bibliographies of materials available relating to
specific units are given, with selected library locations for these.
Some are arranged under the entry for a particular regiment (with
the tabular information), and some separately under larger formations and commands or the names of campaigns and wars, such
as the North-west Rebellion, 1885, or World War II, 1939–45.
Included is a Role of the Regiments as of 1958, and indexes of
authors, periodicals, and distinctive titles. *Lineages of the Canadian Army 1855–1961: armour, cavalry, infantry, 1961,* by the
same author, provides a separate guide to these units, reporting
their history in the dates of embodiment, amalgamation, and
disbandment.

Illustrations of the regimental insignia and corps badges of the
units of the Regular Army and of the Militia of the Canadian
Army along with brief histories of each and their respective battle
honours can be found in vol. 1 of the Canadian Army List,
Regiments and Corps of the Canadian Army, Queen's Printer,
Ottawa, 1964, prepared by the Army Historical Section of the
Canadian Army under the authority of the Minister of National
Defence.

The background and details of the integration of the Canadian
armed services into the Canadian Forces can be studied in the
Canadian Department of National Defence's *White Paper on*

Defence by Paul Hellyer and Lucien Cardin, Queen's Printer, Ottawa, 1964.

The respective periodicals of each service, the *Crowsnest* (RCN), the *Canadian Army Journal*, and the *Roundel* (RCAF) have been superseded by the *Canadian Forces Sentinel*.

The vagaries of Canada's defence policy since World War I are detailed with scholarly exactitude in James Eayrs' *In Defense of Canada*, University of Toronto Press, 1964–5; vol. 1: *From the Great War to the Great Depression*; vol. 2: *Appeasement and Rearmament*.

An introduction to Canada's military history is George F. Stanley's *Canada's Soldiers: the military history of an unmilitary people*, rev. edn., Macmillan, Toronto, 1960. This is a record and analysis of Canada's three and a half centuries of military action, tracing the development of Canada's military traditions and military organization from marauding Amerindians to Korea. It also serves as an outline introduction to the gradual development of Canadian military policy.

More detailed information on Canada's military adventures is contained in the official histories: Gerald W. Nicholson's *Canadian Expeditionary Force 1914–1919: official history of the Canadian army in the First World War*, Queen's Printer, Ottawa, 1962; *Official History of the Canadian Army in the Second World War*, Queen's Printer, Ottawa, 1955–60, edited by Charles P. Stacey— vol. 1: *Six Years of War, the Army in Canada, Britain and the Pacific*; vol. 2: *The Canadians in Italy, 1943–1945*; vol. 3: *The Victory Campaign*; Herbert F. Wood's *Strange Battleground: official Canadian Army history of the Korean War*, Queen's Printer, Ottawa, 1965.

The official histories of the RCN and the RCAF are respectively, G. N. Tucker's *The Naval Service of Canada: its official history*, Ottawa, 1952, and *The RCAF Overseas*, Toronto, 1944–9—vol. 1: *The First Four Years*; vol. 2: *The Fifth Year*; vol. 3: *The Sixth Year*.

Vernon A. M. Kemp's *Scarlet and Stetson: the Royal North-west Mounted Police on the Prairies*, Ryerson Press, 1964, is a collection of personal reminiscences of a retired senior officer of that notable force. It depicts the men who made up the only effective law enforcement agency in the immense, sparsely settled Canadian West and North-west from 1873 onwards during the period 1900–17. Homesteaders, rowdy itinerant farm labour, remittance men, all left their mark on the developing country and all felt the beneficial, often benevolent, frequently unprecedented administration of law in remote and distant regions. The Force, now the Royal Canadian Mounted Police, is still the provincial police for several of the provinces.

The Upper Canada Historical Arms Society has prepared *The Military Arms of Canada*, Museum Restoration Service, West Hill, Ontario, 1963. The firearms used by the militia and armies of Canada from the early seventeenth century until the present time are described and illustrated.

Welfare

The growing role of the Federal Government in national welfare schemes has been apparent in Canada since the end of World War II. There is now a national old-age pension plan, hospital and medical care, social and unemployment insurance, and a variety of other forms of social assistance for individuals in every part of the country. Each provincial government administers welfare services, and local municipalities share to some extent in the responsibility. Some idea of the extent of their services can be gained from the inauguration by the Federal Government of the new *Canada Assistance Plan*, Queen's Printer, Ottawa, 1965, and the various separate measures to combat poverty and increase economic opportunity in urban and rural areas.

The purpose of the Canada Assistance Plan is to replace the existing federal-provincial shared programmes of public assistance with a single comprehensive measure. Under this Plan an Advisory National Council on Welfare has been established to help the Government in various ways so that a co-ordinated system of public welfare can come about in Canada.

The Canadian Welfare Council, 55 Park Avenue, Ottawa, is a non-governmental organization which gives leadership, in co-operation with other national bodies, to social welfare planning in Canada. It provides information on welfare employment opportunities and conducts extensive research on behalf of both government and private business. The Council Family and Child Welfare Division issues a quarterly bulletin and other publications reporting on activities in this field. The Public Welfare Division produces annual and occasional reports on this aspect of Canadian welfare. *Canadian Welfare*, published bi-monthly from 1928 to 1935, contains the annual *Proceedings* of the Council. Since 1936 they have been published separately each year.

A Canadian Committee on Children and Youth was established in 1965, following the Second Canadian Conference on Children, held in Montreal. The *Report of the Ontario Minister of Public Welfare's Advisory Committee on Child Welfare*, Queen's Printer, Toronto, 1965, produced some far-reaching recommendations for changes in the administration of child care and protection services in the Province of Ontario. In New Brunswick, following the Byrne Royal Commission Report, Queen's Printer, Fredericton, 1965, child welfare services, together with all other forms of welfare provision, were included in the provincial government's assumption of responsibility for local government.

Social Problems: a Canadian profile by Richard Larkin, McGraw-Hill, Toronto, 1964, consists of articles on Canada's major social problems written by scholars, officials, and journalists. They are drawn from periodical publications such as *The Canadian Medical Association Journal, Canadian Welfare, Canadian Journal of Corrections, Saturday Night*, and from books. A few are published for the first time.

The problems include French–English separatism, difficulties in ethnic and racial group relations, work, population and immigration, family relations, health services, alcohol and drug addictions, mental illness, sexual deviance, crime, and delinquency.

The dates are from the early 1950's to 1963, but most articles were published from 1960 to 1963. Most have undergone

D*

substantial editing. The statistics are rarely later than 1961 but are usually dated. The bibliographies are good and include 1964 publications. Varying as they do from journalism to documentary, the articles present a balance of fact and opinion, of popular and professional treatment. The work provides background and serves well the purposes of self-examination and national stocktaking.

The International Institute of Metropolitan Toronto has published *Newcomers in Transition*, the Institute, Toronto, 1965, as a report on the way in which immigrants are able to make use of established community services. Various provincial and federal departments of government, such as the Department of Citizenship and Immigration, Ottawa, have worked over the past 20 years to aid in the process of assimilation of newcomers to Canada. Helen Cowan has written *British Emigration to British North America: the first hundred years*, University of Toronto Press, 1961. This book covers the period 1785–1850 and deals with the flow of immigrants westward across the continent. *Strangers within our Gates, or coming Canadians* by J. S. Woodsworth, F. C. Stephenson, Toronto, 1909, is an early account of the impact of European settlers before World War I in western Canada.

Folklore and Customs

Canada has had a rich tradition of folklore which extends both before and after the days of its first discovery by Europeans. The Indian tribes of Canada had many legends and stories which they have retained in various forms, and they make up the richest part of Canadian folklore. Marius Barbeau has collected and published many of them. His work, *Haida Myths, Illustrated by Argillite Carvings*, was issued as Bulletin No. 127, Anthropological Series No. 23, National Museum of Canada, Queen's Printer, Ottawa, 1953. In this volume, several tales are told and illustrated, including *Tlenaman or the Dragon*, *Wasco, the Sea-Wolf*, and *Su'san the Strong Man*. This latter is the Haida equivalent to the story of Samson or that of St. George. Accompanying them are photographs of argillite carvings based on these stories made by the

Indians. The earliest known date of argillite work among the Haida Indians is about 1820. This dark slate was carved to imitate the carvings made by Boston whaling sailors on walrus tusks and whales' teeth. The Haida Indians brought to their work the rich folklore incorporated in their legends, and the resulting carvings illustrate in a marvellous way these heroic fables and myths.

Horatio Hall has prepared *The Iroquois Book of Rites*, University of Toronto Press, 1963, which describes the ceremonies performed in the long houses of the Iroquois in previous generations. No complete collections of Indian tales and stories exist, but there are selective gatherings and some of a regional nature. Hilda Mary Hooke has put together *Thunder in the Mountains, Legends of Canada*, 1947, that provides a selection of Indian stories. Robert Edward Gard collected *Johnny Chinook: tall tales and true from the Canadian West*, 1945, which deals mainly with Alberta and Saskatchewan. Marius Barbeau edited *The Tree of Dreams*, Oxford University Press, Toronto, 1955, which covers stories from the Province of Quebec.

Les Archives de folklore, Laval University, 1946–60, contains documents and reports of investigations on French traditions in North America, and particularly on the manners, customs, stories, songs, and popular arts of French Canada. Among many titles included are *Civilisation traditionnelle des Lavalois*, Quebec, 1951 and *La Vie traditionnelle à Saint-Pierre*, Quebec, 1960. *Readings in Canadian Slavic Folklore* by B. Rudnytski, University of Manitoba Press, Winnipeg, 1961, is a two-volume collection of Ukrainian stories and songs that are to be found in Canada. The Canadian way of life is made up from so many different national and ethnic strands that there is no such thing as a uniform Canadian habit of thought and action. Each new wave of immigration further complicates the picture, and the diversity in Canadian life can be expected to grow and continue for many years to come.

Gertrude Pringle prepared *Etiquette in Canada: the blue book of Canadian social usage*, 2nd edn., McClelland & Stewart, 1949. This is a Canadian "Emily Post" with wide coverage on social custom and protocol with appended foreign words and their meanings and a subject index. Detailed and authoritative, it is comprehensive and incorporates information gathered from many Canadian sources—social, official circles, judicial, literary, etc. This standard work on Canadian etiquette is now, unfortunately, out of print and outdated. Still valuable, however, are its chapters devoted to uniquely Canadian topics not discussed elsewhere. More current coverage of everyday situations may be found in Claire Wallace's *Canadian Etiquette Dictionary*, Harlequin Books, Winnipeg, 1960.

Annie H. Foster and Anne Grierson have prepared *High Days and Holidays in Canada*, Ryerson Press, Toronto, 1956. This is the only Canadian directory of holidays in print, and includes, in chronological order, the Canadian statutory holidays and other days of special interest to Canadians, celebrated in the various provinces. Although written for schoolchildren, the considerable detailing of the history and special customs associated with each day makes it of general interest and value.

Costume

The costumes of the native tribes of Canada are well known through reproductions and descriptions in numerous works of reference and have long been a favourite subject of artists and photographers. Among the artists, Paul Kane has left a vivid record of the costumes of the Indians of the West in his series of paintings and sketches recording his journey through Canada in the 1840's. A number of these are reproduced in colour in *Paul Kane* by A. H. Robson, Ryerson Press, Toronto, 1938. Douglas Leechman, in *The Native Tribes of Canada*, Toronto, W. J. Gage, 1956, includes in descriptive text and sketches a record of the costume of Canada's Indians and Eskimos noting distinctive regional and tribal variations.

No comprehensive work on the costumes of Canada has been written, but the collection of clothing at the Royal Ontario Museum, Toronto, has provided material for two pamphlets—

Women's Costume in Early Ontario and *Women's Costume in Ontario, 1867–1907* by Mrs. K. B. Brett, director of the collection. The many reproductions include photographs of actual garments, drawings, paintings, and photographs from contemporary sources.

With the development of dress manufacture in Canada in the mid 1900's, a basis of the style and fashion industry was laid. One of the principal sources of information on domestic Canadian style are the illustrated mail order catalogues of two of Canada's largest retailing concerns, Eaton's of Toronto and The Robert Simpson Co. Ltd. The firms issued catalogues from 1884 and 1894 respectively, and from 1896 both illustrate a wide range of fashionable and working dress. The catalogues of the Eaton Co. for early years are available on microfilm.

The costumes of the French settlers of Quebec have been recorded in the works of many of her artists. Cornelius Krieghoff (1812–72) specialized in depicting the life of the French Canadian countryman, and *Cornelius Krieghoff* by Marius Barbeau, Toronto, Society for Art Publications, 1962, reproduces a number of his colourful canvases. Barbeau has also written a monograph on the gay French Canadian Assumption sash, *Ceinture fléchée*, Éditions Paysana, Montreal, 1945.

CHAPTER 4

Canadian Education

Primary and Secondary Education

Under the terms of the British North American Act, which established the powers and duties of the Canadian Federal Government, education is a responsibility of each provincial government. Until World War II, each province fixed its own standards, set up its own system of financing, determined its own curricula and aims in education, and drew up its own requirements for secondary school graduation and university entrance. Substantial differences have grown up between the education systems of the ten provinces, and since 1945 there has been continuing pressure to have some degree of standardization and equality of educational opportunity for children in all parts of Canada.

Dr. Charles E. Phillips, in *The Development of Education in Canada*, Gage, Toronto, 1957, has provided a comprehensive history of Canadian elementary and secondary school education. This survey covers the beginnings of education in Canada from the time of Champlain until the middle of the twentieth century. The author describes briefly the social setting in Canada and then discusses the developments which occurred in each of the ten provinces first during the French régime, next under British rule, and, lastly, from 1867 to the mid 1950's. He emphasizes the radical changeover which took place when the administrative control of the educational system passed from the hands of a small portion of the country's population to that of the voting majority. Dr. Phillips concludes his book with an examination of the various influences which have affected teaching and the concept of public education in Canada. An index and lengthy bibliography are provided.

So many changes have occurred since the publication of this work that reference must be made to some of the more recent books and periodicals in the educational field. Of general value are the Reports of the two Canadian Conferences on Education, the first held in Ottawa in 1958 and the second in Montreal in 1962. The Report of this latter was edited by Fred W. Price and published by the University of Toronto Press and Les Presses de l'Université Laval, Quebec, in 1962. This report has part of the text in French only, and includes a bibliography of basic documents on Canadian educational practices and problems.

The Canadian Education Association was founded in 1893 in order to provide a forum for professional and lay persons interested in educational matters. The *Proceedings* of the annual conventions of the Association were published regularly until 1944. Later proceedings are included in the Association's official periodical publication, *Canadian Education*. A valuable source of current information is the *Canadian Education Association's Newsletter*. The Association has also been instrumental in creating a standing committee of (provincial) ministers of education within the Association who regularly discuss educational matters of common concern to all provinces and form an unofficial forum for national education policy.

Another national body concerned with education is the Association canadienne des éducateurs de langue française (ACELF) which in 1952 produced a *Bibliographie analytique de la littérature pédagogique canadienne-française*, Editions de l'ACELF, Quebec. The work of this Association through the years has been a powerful stimulus for the reform of education, particularly in the Province of Quebec. Inquiries into education in this Province have resulted in the publication of the various Reports of the Royal Commission on Education in Quebec headed by Msgr. A. M. Parent and the reports of other bodies. Such documents include *Rapport de la commission du programme de la faculté des arts au conseil universitaire*, 2 vols., 2nd edn., Les Presses de l'Université

Laval, Quebec, 1960; *Rapport de la commission royale d'enquête sur l'enseignement de la Province de Québec*; 1er pt. *Les Structures supérieures du système scolaire*; 2^{ieme} pt. *Les Structures pédagogiques du système scolaire*; 3^{ieme} pt. *L'Administration de l'enseignment*, Ministère de l'Education, Québec.

On the level of federal co-ordination of education, an important role is played by the Education Section of the Dominion Bureau of Statistics in Ottawa. This office has for many years produced an annual and bi-annual survey of education at all levels in Canada. Some of the recent publications of the Bureau include its *Survey of Elementary and Secondary Education, 1962–63*, Queen's Printer, Ottawa, 1966. This bi-annual publication consists of statistical tables and interpretive text on school enrolment, class size, teacher training, experience and salaries, and school-leaving records on a national scale as well as by provinces. A similar report is the *Survey of Education Finance, 1961–1962*, Queen's Printer, Ottawa, 1966. This bi-annual series contains statistical tables with explanations covering all aspects of educational finance from public school through to university. As a general guide the Bureau has also published *The Organization and Administration of Public Schools in Canada*, 2nd edn., Queen's Printer, Ottawa, 1960. This report, which includes some statistics, provides background information in the history, law, and organization of elementary, secondary, special, and vocational education, including finance and teachers salaries. It surveys each province and the Federal Government's activities in relation to education.

The Canadian Council for Research in Education has been active in recent years, linking the research activities of each of the provincial departments of education. In 1965, with the help of the Canada Council, it began the publication of the *Canadian Education Index: Répertoire canadien sur l'éducation* (Fig. 8), the Council, Ottawa, a monthly guide to the contents of Canadian education periodicals and a valuable source of information on current research. The Ontario Institute for Studies in Education, Toronto, has recently begun an expanded programme of education research, and publishes a number of its studies each year.

ABILITY
  See also
kinds of Ability, e.g. Physical ability
  Tests
Problems of testing abilities in non-western cultures. P.E. Vernon. McGill Univ Bul 7:9-10 Ap '65

ABILITY and achievement
"Capacities of children" [Pt. I address] M.C. Reynolds. Special Ed 39:25-7 Ap '65
"Capacities of children" [Pt. II address] M.C. Reynolds. Special Ed 39:11-14+ My '65
  See also
Underachievers

ACADEMIC freedom
Protecting freedom to learn. M.P. Heller. Argus 24:170+ My '65

ACCELERATION
Acceleration [at Sturgeon Falls, Ont.] Brother Frédéric. Ont J Ed Res 7:155-7 Winter '64-'65
Acceleration--design or expedient? J.S. Kobayama. Alberta Sch Trust 35:8-9+ My '65

Relative achievement of pupils in schools of varying sizes [study] Status Committee, Federation of Women Teachers' Associations of Ontario. Toronto [1965] bibliog tabs 49p
[Relative achievement of pupils in small schools] in Two research projects undertaken by the Federation of Women Teachers' Associations of Ontario. L.D. Martin. bibliog Ont J Ed Res 7:179-86 Winter '64-'65
  See also
Ability and achievement
Underachievers

ACHIEVEMENT, Prediction of. See Prediction of scholastic success

ADAMS, Charles J.
Understanding the Muslim world. McGill News 46:8 Je '65

ADAMS, Judy
For school bus riders. Quest 2:23 Mr-Ap '65

ADAMS, W.S.
British Columbia Institute of Technology. 11 Sch Prog 34:34-6 Je '65

Fig. 8. *Canadian Education Index*, 1965.

The Canadian Library Association issued a *Checklist of Canadian Periodicals in the Field of Education*, the Association, Ottawa, 1964, as its Occasional Paper No. 44. One of the most valuable periodicals in the field of general educational information is *School Progress*, Toronto, established 1931, which carries news on education in all parts of Canada.

Adult Education

The Canadian Association for Adult Education (CAAE), 21 Sultan Street, Toronto, is a national voluntary organization financed by memberships, government grants, and private corporations. It receives study and research grants from governments and foundations. It has provincial member sections in British Columbia, Ontario, Manitoba, and the Maritimes and associate groups in Saskatchewan and Quebec. Its bi-monthly publication *Continuous Learning* is a source of current information on adult education in Canada, and the Association also maintains a library and national information office. In 1950 the Association published *Adult Education in Canada*, edited by Dr. J. R. Kidd. This volume contains the history and philosophy of adult education in Canada —how it began, how it works, who sponsors it, who participates in it, and concrete examples of its action. The contribution of radio to rural education, the part played by universities and public libraries in urban centres, the role of labour unions, and business groups are also considered.

OACE, Planning and Purpose in Adult Education in Ontario, CAAE, 21 Sultan Street, Toronto, 1966, is the report of the founding conference of the Ontario Association for Continuing Education. In it are described many of the methods used for the continuing education of adults, and there is a list of persons active in adult education in the Province.

Education of Women

With the growing number of women entering the labour force, the Federal Government has found it useful to provide a directory of social and professional associations for Canadian women; Canada, Department of Labour, Women's Bureau, *National Women's Organizations in Canada, 1964–65*, Queen's Printer, Ottawa, 1964. Entries in French and English define the aims and programmes, list officers, membership figures, publications, and, where it applies, international affiliation of each organization.

Ontario, Department of Labour, Women's Bureau, *What do Women think about Working?*, Queen's Printer, Toronto, 1965, is a concise and well-illustrated report of a survey conducted by the Women's Bureau of the Ontario Department of Labour in 1964. The survey indicated that the trend, at least in Ontario, for women between the ages of 35 and 54, whose children need less intensive care, is to work outside the home usually on a part-time basis. It showed that women form a valuable source of experienced, well-educated labour and that, as a result, more part-time job opportunities and counselling for vocations and family arrangements are needed. Charts dealing with such matters as "the need for low-cost day care centres" or "how to go about trying to find a job" illustrate the results of the survey.

Trevor Wigney has prepared *The Education of Women and Girls*, Ontario College of Education, Department of Educational Research, Toronto, 1965. This is a comprehensive and factual report of the education of women in Canada and the United States. It traces the background of women's education and shows that the problems of continuing education can not be seen in isolation from the early education and social foundations provided for girls in North American society. The report focuses attention on the needs and problems and describes some of the current changes which are taking place in an attempt to relate the existing educational provisions to the new needs expressed by women. Tables, diagrams, and bibliographies are found in the various chapters on "Learning the feminine role", "Womanpower", and "Continuing education: needs and experiments". A useful list of major programmes in continuing education for women offered in North America is appended to the report.

Schools and Religion

Two problems, religious education in the public schools and public aid to separate schools, mainly Catholic, are of long-standing concern in most of the Canadian provinces. In 1965 the Ethical Education Association of Ontario carried its fight against religious education in the public schools before the McRuer Royal Commission on Civil Rights. Charles B. Sissons wrote *Church and State in Canadian Education*, Ryerson Press, Toronto, 1959, which is an historical study of this problem in various parts of Canada. F. A. Walker has prepared 2 volumes dealing with aspects of the church and education: *Catholic Education and Politics in Upper Canada*, Dent, Toronto, 1955, traces the origins of the separate school movement from 1794 and *Catholic Education and Politics in Ontario*, Thomas Nelson & Sons, Toronto, 1964, recounts the history of this question during the past 100 years. The matter of control of the public school system by various bodies was considered by Frank P. T. McKinnon in *The Politics of Education*, University of Toronto Press, 1960, which dealt extensively with the forces affecting the administration of the public schools.

University and Higher Education

In 1951 money was made available for the first time by the Federal Parliament to each of the ten provinces to be used to finance current university costs. In 1960 the Province of Quebec, which had refused up to that date to accept federal grants for universities, began to take them. The amount given each year has risen steadily, and in 1964–5 it totalled $355,000,000. This amount is expected to increase to $1,704,000,000 in 1975–6 according to the *Report of the Commission on Financing Higher Education in Canada*, the Association of Universities and Colleges of Canada, Ottawa, 1965.

In order to distribute the grants, the Canadian Universities Foundation, Ottawa, was set up by the universities and colleges which were members of the National Conference of Canadian

Universities and Colleges. In 1965, by Act of Parliament, the Foundation united with the National Conference of Canadian Universities and Colleges to become the Association of Universities and Colleges of Canada, Ottawa. It publishes annually *Canadian Universities and Colleges,* which gives for each institution the location, enrolment, administrative staff, a brief outline of the history, government and the faculties, courses, degrees, extension services that are provided, and admission requirements and fees. The arrangement is alphabetical by name with affiliated colleges under the parent body. There is a special section devoted to non-member institutions and colleges. The Foundation has also published *Financing Higher Education in Canada,* Studies 1–5, Ottawa, 1961–4. These demonstrate the shift of the financial burden of higher education in Canada from private purse to public treasury. In a single decade, from 1950 to 1960 during which expenditure on higher education trebled, the Federal Government's share of the cost rose from 4 per cent to 24 per cent, with a proportionate drop in the share borne by students, churches, corporate bodies, and provincial governments. The authors of these studies examine the rising costs of education and show the factors—larger student bodies, increased facilities, and expansion of research programmes —that underlie these costs. They offer estimates of future enrolments and of the resources that will be needed to cope with them.

The Bureau of Statistics, Ottawa, contributes a regular bi-annual survey entitled *Canadian Institutions of Higher Education,* Queen's Printer, Ottawa. It is useful for persons planning to attend a Canadian college or university, since it contains names and addresses of all institutions where courses leading to degrees are offered and brief information about courses of study available in each. 359 institutions are listed in the 1960–1 issue of which approximately 50 give degrees in fields other than theology. Most of the remainder are junior colleges or schools affiliated with large universities. The listing is by province. The institutions are also arranged by courses of study offered and by kinds of degrees granted. For detailed information as to entrance requirements and tuition fees, the catalogues of individual institutions should be consulted.

The Department of Education of the Province of Quebec has published an *Education Directory, 1965–66, University and Post-secondary Education,* Department of Education, Quebec, 1965. Quebec has six universities—Bishop's, Laval, McGill, Montreal, Sherbrooke, and Sir George Williams. In addition there are nearly 100 professional and training post-secondary institutions operated under the Departments of Education, Agriculture, and Cultural Affairs. Twenty-four other schools operate under private auspices including seven schools of nursing. There are an additional forty-one schools for training nurses aides, and child care workers. The *Directory* contains a useful subject index in both French and English. All schools listed are complete with postal address and the name of the director of the school. The various affiliations of each school are indicated as well as the ministry or institution which supervises it.

Dr. Robin S. Harris and Arthur Tremblay have prepared *A Bibliography of Higher Education in Canada: Bibliographie de l'enseignement supérieur au Canada,* University of Toronto Press, Les Presses de l'Université Laval, 1960 (Studies in Higher Education in Canada, No. 1).

The title-page and introduction are in English and French. Part I provides references on the Canadian cultural and educational background; Part II includes sections on history and organization of the institutions, curriculum, and teaching (with subdivisions for specific fields of study), the professor, and the student.

This is the first of a projected series of studies on higher education in Canada sponsored by the Committee on the History of Higher Education in Canada established by the National Conference of Canadian Universities. Among its nearly 4000 entries are included the books, pamphlets, theses, dissertations, and articles in journals and magazines which are necessary for a complete understanding of the history of Canadian higher education. A *Supplement,* 1965, was published containing more recent material.

CHAPTER 5

Canadian Economics and Business

Economics

George W. Wilson, Scott Gordon, and Stanislaw Judek have prepared *Canada, an Appraisal of its Needs and Resources*, Twentieth Century Fund, New York, University of Toronto Press, 1965. This work was written by a team of Canadian economists and is designed to give an authoritative look at the economic potential of Canada. The treatment of the issues is non-technical and there is a useful blending of data, analysis, and judgement. Part I sketches the past economic trends since the late 1930's. Part II deals with Canadian resources in land, labour, capital, and entrepreneurship. Part III makes estimates of Canada's economic potential in 1970 and 1975. There is a useful index.

The economic background to present-day Canada is well laid out in *The Canadian Economy: selected readings* by J. J. Deutsch *et al.*, 2nd edn., Macmillan, Toronto, 1965. This book is intended primarily as an aid in the introductory teaching of economic principles in Canadian universities and colleges. There are thirty-three selections divided into eight parts headed: National Income and Employment; Policies for Economic Stability; Federal-Provincial Fiscal Relations; Maintaining Competition; Agricultural Policy; Labour and Industrial Relations; Foreign Trade, the Balance of Payments, and the Canadian Dollar; Growth and Development.

A work that covers the early period and is still of considerable value is H. A. Innis and A. R. M. Lower, *Select Documents in Canadian Economic History, 1783–1885*, University of Toronto Press, 1933. This collection, as well as *Essays in Canadian Economic*

History by H. A. Innis, edited by M. Q. Innis, University of Toronto Press, 1956, was written by one of the most important economic historians of North America. Professor Innis has carefully exposed the economic foundations of Canada, and the insights which he has provided are of value not only to the economist but also to all social scientists attempting to form some basis for future social planning in Canada. Another valuable study is *Canadian Economic Growth and Development from 1939 to 1955* by J. M. Smith, Queen's Printer, Ottawa, 1957. O. J. Firestone has produced *Canada's Economic Development, 1867–1953*, Bowes & Bowes, London, 1958, which is a study over a longer period of the economic growth of Canada.

Earlier works in the economic history of Canada have been closely related to political science and government. Much that was written, although of basic importance, was on subjects which were only marginal to economics. Because they provide valuable sources of information, they are listed here. Dr. Adam Shortt's *Documents Relating to Canadian Currency, Exchange and Finance during the French Period* (Ottawa, 1915), W. B. Munro's *Documents Relating to Seigniorial Tenure in Canada,* 1598–1854 (Toronto, 1908), S. Leacock's *Mackenzie/Hincks* (Toronto, 1926), and O. D. Skelton's *Life and Times of Sir Alexander Tilloch Galt*, Carleton Library, No. 26, (Toronto, 1966) are still useful. In the field of history, H. P. Biggar, *The Early Trading Companies of New France* (Toronto, 1901; reprint University Microfilms, Ann Arbor, 1955); J. S. McLennan, *Louisbourg from its Foundation to its Fall* (London, 1918); G. C. Patterson, *Land Settlement in Upper Canada, 1783–1810* (Toronto, 1921); G. Bryce, *Remarkable History of the Hudson's Bay Company* (London, 1900); H. I. Cowan, *British Emigration to British North America* (Toronto, 1928); Chester Martin, *Lord Selkirk's Work in Canada* (Oxford, 1916); and C. D. Allin and G. M. Jones, *Annexation, Preferential Trade and Reciprocity* (Toronto, 1911) may be cited. Other early contributions to economic history include E. S. Moore, *Mineral Resources of Canada* (Toronto, 1929); R. Drummond, *Minerals and Mining in Nova Scotia* (Stellarton, 1918); B. E. Fernow, *Forest*

Conditions of Nova Scotia (Ottawa, 1912); and H. M. Whitford and R. D. Craig, *Forests of British Columbia* (Ottawa, 1918).

New editions of these and similar works are brought out from time to time. The University of Toronto's series Canadian University Paper Books, of which over 50 volumes have appeared, is an excellent source for some of the basic works.

In the field of economic geography Pierre Camu, E. P. Weeks, and Z. W. Sametz have assembled *Economic Geography of Canada*, Macmillan, Toronto, 1964. This is a study of the way man has applied his talents to the national resources of Canada. Numerous detailed maps, graphs, tables, and photographs are included. The work puts forward a proposal for the establishment of a 68-region economic geography system for Canada, and documents the resources of each region.

The Royal Commission on Canada's Economic Prospects was appointed by the Parliament of Canada in June 1955 to "inquire into and report upon the long-term prospects of the Canadian Economy". The Commission conducted hearings throughout the country and received 330 submissions from governments, organizations, and individuals in all types of economic activity. Its staff included research directors from universities and industry who guided the work as well as preparing individual studies.

The final report, Queen's Printer, Ottawa, 1957, begins with the background to Canada's changing prospects: the world environment, relations with the United States, international trade, and previous Canadian economic development. Next are chapters on the population growth and the probable future growth in particular industries. Productivity and estimated output and estimates of probable changes in the economic structure follow. Separate chapters analyse the supply of capital and foreign investment and regional problems in the Atlantic provinces and the Canadian north. Finally, the role of government policy in maintaining economic stability and promoting economic growth is outlined. Two of the appendixes deal with taxation of the oil and gas industry and municipal finance. Each chapter is amply supported with tables and charts of historical statistics with projections to 1980.

The studies themselves, numbering 33, were made either by the research staff or by independent specially commissioned organizations—banks, insurance companies, labour organizations, management consultants, chartered accountants, or business services. Almost half deal with individual industries, the others with labour problems, trade, finance and investment, and special regional problems. One charts Canada's economic growth from 1939 to 1955. Such diversity of sources and subjects has resulted in diversity of detail and length (10–700 pages each) but the studies are generally thorough and well-written, and many projections made for 1965 and later years are proving to be valid.

The Economic Council of Canada was established in 1963 under the chairmanship of Dr. John J. Deutsch to examine the Canadian economy and advise the Government on how to deal with specific problems such as unemployment, slow growth, and depressed areas. In the first annual review, *Economic Goals for Canada to 1970*, Queen's Printer, Ottawa, December 1964, certain basic objectives were defined and many fundamental questions posed. The five main areas under examination were: employment, economic growth, price stability, the balance of payments, and the problem of the equitable distribution of rising incomes. Questions arose regarding the long-term impact of computer technology on the Canadian economy, labour mobility, price stability—will it be achieved through responsible restraint on the part of both industry and labour or will strict government control be necessary? In this initial report the Council has "attempted to indicate the combination and balance of policies which would be necessary for the achievement of our goals in a free and predominantly private enterprise market economy". The central theme in the second annual review, Queen's Printer, Ottawa, December 1965, is the problem of manpower, and the goal is full employment together with the upgrading of Canadian income and education levels and the eventual elimination of regional disparities in productivity and economic growth.

Other works on Canada's current economic condition include the *Annual Report of the Bank of Canada*, Ottawa, published yearly, as well as the annual reports of the various chartered banks of Canada, the Toronto-Dominion, Royal, Canadian Imperial, Nova Scotia, and others. The Dominion Bureau of Statistics publishes the quarterly and annual *National Accounts, Income and Expenditure*, as well as other statistical bulletins on the various industries of Canada. The École des Hautes Études Commerciales, Service de documentation économique, Montreal, publishes *L'Actualité économique.* In each quarterly issue there is an up-to-the-minute review of the main economic activities and projects of the Province as well as general economic information. There are reviews of recent publications touching on all aspects of economics with particular regard to Canadian questions. There is an annual index. Two cumulated indexes for the years 1925–50 and 1950–60 have been published.

Labour

In the field of Canadian labour, Professor H. A. Logan has prepared *Trade Unions in Canada: their development and functioning*, Macmillan, Toronto, 1948. This is a thorough history of Canadian trade unionism, reviewing its early beginnings, its development industry by industry, the growth of national federations and congresses, with accounts of improvements in conditions of labour by legislation and of the special problem of French Canada.

H. D. Woods, Director of McGill University's Industrial Relations Centre, Montreal, and Professor Sylvia Ostry of the University of Montreal, have produced a study of Canadian labour legislation, *Labour Policy and Labour Economics in Canada*, Macmillan, 1962. This book provides provocative and challenging views on the merits of existing labour legislation and the question of government intervention in labour–management affairs.

The Canada Department of Labour, Economics, and Research Branch has published *Labour Organizations in Canada*, Queen's Printer, Ottawa, annually since 1911. This is a standard handbook of the labour organizations active in Canada. Size, basic structure, and leaders are given. Information includes a directory of organizations, officers, publications, and location of locals in Canada. Three sections cover: I, International and National Unions; II, Independent Local Unions; III, Central Labour Congresses and their Divisions. The same Department publishes the *Labour Gazette*, Queen's Printer, Ottawa, the official journal on industrial relations in Canada, monthly in both English and French. Feature articles treat such topics as trade unions, manpower, technological developments, poverty, and vocational training. Reports on older workers, employment of women, labour–management relations, certification and conciliation, Canadian and foreign labour law, the National Employment Service, and Unemployment Insurance Commission appear monthly. Statistical data, compiled by the Economics and Research Branch of the Department and by the Dominion Bureau of Statistics, is given for the labour force, labour income, prices, strikes, lockouts, and industrial accidents. Federal conciliation board reports, reasons for judgement of the Canada Labour Relations Board, and lists of government contracts, included in the *Labour Gazette* before 1966, are now issued separately.

A valuable work of reference is the *Handbook on Canadian Labour Law*, by Alfred C. Crysler, Carswell Co., Toronto, 1957. This book summarizes federal and provincial labour legislation and decisions of the courts respecting labour relations and trade unions. It has an excellent index.

Money and Banking

A. B. Jamieson's *Chartered Banking in Canada*, rev. edn., Ryerson, Toronto, 1955, is in two parts. Part I, Foundations and Development, is a compact historical outline of those elements of the development of Canadian banking which have a contemporary significance, emphasizing particularly the growth of Canadian banking legislation. This is information which cannot be found readily elsewhere. Specific information pertaining to amalgamations and failures, growth and resources, branches in operation, and similar statistics are in an appendix at the back of the book. Part II, Banking Practice, sets out for both the general reader and the banker a description and analysis of current banking practice, although no attempt is made to deal with monetary or banking theory. It "deals with the way in which banking is carried on in Canada, the different functions performed and with practices and principles which experience has shown it wise to follow and bear in mind". The work covers organization and administration, deposits, loans of all types (both personal and commercial), collateral securities, the analysis of financial statements, letters of credit, foreign exchange, clearing houses, losses, audits and inspections, and the Bank of Canada. A supplement contains the Revision of the Bank Act, 1954, and other legislation affecting banks.

E. P. Neufeld, *Money and Banking in Canada*, McClelland & Stewart, Toronto, 1964, No. 17 in the Carleton Library, contains historical documents and a commentary on the connection between the Canadian medium of exchange and the banking system. The editor has selected those events which he considered the major developments in the history of Canadian banking, and he has assembled documents, review articles, and contemporary comments that illustrated them. An introductory article aids the reader to place the separate developments in historical perspective. A useful brief general review of Canadian banking legislation from 1822 to 1944 is included as an appendix.

A further work of reference is *Canadian Money and Banking*, McGraw-Hill, Toronto, 1964, prepared by J. W. O'Brien. This is a readable survey of money and banking in Canada written by an economist from Sir George Williams University, Montreal. Divided into three sections it covers the principles of monetary and banking systems with specific reference to Canadian institutions, a short summary of Canadian banking history, and an explanation of monetary theory.

The Canadian Banker, Toronto, founded 1899, is a quarterly publication of news and articles dealing with matters of banking interest in Canada.

Business

In a nation that has steadily introduced more and more government control into the way of life of its citizens, the effects of such control have to be considered at the same time that one considers the role of business. In recent years the Canadian Government has adopted a number of policies that have permitted aspects of a free economy to continue, while at the same time there have been deliberate actions taken to ease the impact of foreign competition and the changing manpower situation in Canada itself.

One of the main areas of support offered by government to Canadian business has been tax and tariff policies to develop Canadian industry. Such tax incentives have released money not only for research, but for physical expansion and modernization of equipment. In the same way, every effort has been made by government to stimulate in business and industry an adequate rate of scientific and technological growth so that it can meet competition from industries abroad. This has been accomplished by close co-operation between private industry's research and development programmes and the Canadian Government's extensive public research establishments.

Finally, there has been provision by the Federal Government of more and more social capital in order to build up adequate services of public housing, transport, medical care, and education, particularly at the level of universities and adult manpower retraining.

The Income Tax Handbook, 1962–3, by Arthur W. Gilmour, DeBoo, Toronto, 1963, is a detailed and comprehensive guide written to assist the businessman, accountant, or student in interpreting the complex provisions of the Income Tax Act and its regulations.

The Canadian Tariff Act is constantly undergoing revisions, and a loose-leaf system is provided to persons wishing to be fully informed of changes. This is *The Customs Tariffs and Amendments with Index to Commodities*, published by the Department of

National Revenue, Customs and Excise Division, Ottawa, and available from them.

In order to keep up to date on the impact of governmental influence in Canadian business life, reference should be made to the monthly *Canadian Business*, established 1930, the official organ of the Canadian Chamber of Commerce. This magazine aims to inform and appraise readers within Canada and abroad on current economic problems in Canada. Permanent sections are world news, review of business and economic conditions in Canada, investments, and American reports. These sections are made up of brief retrospective commentaries reflecting the outstanding news items of the month. Articles cover a wide range of topics: commerce, banking, trade unions, biographical sketches, politics, and management. Discussions, letters, theoretical studies, and forecasts written by experts express different opinions on internal and external economic matters. Each issue contains some special material; business appointments, calendars of events, statistical tables, advice on salesmanship, government aid to small business, and other similar practical items.

A further source of information is the National Industrial Conference Board, New York, which regularly issues its *Canadian Studies*. The NICB is an independent non-profit research institution founded in the United States to study major aspects of the operation and environment of industry and responsibilities of business management. It claims that its "approach is objective; its methods are scientific; its findings are factual and thorough". Subscribing associates (4000 in North America and abroad) consist of business organizations, professional firms, trade associations, labour unions, universities, and government agencies; they constitute the sole financial support of the Board. The research staff of the Canadian office participates in all phases of its programme and deals with specific Canadian problem areas. Since 1959 it has published eight numbered and eleven unnumbered reports including *Problems and Policies in Canadian Manufacturing*, *New Patterns in Company-paid Moving Expenses in Canada*, and a *Directory of Canadian Labour Statistics*. Certain studies are repeated when warranted by changing conditions. All studies are well indexed in the excellent 10-year cumulative index of all NICB publications which appears each year.

Industrial Canada, established in 1900, is published monthly by the Canadian Manufacturers Association, Toronto. This periodical contains feature articles on a wide range of general management topics and Canadian industrial problems of interest to Canadian and foreign businessmen. Articles are all contributed and emanate from well-qualified industrial, university, and other sources, briefly described. General features (editorials, business barometer, showcase, trends, and events) appear in a majority of issues. "Buy Canadian news digests" and "New developments in Canadian manufacturing capability" are typical of feature articles. Briefly annotated publications from government and industry, a few book reviews, appointments, industrial news, and "Enterprise in action", a story on one Canadian company, appear regularly. Of particular value is the "Service portfolio"—sales tax rulings, trade developments, "Where in the world" (fairs and exhibits), industrial relations diary, and tariff news of all countries, indexed by author and subject.

The *Financial Post*, Maclean-Hunter, Toronto, is an outstanding financial newspaper, established 1907, which acts as an authoritative source of news, personal and general public views on commerce, industry, national affairs, and investment. It is regarded by many as the *Wall Street Journal* of Canada. Activities of selected Canadian companies, mines, and banks are reviewed in each issue, together with summaries of quarterly and annual reports and financial statements. Records of stock exchange transactions, dividends declared, bond quotations, mutual fund portfolios, annual meetings, all provide invaluable statistics and are used by investors, stock brokers, and executives across the country. Articles and editorial columns appraise the latest financial and political events, both domestic and foreign. Interesting material on diverse topics ranging from travel, health, and scientific research to production, credit, and demographic statistics is included. Practical miscellaneous news items such as appointments, opening of new plants, manufacturing ideas, positions vacant, new projects, opportunities in every section of business and industry, can be helpful for individuals as well as for companies.

Three basic business services are prepared each year by the *Financial Post*. They are the *Survey of Investment Funds*, the *Survey of Industrials* (Fig. 9), and the *Survey of Oils*. The *Survey of Investment Funds* gives detailed information on Canada's leading investment funds whose shares are owned by the public. It also lists the portfolios of several other large investment funds operated by professional investment managers, showing the changes made in the last year. It has been published since 1962. There are helpful comparisons on fund growth, management costs, and the results of various investment policies. There is useful background information on the present financial position of the funds, past development, dividend payments, management, and a calculation showing the fund's investor's profit or loss experience over varying periods of time as well as tables showing the changes net asset value per fund share over these same periods. There is a list of all the Canadian stocks in the portfolios covered by the survey. Under the name of each stock is a list of the funds that own the stock and shares held. The *Survey* covers open-end investment, specialized investment, balanced, common stock, bond, managed, specialty, trust company equity, closed-end investment, trust company equity pension, and life company equity pension funds. There is an alphabetical index by name of fund.

The *Survey of Industrials*, established 1926, is published annually and serves as a comprehensive handbook of Canadian companies. It is used mainly by investors, businessmen, and economists. Reviews of the companies include detailed data on capital stock, earnings, assets, liabilities, dividends, and debentures—information which provides a good summary of the firms' financial position. Addresses of head offices, top personnel, subsidiaries, plant locations, as well as nature of business and dates of annual meetings, are some of the important factual details which make this volume an invaluable accurate source book of company information. The alphabetical index is the key to all large and small

E

Morrison-Lamothe Bakery Ltd.

Head Off. — 95 Echo Drive, Ottawa. **Trans. Agents** — Guaranty Trust Co. of Canada, Ottawa. **Report Appeared** — Sept. 17 in 1965. **Meeting** — At call.

Company — (Dom. 1938). Owns and operates bakery with capacity for 400,000 1½ lb. loaves per week. Also operates catering service for restaurants and retail outlets in Ottawa. A subsidiary produces frozen foods.

Construction of new plant in Ottawa was started in 1964-65.

Directors — G. C. Morrison, pres.; G. W. McKendry, vice-pres. & gen. mgr.; Arthur Pigott, vice-pres.; D. G. Wilson, sec.-treas.; Mrs. A. C. Pigott, J. C. Lamothe, C. Lamothe, Ottawa.

Capital Stock*. — Author. Outstand. Par Pref. 6% cum.   50,000 sh.   50,000 sh. $10
Class A   300,000 sh.   nil   n.p.v.
Class B   100,000 sh.   100,000 sh.   n.p.v.
*At Feb. 27, 1965.

6% Pref. — Entitled to 6% (60c) per sh. p.a. cum. Redeem. at $11.

Cl. A and Cl. B rank equally except that Cl. A entitled to one vote per sh. and Cl. B to ten votes per sh.

Capital Changes — By S.L.P dated Nov. 25, 1964, author. and issued com. shs. reclassified as Cl. B shs., n.p.v.; and 300,000 Cl. A shs., n.p.v., created.

Dividends—Pref.: Entitled to 6% p.a. (60c) cum.; pd. regularly May and Nov. 1. **Class B.** (Com. prior to Nov., 1964): Present rate 20c per sh. p.a. pd. regularly May and Nov. 1, since May 1, 1961. Previous rate was 10c per sh. pd. annually Nov. 1, 1958-60 incl.

Funded Debt—7% **S.F. Debentures, Series A**—Dated Sept. 1, 1964; due Sept 1, 1984. Author. $2,500,000; issued and o/s

Viau Limited

Head Off. — 4945 Ontario St. E., Montreal. **Trans. Agents** — Administration & Trust Co., Montreal. **Report Appeared** — Apr. 25 in 1966. **Meeting** — May 5 in 1966.

Company — (Que., 1925). Mfrs. biscuits and confectionary. Factory at Montreal, warehouses at Montreal, Quebec, Ottawa-Hull, Toronto and Winnipeg.

Directors — Roger Viau, chm. & pres.; Guy Lanctôt, vice-pres. and gen. mgr.; Robert Viau, C. Melancon, Charles Viau, C. A. Geoffrion, Raymond Lanctôt, Montreal. **Sec.** — Abel Fafard. **Treas.** — J. R. Lamouche.

Capital Stock — Author. Outstand Par 1% Preferred 3,000,000 sh. 1,282,104 sh. $1
Common   400,000 sh.   233,108 sh. $2.40
Listed: VO, M.

Dividends—Pref.: 1c p.a. pd. regularly. **Common:** Rate 80c p.a. pd. Jan., Apr., July, Oct. 1. (Jan. 1964 pay omitted owing to strike, otherwise pd. regularly). Com. divds. declared in recent fiscal years have been as follows:

1951	$1.75+1.09	1961 .... {$0.75
1952	2.00+0.50	{10.60 + stk.*
1953-58 ...	2.00+1.00	1962-63 .... 0.60
1959	2.25	1964 .... 0.60
1960	3.00	1965-66 .... 0.80

§Following 4-for-1 split.
*8 1% Pref. shs. $1 par for each new com. sh. held.

VIAU LIMITED
BALANCE SHEET—MAIN ITEMS

As at Jan. 31:	1966	1965	1964
Cash & invests. ..	$485,984	$265,201	$421,132
Inventories	711,663	793,277	787,945
Total curr. assets	1,639,541	1,553,780	1,657,587
Fixed assets†	1,500,531	1,563,541	1,580,093
Total assets	3,161,973	3,119,222	3,239,581
Total curr. liab..	284,706	369,317	283,297
Capital stock	1,841,563	1,841,563	2,191,218
Contrib. surplus ..	79,529	79,529	79,529

Bowes Company Ltd.

Head Off. — 181 Carlaw Ave., Toronto. **Trans. Agents** — National Trust Co., Toronto. **Report Appeared** — In May in 1966. **Meeting** — May 19 in 1966.

Company — (Dom., 1919) Mfrs., importers and wholesalers of confectioners' and bakers' supplies. Factory in Toronto.

Directors — A. W. Baillie, pres.; G. E. Sweet, sec.-treas.; J. W. Walker, Toronto; T. G. Drew-Brook, Hornby, Ont.; Alexander Petrie, B. B. Green, Oakville, Ont.; T. H. Bowes, Winnipeg.

Capital Stock — Author. Outstand. Par 1% Pref. 3,000,000 sh. *137,628 sh. $1
Common   900,000 sh.   605,035 sh. n.p.v.
*After giving effect to redemption on Mar. 28, 1966, of 50% of o/s pref. shs. (without regard to fractions) under offering made to shareholders of record Mar. 18, 1966.
Listed—BOW, T (com. only).

Capital Change—In May, 1965, com. stock split on 5-for-1 basis.

Dividends—Pref.—1c p.a. pd. annually in Dec. **Com. (new)**—Annual divd. of 20c a sh. r.d. May 26, 1966. **Extra** 10c pd. Dec. 29, 1965. **Com. (old)**—Prior to 5-for-1 split, $1 per sh. pd. annually in May, 1957-65 incl.; 50c pd. in 1955-56 incl. Extra 50c a sh. pd. in 1958-64 incl.

Subsidiaries—Chocolate Products Ltd., Toronto. Manufactures chocolate syrups and syrups for soft drinks. Wholly owned.

Watt & Scott Ltd. — Food product distributors. Wholly owned. Owns all o/s shs. of Watt & Scott (Toronto) Ltd.

McNair Products Co. Ltd., Toronto. Wholly owned. Packages and sells dried fruit, nuts and cereal products.

F. Archibald Brokerage Ltd., Winni-

FIG. 9. *Financial Post Survey of Industrials, 1966.*

enterprises, which are arranged by the type of business. Private companies are omitted, but subsidiaries of foreign corporations are included provided they are listed on a Canadian Stock Exchange. Price range of Canadian industrial stocks for several years, stock exchange commission rates, both in table forms, can be readily consulted by laymen or executives. Each issue is a new appraisal of current industrial developments in Canada.

The *Survey of Oils*, established 1960, is useful for reviewing oil and natural gas companies, both active and inactive, oil royalties, maps, production tables, and price ranges. The volume contains an up-to-date review of the oil industry; both present developments and probable resources for the information of both industrialists and students of economics. It is authoritative and well-organized in its presentation, comprising a survey of companies operating in the oil and gas industry, details on property locations, drilling operations and results, production volumes and reserves, capitalization, finances, dividends, royalty liabilities, names of officials and directors. An extensive map section outlines individual oil fields and present holdings in many exploration areas. Tables show annual price range of listed stocks over the past 8 years.

The *Canadian Trade Index* (Fig. 10), Canadian Manufacturers Association, Toronto, has been published since 1900. With over 12,000 listings, this directory is a primary guide to Canadian manufacturing firms and to their products. Companies are listed alphabetically and information provided includes locations of all branch offices, plants, divisions, representatives, parent company, names of top executives, and trade names. The classified list of products indexes more than 10,000 items arranged by keyword with the names of manufacturers who are making them. In addition to the detailed directory section a substantial chapter on export gives brief practical advice on the methods of foreign trade, outlines the export services of the Federal Government, and lists trade commissioners abroad. Useful information is found in advertisements, in the geographical breakdown of companies, and in the French-language index. Businessmen, manufacturers' representatives,

COLOURS, Ink, Printing Ink, etc.
★Dominion Colour Corporation Limited, Toronto, Ont.

COLOURS, Mortar, Cement, Plaster, Stucco.
Ensign Industrials Ltd., St. Catharines, Ont.
Grace, W. R., & Co. of Canada Ltd., Grace Construction Materials Division, Scarborough, Ont.
★Master Builders Co. Limited, The, Toronto, Ont.
★Northern Pigment Co., Limited, Toronto, Ont. (Adv. page 59).

COLOURS, Plastic.
★Dominion Colour Corporation Limited, Toronto, Ont. (and rubber).
★FERRO ENAMELS (CANADA), LIMITED, Oakville, Ont. (Adv. page 132).
★Korlin Limited, Stratford, Ont.
Resco Chemicals & Colours Limited, Toronto, Ont.

COLOURS, Pulped in Water, for Paper Coating.
★Dominion Colour Corporation Limited, Toronto, Ont.

COLOURS, Show Card.
★Carter, H. J., Limited, Toronto, Ont.
Carter's Ink Co. of Canada, Ltd., The, Montreal, Que.
Peerless Products (1954) Ltd., Vancouver, B.C.
★Poole, J. E., Company Limited, Toronto, Ont.
Reardon Company, Ltd., The, Montreal, Que.
★Reeves, L. A., Ink Company Limited, Toronto, Ont.

COLOURS, Water.
Reardon Company Ltd., The, Montreal, Que.
Wesco Paints Limited, Clarkson, Ont.

COLOURWORK, Fired on Glass.
Cutler Brands, Limited, Toronto, Ont.
★De Paoli Industries, Windsor, Ont. (also screen-processed).

COLUMBIUM CONCENTRATES.
★St. Lawrence Columbium and Metals Corporation.

COMBINES, (Combined Harvester and Thresher).
Agristeel Fabricators Ltd., Minnedosa, Man. (Cabs).
★Cockshutt Farm Equipment of Canada Limited, Brantford, Ont. (Self-propelled).
Diamond Manufacturing Company Limited, Claresholm, Alta. (Chaff savers).
Fibro Industries Ltd., Regina, Sask. (Cabs only).
★International Harvester Co. of Canada Limited, Hamilton, Ont. (for cereal, grain and rice).
★Massey-Ferguson Industries Limited, Toronto, Ont.
McCoy-Renn Mfg. Ltd., Calgary, Alta. (Nylon tine pick-up attachment).
★Versatile Manufacturing Ltd., Winnipeg, Man. (Pull type and self propelled).

COMBS, Curry, Rubber.
Griffith, G. L., & Sons Div., Federal-Mogul (Canada) Ltd., Stratford, Ont.

COMBS, Dressing and Fine. See also Toiletware.
BOW Plastics Limited, Montreal North, Que.
Dent & Vallis (Canada) Limited, Toronto, Ont.
★Dominion Comb & Novelty Co., The, Warwick, Que.
★F. & H. Plastics Limited, Scarborough, Ont.
Lord Plastics, St. Jacques, Que.
★Midland Flambeau Limited, Midland, Ont.
★Payge Manufacturing Ltd., Montreal, Que.
★Tilco Plastics Limited, Peterborough, Ont.
★Wintrob, M., & Sons, Canada Limited, Toronto, Ont. (Pocket).

COMBS, Fancy. See also Combs, Dressing and Fine.
BOW Plastics Limited, Montreal North, Que.
Kay-Cee Products Ltd., Montreal, Que. (Aluminum).
Solo Products Limited, Montreal, Que.
Tilco Plastics Limited, Peterborough, Ont.
★Wintrob, M., & Sons, Canada Limited, Toronto, Ont.

COMBUSTION CONTROL EQUIPMENT.
★Bailey Meter Company Limited, Pointe Claire, Que.

FIG. 10. *Canadian Trade Index*, 1966.

exporters, and importers keep this compact reference book for verifying, searching, checking names, addresses, and products. Each year information is brought up to date making it a dependable and accurate handbook for its users.

The *Canadian Mines Handbook*, Northern Miner Press, Toronto is an annual handbook of Canadian mining companies established since 1932 and summarizes their activities for the year. It gives a review of the Canadian metal production statistics. There are maps showing the location of the various principal mining areas in Canada, and an index by company. Also of value is the *Financial Post Survey of Mines*, Toronto, issued since 1925 on an annual basis.

As an aid to the identification of various associations in Canada, *Canadian Business* published a *Directory of Business, Trade and Professional Associations in Canada, 1961–2*, 2nd edn., Montreal, 1961. This directory contains alphabetical listings for approximately 3500 associations and societies together with a subject index which classifies them according to activity or service. In addition there are lists of some 1400 boards of trade, chambers of commerce, and junior chambers of commerce in Canada arranged by province and then alphabetically by place. The alphabetical listings give the address and the name of the chief officer of the group. The list contains national, regional, provincial, and local associations, with special emphasis on the larger metropolitan areas, and includes labour federations and councils, major civil service associations, research councils, and marketing boards.

The *Financial Times* is a Montreal-based financial weekly established 1912, devoted predominantly to the field of banking, trade, taxation, and investment. The latest monetary events in Canada, the United States, and around the world are covered. In particular, stock exchange records, mutual funds, bond quotations, earnings, dividends, high, low, and average prices of securities, are published each week in comprehensive table form. Government actions, export, import opportunities, mining, and manufacturing developments are summarized and commented on in brief or in feature-length articles. It is useful for investors, directors, bankers, manufacturers, small exporters, and many others in business.

Two periodicals which provide information on management matters are *Plant Administration and Maintenance*, Toronto, published monthly since 1941, and *Quebec Industrial*, Montreal, established 1946. The *Canadian Underwriter*, Toronto, established 1934 and issued semi-monthly, deals with matters in the field of insurance. *Office Administration*, Toronto, established 1955, is a monthly magazine dealing with the application of administrative techniques to Canadian business.

Marketing and Advertising

Edward J. Fox and David S. R. Leighton are editors of *Marketing in Canada*, a publication sponsored by the American Marketing Association and published by Irwin, Homewood, Illinois, 1958. It consists of a series of essays divided into seven broad parts —history and background, regional markets, distribution channels, auxiliary marketing services, government regulation, managing the sales force, and selected case histories. An appendix contains a useful guide to sources of marketing information. Although the data is somewhat outdated, the book contains considerable reference material of value.

The Institute of Canadian Advertising, which is the national organization of Canada's 200 advertising agencies, is involved in many projects aimed at improving the effectiveness of Canadian advertising. It publishes *Stimulus*, a monthly magazine about advertising for those inside and outside the business.

Canadian Advertising, published bi-monthly since 1928 by Maclean-Hunter, Toronto, contains a comprehensive listing of advertising agencies, Canadian printed media which accept advertising, radio, and television stations by provinces, domestic and international media representatives, and other directory and statistical items related to the Canadian advertising business. Originally designed to serve as a media guide for advertisers and advertising agencies, still its primary function, *Canadian Advertising* is also used by a wide range of interested groups and individuals as a source of current detailed directory information about Canadian periodical publications. Included are daily newspapers, weekly newspapers, weekend supplements, foreign language publications, consumer magazines, farm papers, and business papers, which includes financial, professional, and trade journals. Each entry contains complete directory information, regional market data where applicable, a full listing of advertising rates and related technical information, personnel roster, sales representatives in other cities, and a recent circulation tabulation. Radio and television station listings include similar information—location (studio and transmitter), wave, power and time, operating schedule, advertising rates, personnel, and representatives.

Marketing, Maclean-Hunter, Toronto, is Canada's national weekly newspaper for business, advertising, and sales executives which has appeared since 1908. By reporting recent developments in advertising, selling, and media evaluation, it has become an important source of market, sales, and merchandising information for advertisers and their agencies. It includes feature articles, advertising agency reports, appointments, a calendar of weekly events, national expenditure, radio and television expenditures, and classified advertisements. Special issues each year are devoted to such areas as sales and advertising forecasts, conventions and exhibits, media reports, area market reports, and the allied interests of packaging and graphics.

Canadian Market Data, Maclean-Hunter, Toronto, appears yearly and provides an analysis of Canadian industries—national and regional, their current and growth trends, buying pattern, and the publications that appear in connection with each industry.

A number of guides to specialists in the business world are published. One, such as the *Directory of Canadian Chartered Accountants*, is produced annually by the Canadian Institute of Chartered Accountants, Toronto. It gives officers and council members and the list of affiliates of each provincial institute in ten alphabetical arrangements. Appended is a geographical list of firms of chartered accountants and practitioners in Canada.

Transportation

Transportation in Canada is a rapidly changing affair. New methods of public and private transportation are constantly being developed as the increase in the Canadian population renders older methods of transportation inadequate. Sea, rail, road, airline, bus, dog sled, and hydrofoil transport are all employed in Canada as well as many other forms. Pipelines, aerial tramways, and helicopter services are some of the newer methods that have come into being. One basic work of reference is *Economics of Canadian Transportation* by A. W. Currie, 2nd edn., University of Toronto Press, 1959. This volume summarizes the state of development of transportation services and deals with attendant problems such as labour, freight rates, government ownership, and commodity movements.

Because transportation is a basic feature of the Canadian economy, there are many accounts of individual forms of transportation. Especially valuable in identifying these is G. P. de T. Glazebrook's *A History of Transportation in Canada*, Ryerson Press, Toronto, 1938. This has been reprinted in 2 volumes by the Carleton Library, 1964, with a new preface by the author. Volume 1 covers the history of transportation from the French régime to the first railway era and 1867. Volume 2 deals with Canadian transportation from 1856 to the late 1930's.

H. A. Innis's *A History of the Canadian Pacific Railway*, London, appeared in 1923. More recently A. W. Currie has prepared *The Grand Trunk Railway of Canada*, University of Toronto Press, 1957. This railway played an important part in the economic development of Canada from 1852, when it was first considered, until 1919 when it was acquired by the Government of Canada. It formed part of the financial link between Britain, the United States, and Canada, and gave Canadians one of their earliest experiences with "big business". The volume documents the progress of negotiations for construction, the building, operation, and subsequent amalgamation of the Grand Trunk with other railway lines. G. R. Stevens's *Canadian National Railways*, vols.

1–2, Clarke Irwin, Toronto, 1960–2, is the history of a colony and a nation in the years 1836–1922, during which time 214 individual railway companies and 60 related concerns (communications, shipping, accommodations, land sales, and colonization) were absorbed by the company, thereby forming a national transportation network of enormous power and importance. It became a national institution which today exerts a very considerable influence on all phases of Canadian political and economic life. Drawings, photographs, maps, and tables illustrating these carefully documented volumes add to their value as a major reference source in the field of Canadian economic history.

The development of automobile transportation and its effects are considered in J. C. Leosard's *Transportation in Canada*, Queen's Printer, Ottawa, 1956. Subways, buses, and taxis have all increased the urban transportation problems, and greatly changed the nature of Canadian cities. *The Story of Canadian Roads*, by Edwin C. Guillet, University of Toronto Press, 1966, is a comprehensive account of the growth of surface routes from portage trails snaking their way through the wilderness to super-highways carrying the raw materials and produce of an industrial nation. Canada's roads are described in some detail in this well-illustrated volume which contains nearly 200 sketches, engravings, paintings, and photographs, most of them contemporary, gathered from archives and libraries across the country. Street railways were popular in Canada at the turn of this century. The Canadian Railroad Historical Association, Box 22, Station B, Montreal, was founded in 1932 and incorporated in 1951 in order to provide a meeting ground for those interested in various aspects of the early history of transportation in Canada. It publishes a *Bulletin* and has aided in the distribution of such studies as Omer S. A. Lavalee's *The Montreal City Passenger Railway Company*, 1961. The Upper Canada Railroad Society *Newsletter*, Marine Museum, Toronto, includes brief essays on a wide variety of topics dealing with railways in Upper Canada since 1851.

One of Canada's largest transportation endeavours is described by Lionel Chevrier, *The St. Lawrence Seaway*, Macmillan, 1959.

E*

This volume written by the man who was president of the Seaway from 1954 to 1957 and associated with the project for over 12 years, covers the entire history of the project. It is well illustrated with maps and pictures of each of the separate sections of the Seaway, and has an index.

William R. Willoughby has written *The St. Lawrence Waterway: a study in politics and diplomacy*, University of Wisconsin Press, Madison, 1961. This is a scholarly account of the efforts from 1700 to improve the navigation of the Great Lakes–St. Lawrence waterway, particular emphasis being placed on the many intricate negotiations relative to construction of the present seaway during the years since 1920.

One of the leading periodicals dealing with water transport, *Canadian Shipping and Marine Engineering News*, Toronto, was established in 1911 and appears monthly. It provides current information on events in the Canadian shipping world. A further guide to shipping is the *Canadian Ports and Seaway Directory*, Gardenvale, Quebec, which since 1934 has provided an annual alphabetical guide to Canadian ports and the activities and persons associated with shipping and marine transport. It is a useful manual for mariners, transportation, and shipping companies. Pertinent data includes location, port authorities, approaches, pilotage, accommodations, available services, names of marine firms, and agents. Detailed information about the St. Lawrence Seaway such as charges, tolls, and navigation facilities, has been featured since 1962.

Broadcasting and Postal Services

The official Canadian government organizations concerned with broadcasting are the Board of Broadcast Governors and Radio Canada/the Canadian Broadcasting Corporation (CBC), with headquarters in Ottawa. The CBC is a publicly owned organization operating in both French and English to provide national broadcasting service in radio and, since 1952, in television.

Since broadcasting is under federal government jurisdiction, there are various reports of special parliamentary committees on broadcasting, the most recent being the *Report of the Committee on Broadcasting, 1965*, Queen's Printer, Ottawa, 1965. This document deals with the present state of both the public and private sectors in Canadian broadcasting. It describes the existing programme arrangements and future possibilities in both public and private broadcasting, and includes a section on financing. There is a detailed index particularly with regard to the various services provided by the CBC.

The Canadian Association of Broadcasters, Toronto, represents most of the private broadcasting companies, both radio and television. It was founded in 1926 and reorganized in 1936. With it are linked several regional associations of broadcasters: WAB—Western Association of Broadcasters; CCBA—Central Canada Broadcasters' Association; ACRTF—Association Canadienne de Radio et Television de Langue Française; and AAB—The Atlantic Association of Broadcasters. The CTV Television Network Ltd. is a private Canadian television network with headquarters in Toronto.

News of broadcasting and professional articles are to be found in two trade papers, *The Canadian Broadcaster*, established 1942, and *Canadian Sponsor*, established 1959, both published in Toronto.

The Official Postal Guide, Queen's Printer, Ottawa, has been published annually since 1854. It is the official guide to post office names and addresses, and is presently printed by computer in loose leaf form as *List of Post Offices in Canada*.

Patrick and Mary Douglas have prepared *Canada's Postage Stamps*, McClelland & Stewart, Toronto, 1964. This book gives a detailed account of Canadian postage stamps, including a postal history, and the background and philatelic characteristics of every issue from the first Province of Canada stamps in 1851 to the present. There is a bibliography and glossary of stamp-collecting terms.

CHAPTER 6

Language

APART from the few vocabularies appearing in the accounts of early explorers and the requirements of the fur trade, interest in the Indian and Eskimo languages in Canada originally centred mainly on the use of these languages in Christianizing and educating the native races. From the mid eighteenth century translations of biblical texts and devotional manuals in Indian languages for the use of French and later English missionaries were published. By the third quarter of the nineteenth century, various works on the languages themselves were beginning to appear.

Father Albert Lacombe, OMI, prepared the *Dictionnaire de la langue des Cris*, Beauchemin, Montreal, 1874, and the Rev. Silas T. Rand compiled a *Dictionary of the Language of the Micmac Indians*, Nova Scotia Printing Co., Halifax, 1888. Father J. A. Cuoq issued the *Lexique de la langue iroquoise*, Chapleau, Montreal, 1882, having published at an earlier date various studies on the Iroquois language. A *Cheap and Concise Dictionary of the Ojibway and English Languages* in two parts, *English–Ojibway* and *Ojibway–English*, appeared in a second edition in 1912, International Colportage Mission, Toronto.

For over 100 years the Eskimo language has been a source of study by Canadians and others. In 1925 Rev. E. J. Peck produced *Eskimo–English Dictionary*, the General Synod of the Church of England in Canada, Hamilton, as well as an *Eskimo Grammar*, Department of Interior, Ottawa, 1919, reprinted 1931. This latter volume was issued by Maurice S. Flint as *Revised Eskimo Grammar*, Ottawa, 1954. Recently, Arthur Thibert, OMI, has prepared a *Dictionnaire, Français–Esquimau–Français*, University of Ottawa,

1955; and an *English–Eskimo, Eskimo–English Dictionary*, rev. edn., Ottawa, 1958. Both these works contain practically all of the words commonly used by Canadian Eskimos.

In the past 50 years major attention has been on English and French. Jean-Paul Vinay, in co-operation with Pierre Daviault and Henry Alexander, edited *The Canadian Dictionary, French–English, English–French*, McClelland & Stewart, 1962, which was an attempt to present the combined results of research in both languages. This dictionary, prepared in the Centre de recherches lexicographiques de l'Université de Montréal, includes, in both English and French, those words and phrases that are uniquely Canadian, as well as containing all the words normally found in a dictionary of this type. It does not concern itself with regional dialects, but with the terminology peculiar to the French and English spoken throughout Canada.

A valuable part of this work is the preliminary section, especially the *Notes on the Phonology of Canadian French* and the *Notes sur la phonologie de l'Anglo-Canadien*. The editors point out that the distinctive features of Canadian French are not numerous when one considers the time and space separation from France. They also call attention to the middle-of-the-road quality of the present-day pronunciation of both English and French. The English pronunciation guide is based on linguistic studies in three densely populated areas—Montreal, Toronto and southern Ontario, and Vancouver.

This dictionary has attempted to establish for the first time a Canadian standard of spelling, pronunciation, and correct usage.

Louis Alexandre Bélisle's *Dictionnaire général de la langue française au Canada* (Fig. 11), Bélisle Editeur, Quebec, 1957, was prepared by Mr. Bélisle of the Société du Parler Français au Canada and contains over 50,000 articles and 3000 illustrations. It is based on the dictionary of Littré, but has been supplemented with words from Larousse, Quillet, Simon, and other works. For each word, several acceptable usages may be given, each with an explanation, definition, and example. A special feature is that

French-Canadian usage is marked by the symbol of a fleur-de-lis along with the literary French equivalent, and an example, e.g. châssis (fleur-de-lis), fenêtre; *régarder par le châssis*. By this method, Mr. Bélisle has identified nearly 5000 popular French-Canadian usages which the Academy in France does not acknowledge. Many of the words first appeared in the *Glossaire du parler français au Canada* published by the Société du Parler Français au Canada, Quebec, in 1930. Other preliminary works on the subject are Sylva Clapin, *Dictionnaire canadien-français, ou lexique glossaire des mots, expressions . . .*, Beauchemin, Montreal, 1902, and Narcisse-B. Dionne, *Le Parler populaire des canadiens-français*, Laflamme, Quebec, 1909.

The illustrations are plentiful, and include examples of Canadian usages and Canadian objects, e.g. *Canot d'écorce*, a birch bark basket.

The editor has taken great pains to incorporate the popular usage of many French words into his dictionary. He has also included many words that are passing out of the language, so that the dictionary has an important historical value. On the matter of anglicisms, the editor considers that many of the English words adopted in French Canada should have the same status as other English words adopted in France. For example, *ploguer*, to plug, from the English *plug* is considered by Mr. Bélisle to be as acceptable in French as *redingote* from the English *riding coat*. This view has met with some criticism in Canada.

Because this dictionary covers so many popular usages, as distinct from slang, it gives an accurate picture of colloquial usage in French Canada, although this usage is rapidly disappearing. The language of French-Canadian radio and television has affected popular speech, especially in urban areas. At the same time radio has spread popular French-Canadian terms throughout Canada. This is particularly noticeable in humour and stories, where much of the point is based on the usage of terms peculiar to French Canada contrasted with usage elsewhere.

A work of some interest is the *Petit dictionnaire du "Joual" au français* by Augustine Turenne, Édition de l'Homme, Montreal, etc.+ Four à réverbère, construction en maçonnerie pour la fusion des métaux dans laquelle la voûte réfléchit la très haute température qu'on y entretient.+ Four électrique, four chauffé par un ou plusieurs arcs voltaïques.+ Four crématoire, voy. crématoire.+ Four à poulet, endroit clos où l'on entretient une température suffisante pour faire éclore les œufs.+ Faire four, se disait des comédiens qui refusaient de jouer, quand la recette ne couvrait pas les frais.+ Aujourd'hui, se dit d'un comédien ou de tout autre qui échoue, d'un livre, d'une entreprise qui ne réussit pas.+ On dit dans le même sens: c'est un four.+ Prov. Vous viendrez cuire à mon four, vous aurez besoin de moi, et je me vengerai.+ Ce n'est pas pour vous que le four chauffe, la chose, l'affaire n'est pas pour vous.

Four électrique.

fourbe (ital. furbo) adj. Qui a recours, pour tromper, à des moyens odieux.+ N.m. et f. Un fourbe.

fourbe n.f. Caractère du fourbe; habitude de fourber: la fourbe n'est le jeu que des petites âmes, Corn.+ Acte de fourber: sa fourbe fut bientôt découverte, Boss.

fourber v.a. Tromper en fourbe: oui, oui, fourber un fourbe est une œuvre louable, Destouches.+ Absol. Prendre plaisir à fourber sans dessein, Corn.

fourberie n.f. Action de fourber.+ Par extens. Penchant à fourber.

fourbi n.m. Objets divers: il a empaqueté tout le fourbi et s'en est allé.+ On dit aussi fourniment, en ce sens.

fourbir (anc. h. all. furban) v.a. Polir par le frottement, en parlant d'ustensiles de fer, de cuivre, et des armes.+ Se fourbir, v.pr. Être fourbi.+ Se fourbir, se dit de cuirassiers ou autres qui nettoient leur armure.

se séparent.✲ Enfourchure; partie du corps qui est entre les deux cuisses: il a reçu un coup de pied dans la fourche.+ Bifurcation.

fourché, ée adj. Qui fait la fourche, qui se bifurque: pied fourché; chemin fourché.+ En blas. Croix fourchée, celle dont les branches sont terminées par trois pointes.+ Pied fourché, bureau où l'on payait les droits d'entrée sur le bétail qui a le pied fendu.

fourchée n.f. La quantité de fumier, de foin, de fourrage qu'on enlève d'un coup avec une fourche.

fourche-fière n.f. Fourche à deux dents longues, aiguës et solides.

Fourchettes.

fourcher v.n. Faire la fourche: un arbre qui fourche.+ Être bifurqué: le chemin fourchait.+ Fig. Cette famille, cette race n'a point fourché, elle n'a formé qu'une seule branche.+ Fig. La langue fourche, quand elle prononce un mot pour un autre.+ Se fourcher, v.pr. Prendre une disposition fourchue.+ Se bifurquer.

fourchet n.m. Maladie inflammatoire du pied des moutons.+ Fourche à deux fourchons.+ Endroit où une branche se divise.

fourchetée n.f. Ce qu'on peut prendre en une seule fois avec une fourchette.✲ Ce qu'on peut prendre en une seule fois avec une fourche: une fourchetée de paille.

fourchette (dim. de fourche) n.f. Ustensile de table à trois ou quatre dents dont on se sert pour prendre les morceaux dans son assiette.+ Grande fourchette, la fourchette à découper.+ Déjeuner à la fourchette, manger de la viande en déjeunant.+ Fig. et famil. On dit aussi: une bonne fourchette, un homme qui mange bien. Il a un joli coup de fourchette.+ La fourchette du père Adam, se dit par plaisanterie quand on prend avec les doigts ce qui se mange ordinairement avec une fourchette.+ Au hasard de la fourchette, se disait de ces établissements où l'on plongeait la fourchette dans le pot pour un sou, avec droit de garder ce qu'on amenait, et fig. sans choix, sans discernement.+ Sorte de pieu fourchu dont les arquebusiers se servaient pour appuyer leur arme en tirant.+ En mécan. Organe servant à manœuvrer un embrayage ou à déplacer une courroie d'une poulie folle à une poulie motrice ou vice versa.+ Le petit os divisé en deux branches

FIG. 11. Dictionnaire général de la langue français au Canada.

1962. The distinctive way of speaking French by many Canadians has been termed "Joual" (from their pronunciation of the word *cheval*). This book is a glossary of "Joual" words and expressions with their French equivalents. The arrangement is alphabetic under topics, e.g. Alimentation, Armée, Cuisine, Voyage, etc. It is the author's purpose to discourage the use of "Joual" and to promote the substitution of better French.

Words are judged objectionable for a variety of reasons: because they are English (crew, newsreel, haircut), because they are anglicized (Discompte, réparage, liste des vins), because they are gallicized (bitcher, watcher, pitcheur), or although they are French, their original meaning has changed (baraque, tranche, col). There is no index and before locating a word its subject must be defined first.

Gaston Dulong has prepared the *Bibliographie linguistique du Canada français*, Presses de l'Université Laval, Quebec, 1966, which continues and brings up to date an earlier work by Geddes and Rivard, *Bibliographie du parler français au Canada*, 1906. This more recent work lists all articles and books that have appeared which contain any references to the syntax, vocabulary, structure, and pronunciation of the French language in Canada.

The Société du Parler Français au Canada has carried on many studies and investigations in the use of French in Canada and has published the results of its inquiries. A comprehensive account of work done is *Études sur le parler français au Canada*. Since then many other bodies have shown concern over the French spoken in Canada. One organization is described by Victor Barbeau in *L'Académie canadienne-française*, 2nd edn., Atelier de Pierre des Marais, Montreal, 1963. The Académie Canadienne-française was founded in 1944 with the object of serving and upholding the French language and culture in Canada. In this study, first published in 1960 and revised 3 years later, M. Barbeau, the founder of the Academy, examines its role in Canadian intellectual life and history.

Particularly useful is a section on the twenty-four Academicians. There is a full-page photograph of each, brief biographical data, and a bibliography of published works of each.

The rules of the Academy, a list of award winners, and a full bibliography of publications complete this detailed study.

Of interest also is the Office de la Langue Française, Quebec, under the Quebec's Department of Cultural Affairs. The purpose of this Office is to work toward the correction and the enrichment of the spoken and written language in the Province of Quebec.

The Canadian Broadcasting Corporation has published a *Guide to the Pronunciation of Canadian Place-names*, rev. edn., Toronto, Canadian Broadcasting Corporation, 1959, 32 pp. The main purpose of this guide is to enable CBC announcers to pronounce place-names that occur in news bulletins without giving offence to listeners who know places mentioned, but it is of use to teachers, students, and members of the general public interested in using the correct pronunciation of more difficult Canadian place-names. The system of indicating pronunciation is one of simple transliteration; stress is indicated by accent placed after the syllable to be accented. In cases where scholarly opinion about pronunciation is at variance with general usage, the latter has been adopted.

A useful guide to Canadian language and usage is the volume by Robert Hamilton, *Canadian Quotations and Phrases*, published originally by McClelland & Stewart, Toronto, in 1952, but reissued in a paperback edition in 1965. This book was designed primarily as a guide to what Canadians have said about themselves in the past, about things Canadian, and on subjects distinctively Canadian. It includes quotations by both Canadian and non-Canadian writers, historians, speakers, and politicians. There are phrases from such varied sources as Sir John A. Macdonald and Walt Whitman to Sir Winston Churchill. Covering the whole period from the sixteenth century to the time of publication, selected passages illustrate the full flavour of Canada's life and people. Quotations such as Stephen Leacock's "In Canada we have enough to do keeping up with two spoken languages without trying to invent slang, so we just go right ahead and use English for literature, Scotch for sermons, and American for conversations", demonstrate the Canadian characteristics both in politics and culture. The work is arranged under broad topics beginning with "Ability", continuing to "Montreal, Que.", and ending with "Yukon". The index has no cross-references, but is an alphabetical listing of those whose quotations are found in the work.

The latest attempt to deal with the question of Canada's founding languages and cultures is to be found in the *Report of the Royal Commission on Bilingualism and Biculturalism*, Queen's Printer, Ottawa, 1967. This report summarizes more than 1300 individual briefs from individuals and groups across Canada which were presented to the Commission in 1964 and 1965. In addition, separate studies were made by the research staff of the Commission on such topics as Canadian education, family life, employment, economic development, technical training, and a wide range of topics. The report indicates the need for more effective communication in both of Canada's major languages as well as in other languages in order to achieve the growth and development that the physical resources of the country make possible.

CHAPTER 7

Science in Canada

Scientific Research

A profound transformation of the way of life of Canadians has been brought about by scientific developments of the twentieth century. Canadian science has shared in scientific discoveries that have taken place in other countries, and scientists within Canada have made many contributions. The impact of scientific development in Canada may be best illustrated by the fact that in 1980 it is expected that the Ontario Hydroelectric Power Commission will require 20 million kilowatts capacity, and of this, only 6 million kilowatts will be provided by water power, once the great source of industrial and domestic energy in Canada. The remainder will be provided by nuclear power through the use of Canadian natural uranium as fuel and heavy water as a moderator.

In the development of metal alloys, electron microscopes, disease-resistant grains, and many other products, the Canadian scientist has materially changed the living standard of his fellow Canadians.

Scientific research in Canada is taking place in government corporations, in universities in every province, in industry, and private research associations. Postgraduate enrolment in science and engineering faculties in Canadian universities has gone up from less than 600 students in 1950 to more than 3000 in 1966. Expansion of science departments in Canadian universities has increased greatly in the 1960's, and the end of the increase is not in sight.

Space technology and astrophysical exploration is being shared in Canada with the programmes of the United States and the

Soviet Union. Since 1956 world congresses on entomology, crystallography, geology and geophysics, genetics, physics, botany, and many other subjects have been held in Canada. The American Association for the Advancement of Science and various international organizations such as the member bodies of the International Council of Scientific Unions have also met here.

All of this activity has its direct effect on Canadian scientific research. In 1966 the Government of Canada established a Science Council consisting of representatives from the universities, government organizations, private organizations, and industry. The purpose of this Council is to act as the national advisory body for the organization and development of scientific work. Its annual report, Queen's Printer, Ottawa, 1967, indicates the functions that it is carrying out.

The National Research Council, Ottawa, established in 1917, conducts research and publishes the following: *Canadian Journal of Biochemistry*, monthly; *Canadian Journal of Botany*, monthly; *Canadian Journal of Chemistry*, semi-monthly; *Canadian Journal of Earth Sciences*, bi-monthly; *Canadian Journal of Microbiology*, bi-monthly; *Canadian Journal of Physics*, monthly; *Canadian Journal of Physiology and Pharmacology*, bi-monthly; and *Canadian Journal of Zoology*, bi-monthly.

To ensure Canadian scientific progress, the Council maintains a balance between fundamental and applied research. This is done in a wide range of fields in the various divisions: Building Research, Mechanical Engineering, National Aeronautical Establishment, Radio and Electrical Engineering, Pure Chemistry, Applied Chemistry, Pure Physics, Applied Physics, Biosciences, Radiation Biology, all in Ottawa; the Atlantic Regional Laboratory at Halifax, Nova Scotia, and the Prairie Regional Laboratory at Saskatoon, Saskatchewan. However, this Research Council did not include medicine, agriculture, or geology and geophysics, and separate organizations exist to co-ordinate and finance scientific research in these fields.

An important scientific agency is Atomic Energy of Canada Limited (AECL), a government corporation that has the responsibility for much of the Canadian work in the nuclear energy field. The Chalk River Nuclear Laboratories of AECL in Ontario form the largest establishment. The work there covers basic research and engineering development directed toward peaceful applications of nuclear energy. Reactors, particle accelerators, and other facilities are used in the fields of engineering, chemistry, physics, material science, medicine, biology, and meteorology.

The Company's Commercial Products group in Ottawa processes and markets radioisotopes produced in AECL nuclear reactors and designs and manufactures equipment and facilities using these isotopes. Over 90 per cent of the business is export. AECL pioneered the use of isotopes in cancer therapy, food preservation, and other applications.

The economic production of power from nuclear sources has been developed so successfully by AECL that Canada ranks as one of the world's leaders in this field. The Power Projects group of AECL, located in Toronto, is responsible for the engineering design of nuclear power stations and for managing the construction of AECL-owned nuclear power station projects. Canada's first full-scale nuclear power station, at Douglas Point on the eastern shore of Lake Huron, went into commercial operation in 1966. The second, which initially will be the third largest nuclear power station ($2 \times 500,000$ kW) in the world, is to be built in Pickering Township, 20 miles east of Toronto.

The Whiteshell Nuclear Research Establishment (WNRE), which extends the research and development facilities of AECL, is the newest and a rapidly expanding part of the Company. Located 65 miles north-east of Winnipeg, Manitoba, WNRE is primarily engaged in furthering nuclear power development and at present conducts research projects in chemistry, chemical engineering, metallurgy, nuclear fuels, special construction materials for reactors, and medical research.

The Defence Research Board, a branch of the Department of National Defence, Ottawa, is the government agency responsible for scientific research, both basic and applied, as it relates to the defence of Canada. The Board not only carries out research in a variety of fields in its own laboratories but must, as well, keep abreast of advances elsewhere, since it must always be prepared to advise the Department on scientific matters. The Board works in collaboration with the armed forces and industry and with research agencies in other countries. Research programmes extend into most of the major fields of science associated with defence, with emphasis on programmes having special relevance to Canadian defence problems.

Work is being carried out in such fields as radio physics, upper atmospheric physics, radio and radar propagation, radiation physics, aerophysics, missile electronics and engineering, transistor circuitry, rocket and satellite instrumentation, physics of shock and blast, marine physics and propagation of sound in water, digital and analogue signal processing systems, weapons systems evaluation, operational research, and on investigation of the physiological effects of heat, cold, acceleration, noise, and the increase or decrease in ambient pressure. Projects under study include design and development of rocket-propelled test vehicles, weapons, and armament, and hydrofoil craft. Physical and organic chemists are engaged in development of rocket propellants and, together with biochemists and physiologists, are also employed on problems of protection, prophylaxis, and therapy relating to radiation, and to chemical and bacteriological agents. Three of the defence research establishments are in Ontario: the Telecommunications Establishment and Chemical, Biological, and Radiation Laboratories, Ottawa; and the Medical Laboratories, Toronto. The Operational Research Establishment is also in Ottawa, with small groups at St. Hubert, Quebec, and Halifax, NS, as well as Trenton and North Bay in Ontario and Victoria, BC. Other establishments are the Canadian Armament Research and Development Establishment, Valcartier, Quebec; the Naval Research Establishment, Halifax, NS; the Suffield Experimental Station, Ralston, Alberta; and the Pacific Naval Laboratory, Victoria, BC.

Scientific and Technical Societies and Institutions in the United States and Canada (Fig. 12), National Academy of Science,

History: Organized 1907 as the Actuaries Club; present title adopted 1946. Standing committees: education; public relations; social security; mortality; promotion of mathematical careers; expenses; papers; group matters.

Purpose: To promote actuarial knowledge among its members.

Membership: Active 411; retired 34. Fellowship or Associateship in one of the Institute of Actuaries (England), The Faculty of Actuaries (Scotland), or the Society of Actuaries (Canada and U.S.A.) required.

Meetings: 7 meetings yearly.

58. **Canadian Association of Anatomists.** *President:* R. Altschul, University of Saskatchewan, Saskatoon, Sask. Term expires June, 1961. *Secretary:* L. F. Belanger, University of Ottawa, Ottawa, Ont. Term expires 1963.

History: Founded 1956 in Montreal. Incorporated 1957 into Canadian Federation of Biological Societies.

Purpose: To advance knowledge of anatomy and to represent anatomical sciences in Canada.

Membership: 1 honorary; 83 charter and elected; 31 associate. Candidates for elected membership must be proposed by two members, and adjudged at annual meeting on basis of membership. Student—full-time university or college student. Organizations wishing to support the Association may apply for a sustaining membership.

Meetings: Annual.

Professional activities: CAG Book Prize given annually to the best student in each department of geography at Canadian universities. Sponsors Canadian Committee of the International Geographical Union.

Publications: The Canadian Geographer—Le Géographe Canadien, three yearly, current volume: 14, $5. Editor: W. G. Dean, University of Toronto, Toronto, Ont.

60. **Canadian Association of Medical Bacteriologists—Association Canadienne des Médecins Bactériologistes.** *President:* P. H. H. Grey, University of Toronto, Toronto, Ont. Term expires December, 1960. *Secretary:* R. W. Reed, McGill University, Montreal, Que. Term indefinite.

History: Formed 1957 to give the medical bacteriologists of Canada an opportunity to speak with a common voice on matters of interest to the specialty.

Purpose: To assure a high degree of professional competence; to contribute to the pro-

Fig. 12. *Scientific and Technical Societies and Institutions in the United States and Canada,* 1961.

National Research Council, Washington, DC, 1961, 7th edn., lists in its Part II 240 societies in Canada that are concerned with various fields of science and technology.

These societies generally function on a national or regional basis. Many of them are provincial in scope, and many of the national societies are made up of regional or provincial affiliates. In most cases these societies have established relations with international federations in the fields of their special interest, and Canadian scientists take an active part in the international exchange of scientific and technical information.

Volume 4, Report 23, *Scientific Research and Development*, Royal Commission on Government Organization, Queen's Printer, Ottawa, 1963, is a study of the research work done by all of the Canadian government departments and agencies. The amount of money spent by governments on scientific research is increasing each year. The 1966 expenditures have variously been established at about 0·85 per cent of the gross national product, or about $425 million. This study was made in 1961 as part of a general review of federal government functions by the Glassco Commission. It documents a considerable activity and includes fourteen appendixes giving financial and staffing information about each agency which carried out scientific research, for the decade ending 1960–1.

In addition to federal government research and development, work is carried on by the provincial governments. In March 1966 the Ministre de l'industrie et du commerce of Quebec presented to the Legislative Assembly a project for the establishment of a "Conseil de la recherche scientifique" and also for the establishment of a "Centre de recherche industrielle du Québec". The main function of the "Conseil" will be to assist the Quebec Government in developing policies in the field of scientific research. It will be concerned with both pure and applied scientific research. The function of the centre will be different. It will carry out its own research, mainly in industrial matters, by means of its own laboratories, or through laboratories already established in industries or universities in the province.

The Nova Scotia Research Foundation was created by the Government of Nova Scotia in 1946 to give that province scientific and technical assistance in finding new and better ways to utilize the resources of the forest, the sea, the farm and the mine. It assists universities, colleges, research groups, industries, and individuals by loans of equipment, grants, scholarships, laboratory and summer assistants, library, cartographic, photogrammetric, and translation services, and technical information.

The New Brunswick Research and Productivity Council, established by an Act of the Legislature in 1962, "promotes, stimulates and expedites continuing improvements in productive efficiency and expansion in the various sectors of the New Brunswick economy". The Council receives an operating grant from the provincial government and support in specific areas from federal sources.

The Manitoba Research Council was created by the Government of Manitoba in 1963 under the sponsorship of the Department of Industry and Commerce. The Council operates as an agency of the provincial government and is financed by provincial government appropriations, although fees and service charges may be levied on specific firms or individuals who use the services of the Council. The objects of the Council are both to promote and carry on research and scientific inquiries in the field of agriculture, other natural resources and industry and to help secure for the Manitoba economy the benefits of research carried on elsewhere.

The Saskatchewan Research Council was set up in 1947 under an Act of the Government of Saskatchewan. The Council carries out research in the physical sciences, both pure and applied, with the aim of improving the provincial economy. A large part of the programme is carried out by the permanent staff, now numbering about 60, but some of the Council's research is promoted by grants to university staffs. The members of the controlling body are appointed by the Lieutenant-Governor in Council and consist of representatives of the Government, industry, and the university.

The Province of Alberta set up a Scientific and Industrial Research Council in co-operation with the University of Alberta in

1921, the promotion of mineral development within the Province being the chief purpose leading to its establishment. The Council operates under an Act somewhat similar to that which set up the National Research Council in Ottawa and it is principally financed by provincial government appropriations.

The Ontario Research Foundation, established in 1928, operates as an independent corporation, deriving its powers from a special Act of the Legislature and governed by a Board of Governors appointed by the Lieutenant-Governor in Council of Ontario. The organization was financed initially by an endowment fund composed of subscriptions from commercial and industrial corporations, from private individuals, and a grant from the provincial government. However, most of its current income is derived from contract research undertaken for industry, although income is also obtained from the various government departments for research and other work undertaken on a contract basis. The Foundation is concerned primarily with the development of industry and of Ontario's natural resources through the application of scientific research.

The British Columbia Research Council is a non-profit, industrial research institute with offices and laboratories at the University of British Columbia. Its function is to enable firms to improve their competitive position in Canadian and world markets by the use of the most up-to-date scientific knowledge. The Council provides a free technical information service in collaboration with the National Research Council, carries out contract research for clients, and initiates research programmes designed to promote and utilize the resources of the province.

The Royal Society of Canada, formed in 1882, and the Association canadienne française pour l'avancement des sciences (Acfas), founded 1924, have been the major learned bodies concerned with science in Canada, and for many years have published reports and transactions describing the various developments in Canadian science. The Association is a federation of fifty societies and is concerned with the promotion of science and scientific education in the French language. It publishes the *Annales de l'Acfas* and the

monthly *Bulletin de l'Acfas*. The Royal Society has three sections
grouping the pure sciences. Section III: Mathematical, Chemical,
and Physical Sciences. Section IV: Geological Sciences. Section V:
Biological Sciences. In addition to the *Transactions* of each section
it publishes *Studia Varia*, mainly through the University of
Toronto Press, on a wide range of topics.

In 1965 *Science in Canada: selections from the speeches of
E. W. R. Steacie* was edited by Dr. J. D. Babbitt and published by
the University of Toronto Press. In these speeches Dr. Steacie, who
died in 1962, had put forward definite and sometimes controversial theories regarding the role of scientific research in Canada's
national development. These excerpts from speeches given between 1952 and 1962 present the views of a skilled, imaginative
scientist and administrator. He discussed topics such as science
and the humanities, science and society, industrial, academic, and
international science, science and the National Academy. Particularly significant are the author's views regarding the role of
government in fostering scientific research. Dr. Steacie was concerned that the tendency towards centralized control in governmental administration should not be allowed to stifle creative
scientific work.

Mathematics and Astronomy

The Canadian Mathematical Congress, 984 Sherbrooke St. W,
Montreal, organized in 1924, publishes the bilingual *Canadian
Mathematical Bulletin* and *Canadian Journal of Mathematics*.

The Royal Astronomical Society of Canada, 252 College St.,
Toronto, publishes an annual *Observer's Handbook* and a bi-
monthly *Journal*. There are sixteen centres of the Society across
Canada, and membership is open to amateur as well as professional astronomers.

Canada possesses a number of major observatories devoted to
one phase or other of astronomical research. The Department of
Mines and Technical Surveys of the Government of Canada operates three of these: the Dominion Observatory at Ottawa, the

Dominion Astrophysical Observatory near Victoria, BC, and the Dominion Radio Astrophysical Observatory near Penticton, BC.

The University of Toronto operates the David Dunlap Observatory at Richmond Hill, Ontario. Among its research activities are astronomical spectroscopy, studies of star clusters and galaxies, and radio astronomy. The National Research Council conducts meteor research at the Spring Hill Observatory near Ottawa and research in radio astronomy at the National Radio Laboratory at Lake Traverse in Algonquin Park, Ontario.

Physics and Geology

The Canadian Association of Physicists publishes *Physics in Canada*, a quarterly, University of Toronto Press, begun 1944.

The Geological Association of Canada was founded in 1947 with headquarters in Toronto and publishes its annual *Proceedings*. This Association was established to aid in the dissemination of information on geology and to encourage and promote the mineral industry of Canada. Much work in geology is done by the Geological Survey of Canada, a branch of the Federal Government. *Geology and Economic Minerals of Canada* was prepared by officers of the Geological Survey and edited by C. H. Stockwell and published by the Queen's Printer, Ottawa, 1963. It provides information about recent geological explorations in Canada, current developments in the mineral industry, physical features, and information on the geology and economic geology of Canada's five major geographical regions. A list of the geological exploration being carried out in each of these regions is included.

A Guide to Geology for Visitors in Canada's National Parks, by David M. Baird, Department of Northern Affairs and National Resources, Queen's Printer, Ottawa, 1963, has been issued by the National Parks Branch to provide visitors to Canada's National Parks with an understanding of basic geology in general and Canadian geology in particular. The formation of various geological features, such as mountains, lakes, rivers, and islands are explained, and the changes brought about on the landscape by glaciers and erosions are emphasized. Photographs, mainly of scenes from the National Parks, are used to illustrate the text. A table for the identification of the more common minerals is included.

Rocks and Minerals of Ontario by D. F. Hewitt, Geological Circular No. 13, Ontario Department of Mines, Queen's Printer, Toronto, 1965, is a well-illustrated publication covering various aspects of geology in the Precambrian shield. Part I deals with the rocks and common minerals of the Province; Part II discusses the geology of Ontario; and Part III describes the economic mineral deposits found there. A history of production is given for each mineral, as well as the amount of annual output, generally up until 1962 or 1963.

Geochronology in Canada, edited by F. Fitz Osborne, Royal Society of Canada Special Publication No. 8, University of Toronto Press, 1964, is a collection of papers presented at a colloquium of the Geology Division of Section III of the Royal Society of Canada in 1963. These papers discuss various aspects of the geological time scale in Canada, and several of them deal with the time scale in specific areas from Precambrian to recent date.

The National Research Council, Building Research Division, has prepared a *Climatological Atlas of Canada*, a joint publication of the Division of Building Research, National Research Council, and the Meteorological Division, Department of Transport, Canada, Ottawa, National Research Council, 1953. The *Atlas* provides general coverage of climatic variations throughout Canada. Charts and tables are grouped into nine sections, each preceded by short explanatory notes. The sections cover temperature, humidity, wind, rainfall, snow fall, hours of sunshine and isolation, seismological disturbances, and permafrost. A section of special graphs is included.

Biological Sciences

The Canadian Federation of Biological Societies was formed in 1957 by alliance of the Canadian Physiological Society, the Pharmacological Society of Canada, the Canadian Association of

Anatomists, and the Canadian Biochemical Society. On behalf of its constituent societies the Federation publishes annually *Canadian Federation News* and *Proceedings*.

The Canadian Journal of Genetics and Cytology is published quarterly by the Genetics Society of Canada, founded in 1956, and the Entomological Society of Canada has produced the monthly *Canadian Entomologist* since 1950 and acted as a link between the various regional societies in the field of entomology.

One of the most active agencies of the Federal Government in biological work is the Fisheries Research Board of Canada, with headquarters in Ottawa. The Board conducts oceanographic research through the following subordinate agencies: Nanaimo Biological Station, BC, Pacific Oceanographic Group, Vancouver, St. Andrew's Biological Station, NB, Atlantic Oceanographic Group, St. John's Biological Station and Arctic Unit. Work is carried out in all phases of oceanography with emphasis on marine biology.

In addition, the Bedford Institute of Oceanography, Dartmouth, NS, studies deep-ocean circulation, air–sea interaction, arctic oceanography, ice physics, submarine geophysics, geology, and chemical oceanography. The Great Lakes Institute, University of Toronto, conducts research in physics, geology, geophysics, botany, zoology, and meteorology dealing with the Great Lakes.

Natural Science

A Naturalist's Guide to Ontario, edited by W. W. Judd, University of Toronto Press, 1964, has been prepared by members of the Federation of Ontario Naturalists and other allied agencies and provides invaluable information for the naturalist planning a trip in Ontario. The first two sections are devoted to general descriptions of the geology, vegetation, and fauna of the province, and includes maps, charts, and sources of further information. The remainder of the book is devoted to regional guides. Under each heading will be found directions for reaching the region, localities within the region which are of particular interest, and descriptions of the geology, plants, trees, birds, and mammals that are typical of the area. If any rare or unique species may be found in the region they are listed. Sources of further information for each region are given, e.g. the local naturalist or nature clubs and the titles of any regional natural history publications.

The Research Branch, Department of Agriculture, has prepared *Edible and Poisonous Mushrooms of Canada*, Queen's Printer, Ottawa, 1962. This is a detailed guide to the identification of various genera of mushrooms, but it is not intended only for the general reader. The technical description of each mushroom would not be familiar to a person unacquainted with scientific terms. The classification of the genera is discussed, and there is a useful glossary for the botanical terms used. Colour photographs are used extensively as an aid in identification, and there are black-and-white photographs showing the structure of each plant. There is a detailed index.

F. H. Montgomery has prepared *Native Wild Plants of Eastern Canada and Adjacent Northwestern United States*, Ryerson Press, Toronto, 1966. This book is meant for the amateur botanist. It contains information on about 400 of the more common species of wild flowers and plants of the region, an area in which over 4600 species occur. Physical descriptions of each plant includes details about its flowers, leaves, stem, root system, and habitat. Each plant is illustrated with a line drawing, and there are 24 colour plates. By means of a simply organized reference key, a plant chosen for identification can be placed in 1 of 7 sections. When it has been placed in the proper section, progressively more careful observations have to be made, and each step refers to the next until the plant or the family has been identified. Scientific and common names are given in the index.

In 1967 the Federal Department of Forestry, Ottawa, published a seventh edition of *Native Trees of Canada*, Queen's Printer, Ottawa, based on its earlier edition (Fig. 13). This work serves as a source of identifying the various species of trees native to Canada. Divided into two general sections, Coniferous and Broadleaf, the trees are further subdivided into family groupings. Each specific type of tree within the family is then fully described according to

GRAND FIR

Abies grandis (Dougl.) Lindl.

Lowland fir, white fir, western balsam, silver fir, larch, giant fir, lowland white fir.

The grand fir is the largest of the Canadian firs, attaining heights of 100 to 125 feet and diameters of 2 to 3 feet. The trunk is tall, straight, and clear, except when growing in the open. The crown is narrow and spire-shaped in young trees, but with age becomes rounded and dome-like, also the lower branches have a tendency to droop and this makes the crown appear wider in the middle than at the

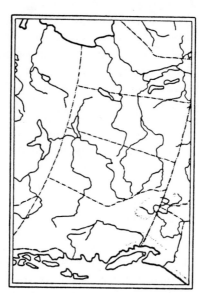

LEAVES—Needle-like, flattened or occasionally 4-sided in cross-section, appearing distinctly 2-ranked on lower branches, 1¼ to 2¼ inches long, blunt, grooved above;

FIG. 13. *Native Trees of Canada*, 1963.

its unique physical structure. Commercial use is also indicated. For each tree, a small map of Canada is inserted in the text. This map is marked to indicate the geographical location of the tree. The textual matter expands and elucidates facts pertaining to location. Clear black-and-white photographs are used to illustrate important physical characteristics of each tree. These photographs, which complement and clarify the text, range from small detailed pictures to full-page plates. A check-list of native trees precedes the main section of the book. This check-list, arranged also by species, indicates botanical and common names (both English and French) of each tree included in the text. An alphabetical index is a further key to locating points of interest.

Roger Tory Peterson's *A Field Guide to Western Birds*, 2nd edn., revised and enlarged, Houghton-Mifflin, Boston, 1961, is a standard book of bird field identification. The marks of all species found in North America west of the 100th meridian are given. More than 700 species are included, exclusive of subspecies.

The "Peterson System" is based on patternistic drawings that indicate the key bird marks with arrows. Of the 60 plates, 36 are in full colour; black and white is used when it is of more aid in identification than colour would be. The plates and line cuts throughout the text are intended as diagrams, arranged for quick comparison of the species most resembling each other.

The text gives additional information such as manner of flight, range, season, habitat, etc. Information on recordings of bird songs, checklists, and regional works is included. The index uses the names of birds officially designated in the fifth edition of the American Ornithological Union *Check-list* (1957). The page numbers for the illustrations are placed only after the common English names, not after the scientific names.

Field Guide of the Birds . . . East of the Rockies, also by R. T. Peterson, Houghton-Mifflin, Boston, 1959, is a guide to the field marks of eastern birds, wherein birds may be identified by impressions, patterns, and distinctive marks. A total of 440 species are included in the main part of the book, plus 7 hybrids and

F

varietal forms. In the Appendix there are 74 accidentals and 181 additional subspecies. Peterson suggests that in the field it is most practical to go directly to the illustration. The plates and cuts are arranged so that comparisons can be made of the species that most resemble one another. Shore, roadside, and flight silhouettes are a useful feature of the line illustrations.

P. A. Taverner has produced *Birds of Canada*, Musson, 1949. This scholarly but out-of-print work was published in order to stimulate an interest ". . . both aesthetic and practical . . ." in the study of Canadian birds. A classic reference work, it attempts to encompass all birds which are known to occur in Canada.

The Birds of Canada, by N. Earl Godfrey of the National Museum of Canada, Queen's Printer, Ottawa, 1966 (Fig. 14), covers essentially the same material. For 518 species, description, measurements, field marks, habitat, nesting, range, subspecies and general remarks are given. Reproductions of paintings by artist–naturalist J. A. Crosby, several to a page in colour, are given for 431 species. A map showing breeding distribution is given. Also included are a glossary, a bibliography of selected references and indexes arranged by English, French and scientific names.

Arctic Birds of Canada by L. L. Snyder, University of Toronto Press, was published in 1957. Each chapter of the book is devoted to one type of bird and describes its distinguishing characteristics and natural habitat. The descriptive text is illustrated with a drawing of the bird and a graphic illustration of its range. Background information of the area under study is well documented in the introduction.

The Freshwater Fishes of Canada by E. P. Slastenko, Kiev Printers, Toronto, 1963, contains information gained from many sources. It is a scholarly work, but can be used by the game and commercial fisherman as well as by the research worker. The total number of kinds of freshwater fishes, both native and introduced, is 185, including subspecies. These belong to 13 orders, 27 families, and 87 genera. Authorities are cited before each of the species is described in complete detail. A list containing explanations of terms and methods of counting and measuring is given. A table of

Order **Falconiformes**—Diurnal Birds of Prey—Vultures, Hawks, and Falcons ·

Family **Cathartidae**—American Vultures

Number of Species in North America 4, in Canada 2

Large, long-winged birds *with the head bare of feathers;* a strongly hooked bill with large open nostrils; toes rather long (the hind one elevated), but weakly hooked and unsuitable for grasping and holding prey. They feed on dead animals and thus serve a useful purpose as scavengers. Flight, on long, broad wings, with much protracted sailing and circling, is extremely graceful.

TURKEY VULTURE

Le Vautour à tête rouge. *Cathartes aura* (Linnaeus)
Plates 15, 20. L. 26.5 to 32.0 in.

Head and extreme upper neck bare except for sparse hair-like bristles. Bill rather long, hooked, with very large broad nostrils. Wings long. *Adults:* Naked head and upper neck, red. Upper body, wings, and tail black, the feathers of back and wing coverts edged with brown. Neck and under parts black. Eye brown. Bill whitish, red basally. Legs, flesh colour. *Juvenal:* Similar to adults but bare skin of head blackish.

Measurements (*C. a. septentrionalis*). *Adult male: wing,* 518–550 (535.9); tail, 252–298 (271); culmen from cere, 24–25 (24.4); tarsus, 65–71 (68.1). *Adult female:* wing, 527–559 (545.8) mm (Friedmann).

Field Marks. A large long-winged (wingspread to 6 feet) black bird with small red (blackish in young) head and longish hooked bill. In flight it soars effortlessly for long periods with wings held definitely above horizontal in a road V; often tilts gracefully from side to side; black under wing coverts contrast with paler flight feathers.

Habitat. Inhabits various types of terrain, except heavy unbroken forest. Spends long periods on the wing, often at considerable heights.

Nesting. No nest. *Eggs* (usually 2) are laid on the ground among rocks, under logs, on cliffs, or in caves. They are ellowish white with bold irregular blotches of browns and ten sparse spots of pale lavender. Incubation period variously reported: 30 to 41 days (*in* Bent, 1937).

Range. Southern Canada, south through the United ates to the West Indies, Central America, and to southern uth America.

Range in Canada. Breeds in small numbers in southern itish Columbia (Comox, Pender Island, Harrison, Oliver),

central and southern Alberta (locally north to near Ashmont), southern Saskatchewan (Moose Jaw, Rush Lake, mouth of Old Wives Creek, Qu'Appelle Valley; possibly north to Saskatchewan River), southern Manitoba (Duck Mountain, Elk Island, Long Lake), western Ontario (Poplar Bay, Kenora), southern Ontario (north to Bruce Peninsula, Credit Forks, Georgetown). Rare visitor to southern Quebec (Lac Raymond, Wright, Barrington, Hatley, Pointe des Monts), New Brunswick (some eighteen records at various points), and Nova Scotia (well-spaced records at various points including Cape Breton Island). Casual in northern

Breeding Distribution of Turkey Vulture

Ontario (Fort Severn, Moose Factory). Accidental in Labrador (Nain, West St. Modeste) and Newfoundland (St. Anthony, Renews). Winters occasionally in southern British Columbia (Comox, Oyster River, Okanagan Landing).

Subspecies. (1) *Cathartes aura septentrionalis* Wied is the breeding subspecies of s. Ont. and e. U.S. Most wanderers to other parts of e. Canada are probably referable to it. (2) *C. a. teter* Friedmann, with an average shorter tail and wings, inhabits w. Canada including w. Ontario. (Wetmore, 1964, *Smithsonian Misc. Collections* 146 (6): 1–18, maintains that *meridionalis* is an older name for *teter* Friedmann.)

85

FIG. 14. *The Birds of Canada*, 1966.

the number of species by provinces and in the drainage basins of the Great Lakes, the Atlantic, Arctic, and Pacific oceans has been included. There are separate indexes for the scientific and common names.

W. B. Scott has written *Freshwater Fishes of Eastern Canada*, University of Toronto Press, 1954. This work intended to present the information available at time of publication about Canadian freshwater fish occurring east of Manitoba, in order to assist in correct identification. For each of the fish there is a brief description, in most cases accompanied by a small black-and-white photograph. Information given includes common and scientific names, a description of distinguishing features, average size, occurrence, life history and habits, the food of the adults, and comments on its flavour and importance as a game, commercial, or bait species, or as a forage fish. The index, minimum of technical language, and brief descriptions make this a quick reference book for game and commercial fishermen, as well as others interested in locating a few general facts about a specific fish.

The Angler's Book of Canadian Fishes by F. H. Wooding, Collins, 1959, is a readable descriptive book about Canadian freshwater game fish, of interest particularly to anglers, but also to anyone wishing to learn about Canadian fish. The book begins with a description of the general characteristics of all fish (body structures, physiology, etc.). The second part describes the various game fish by family, giving a general description and comparison, of the different family members, as well as a discussion of methods and need for conservation. Individual species are then described in more detail. Topics covered are description, distribution, characteristics, and how they are caught, both commercially and by the angler. A number of small black-and-white drawings and a few coloured illustrations are included, as well as a brief list of references, and a detailed index.

Claude Melançon has produced *Les Poissons de nos eaux*, 3rd edn., with additions, Société zoologique de Québec, Quebec, 1958. This is a guide to the fish of the Province of Quebec. The arrangement is systematic following the scientific order of the various species. Precise descriptions of shape, colour, size, and markings for each fish are given, and there are useful identifying sketches. Names are given in Latin, English, and French, and there is a French alphabetical index to the names and a useful list of fishing terms and expressions.

Austin W. Cameron in *Canadian Mammals*, rev. edn. (National Museum of Canada), Queen's Printer, Ottawa, 1964, describes and illustrates over sixty familiar and widely distributed Canadian mammals. Information on individual species includes feeding and breeding habits, habitat, natural enemies, economic value and problems of conservation. Each account is accompanied by a black-and-white illustration by John Crosby, and a small map of Canada showing the distribution or range of each mammal.

W. H. Burt's *A Field Guide to the Mammals*, 2nd edn., revised and enlarged, Houghton-Mifflin, Boston, 1964, contains the field marks of all species north of Mexico. There are 291 range maps for land mammals and details on habitat, habits, young, and economic status are given for 378 species. The illustrations include Grossenheider's superb colour plates, line illustrations of tracks, and photographs of mammal skulls.

CHAPTER 8

Technology in Canada

Engineering

In spite of short-term recessions and competition from European and Asian manufacturers, the industrial production of Canada, since the end of World War II, has been favourable as a whole. The long-range forecasters of Canadian business and industry have maintained that the needs of the world's expanding populations in Asia, Africa, and the Middle East will result in an increasing need for both Canadian finished products and for Canadian natural resources in the decades that lie ahead.

The major industrial and technical developments in Canada have come about by bringing in expert help and machinery and by introducing foreign processes to handle both raw materials and secondary manufacture. The main source of technical information for Canadian industry is provided by the parent United States companies of Canadian plants, and by United States suppliers of equipment who dominate the Canadian market. While some British and European, particularly French goods and processes are to be found in Canada, the overall picture is that of a nation heavily dependent on the manufacturing processes of the United States of America as far as improvements in technology are concerned.

For this reason, most information on Canadian technology is similar to that which is available from United States sources, and publications of many American concerns cover to a large extent the activities of their Canadian subsidiaries. Canada is absorbing a growing population, including about 200,000 young people who enter the labour market each year. Efforts are constantly being made in each province by government to stimulate the growth of industry. Such organizations as the Ontario and Nova Scotia Research Foundations are active in providing for the development of private industry, plants, and processes. A major research and development centre for North America is being established at Sheridan Park, midway between the Canadian industrial centres of Hamilton and Toronto, Ontario.

The development of Canadian industry has required extensive growth in all of the branches of professional engineering. Most important have been the contributions in the mining, construction, electrical, and civil engineering fields. Various Canadian periodicals provide an up-to-date picture of what is happening in Canadian engineering. These are the *Engineering Journal*, Montreal, published monthly since 1919, and *L'Ingénieur*, Montreal, established 1915 and issued 4 times a year. *Electrical News and Engineering*, Toronto, was established in 1891 and appears monthly with an annual *Buyers' Guide and Directory*. *Canadian Electronics Engineering*, Toronto, monthly, was established in 1957, and *Engineering and Contract Record*, Toronto, established since 1888, provides a record of events in various fields of construction and installation.

Mining and Prospecting

The Canadian Institute of Mining and Metallurgy, Montreal, has produced *Mining in Canada*, the Institute, Montreal, 1957, which gives a general background of historical developments in this important area of technical services. The Department of Mines and Technical Surveys has published the *Digest of the Mining Laws of Canada*, 5th edn. (Fig. 15), Queen's Printer, Ottawa, 1957. This publication was issued first in 1924. The authors point out that it is meant only as a digest and general guide to the mining laws and regulations, and reference should be made to other sources for the latest information. The book is divided into sections which cover the basic conditions governing the mining

PLACER-MINING ACT

(R.S.B.C. 1948, Chapter 214; 1953, 2nd. sess. Chap. 18)

Section   Section 27 of this Act specifies that a free miner shall have all the rights and privileges granted by the Mineral Act.

The Act, however, differs from the Mineral Act with respect to claims. The dimensions laid down for these are:

37   Creek Diggins: 250 ft. along stream bed and 500 ft. on either side of centre of stream.

Bar Diggings: a piece of land 250 ft. square or a strip of land 250 ft. long extending from high to low water.

Dry Diggings: a piece of land 250 ft. square.

In the case of discovery of a new placer-mining locality, the following special provisions apply:

38   One discovery claim: a claim 600 ft. in length.

Party of two: two claims each 500 ft. long.

Parties over two: one claim of standard size to each.

In all cases, the width of the claims shall be as for standard claims of the same class.

52   Except during the close season, lay-over, leave of absence, absence on account of sickness, or other acceptable reason, claims must be

FIG. 15. Digest of the Mining Laws of Canada, 1957.

rights in various jurisdictions. The section on the Federal Government includes laws and regulations relating to Indian reserves as well as federal lands in the Yukon and the North-west Territories. A section is devoted to each of the provinces. Included is a brief history of the mining legislation and a digest of the various acts and regulations. Topics covered include obtaining a miner's licence, staking a claim, forfeiture of claims, schedule of fees, and information on the laws. Included are a list of Acts and Regulations, and where to write for detailed information or for copies of the Acts and Regulations.

A. W. Lang has prepared *Prospecting in Canada*, 3rd edn., Queen's Printer, Ottawa, 1956. This is an almost completely re-written edition of a book which had been prepared in previous editions by other writers. The work covers prospecting and geology, mineral deposits, an outline on Canada's geology, how to obtain instruction and courses in mineralogy, and methods of prospecting. It tells how to explore and appraise mineral deposits and gives notes of specific metals and minerals. *Canadian Minerals Yearbook*, Queen's Printer, Ottawa, 1966, reviews some 60 of the most important metals and minerals found in Canada, including latest available data on exploration, development, production and use. This is a basic work for those interested in the Canadian mineral economy.

The *Canadian Mining and Metallurgical Bulletin*, Montreal, published monthly since 1898, provides a coverage of the development of technical processes in Canadian mining. Another periodical of value which also contains business information is the *Northern Miner*, established 1915 and issued weekly from Toronto. The *Canadian Mining Journal*, Gardenvale, Quebec, was established in 1879 and carries regular news on developments in mining in Canada.

Uranium in Canada by Gordon C. Garbutt was published by Eldorado Mining and Refining Limited, Ottawa, 1964, and describes the history and operations necessary to produce refined uranium in Canada. Canada is the second largest producer of this metal in the world, and the work of the companies which is described covers every stage of the process, from exploration to final sale. Part II of the volume gives details of the companies that make up the Canadian uranium industry, and is illustrated by photographs of mining installations and diagrams of property locations and ore formations. The book is a comprehensive and factual account of uranium production in Canada and a companion volume to *Nuclear Fuels in Canada* and *Nuclear Power in Canada* published by Atomic Energy of Canada Limited, Ottawa.

A valuable source of current information on nuclear engineering is the quarterly *Canadian Nuclear Technology*, Maclean Hunter Co., Toronto, first issued in 1961.

Railways and Roads

The operation of Canada's vast trans-continental rail and road systems has been part of the life of the country for many decades. The growth of these enterprises can be seen from the various historical accounts which trace the evolution that has taken place in road and rail transport in Canada. Such changes are still going on, and are described in the current national transportation journals and periodicals. *Bus and Truck Transport in Canada*, Maclean-Hunter, Toronto, has been published monthly since 1925. It records the expansion of the methods of freight and passenger transport that have completely transformed the role of the national transportation systems. Routes and schedules of the latter can be found in the *Canadian Official Railway Guide, with Airlines*, Montreal, issued monthly. *Canadian Transportation*, Don Mills, Ontario, established 1898 is a periodical account of the current developments in all branches of the transport industry.

Aviation

In Canadian Skies by Frank H. Ellis, Ryerson Press, Toronto, 1959, records 50 years of progress in Canadian aviation and was issued for the golden anniversary of flight in Canada. The work is illustrated with photographs of many of the early aircraft and pioneer pilots. It includes a description of the exploration of northern Canada by air, and accounts of the first trans-Atlantic crossings. There is a detailed index.

C. A. Ashley, *The First Twenty-five Years*, Macmillan, 1963, is the story of the growth of Air-Canada, founded as a Crown Corporation by the Canadian Government in 1928 in order to provide a national air transportation system for Canada. This study traces the evolution of the air-line system and shows the degree of autonomy which the corporation possesses, the sources of its capital, and the powers of the minister responsible for it to Parliament.

From the Ground Up, 14th rev. edn., Aviation publishers, Port Credit, Ontario, 1963, by A. F. MacDonald, is a standard text for Canadian flying instruction. This book is designed for Canadian students and as such contains Canadian flying regulations, radio information, and "bush sense" in addition to standard subjects of instruction, all of which are oriented to Canada. An index is provided to subjects and the book is amply illustrated. News of developments in flying has appeared in *Canadian Aviation*, Toronto, monthly since 1928. Another important periodical in this field is *Canadian Flight*, published in Ottawa since 1955.

J. H. Parkin has written *Bell and Baldwin*, University of Toronto Press, 1964, which is a description of the work of the Aerial Experiment Station at Baddeck, Nova Scotia, of which Dr. Alexander Graham Bell was chairman, and Frederick Walker (Casey) Baldwin was chief engineer. The group, which was "founded, inspired, and financed by Mrs. Bell", included also John A. D. McCurdy, Lt. Thomas Etholan Selfridge, and Glen H. Curtiss. The station's experiments ran from 1907 to 1909. The first part of the book gives details of work done before 1907. Part II deals with the work after that date. Powered, man-carrying, heavier-than-air machines, 1893–1909, are described in Part III. The remaining parts of the book cover the Bell Laboratory at Beinn Bhreagh, Nova Scotia, 1909–22, and hydrofoil targets, hydrofoil craft, and aircraft. The author shows how Dr. Bell and Casey Baldwin contributed to the development of the aeroplane and hydrofoil craft that we know today. He describes how Dr. Bell recorded, in detail, the operations of his group. He also kept the press informed, possibly because of the unpleasantness surrounding his earlier experiences with rival claims to the invention of the telephone. The book is indexed, well illustrated, and has separate bibliographies for each of Dr. Bell's associates and for each of the research projects. Fold-out tables are provided to give data on experiments.

Agriculture

From a country once predominantly agricultural, Canada has been transformed into one that is daily becoming more urban, and Canadian life is dominated by the metropolitan centres that have grown up in every province. In 1961 only 12% of Canada's population were living on farms in contrast to 1931 when almost one-third of the nation were farm dwellers. The farm labour force in 1966 amounted to only 7% of the total labour force. However, farming provided employment for more than three times as many workers as all other primary industries combined. As an industrial group, it ranked fourth in importance as an employer, after manufacturing, service (excluding government), and trade.

Wheat, livestock, and dairying produced on large agricultural establishments, now account for nearly three-quarters of the Canadian farmer's cash income. Canadian wheat, like newsprint, uranium, and other natural resources, is sold primarily on international markets. Wheat sales have been a major factor in Canadian political and economic life for many decades and will probably continue for some time to come. At the end of 1958 there were 540 million bushels of surplus grain in western Canada, much of it stored on farmer's fields. Recently the Canadian Government, by means of sales of wheat abroad, has been able to dispose of most of the immense surplus which had accumulated in the 1950's and early 1960's on the Canadian prairies. The trans-continental movement of grain has accounted for some of the prosperity in the seaports of British Columbia and eastern Canada, and indicates how the maintenance of the urban living standard of the majority of Canadians is still closely associated with the prosperity of Canadian agriculture.

G. E. Britnell and V. C. Fowke have written *Canadian Agriculture in War and Peace*, 1935–50, Stanford University Press, Stanford, Calif., 1962, which documents the changes that have taken place over a 25-year period. The Canadian Federal Department of Agriculture has had an important role to play in the life of the nation for the past 100 years. The Information Division of the Department produced *75th Anniversary, Progress through Research, 1887–1962*, Queen's Printer, Ottawa, 1962, an account of the work of the Dominion Experimental Farms from coast to coast. These experimental farms have been one of the main means of improving and developing agriculture in Canada, and have conducted research on a wide range of topics. Included in the Department's programme have been animal, plant, genetics and plant breeding, soils, entomology, microbiology, and food research.

In the field of production and marketing the Department deals with livestock, poultry, fruits and vegetables, dairy products, plant products, and control of disease in plants.

The Agricultural Institute of Canada, Ottawa, has published a bi-monthly *Review* since 1945 and the quarterly *Canadian Journal of Plant Science* which began publication in 1952 and superseded in part the *Canadian Journal of Agricultural Science*.

The Canadian Society of Technical Agriculturists, Ottawa, published its *Membership Directory*, Ottawa, 1957. The *Proceedings* and the *Canadian Journal of Agricultural Economics* have been produced regularly by the Canadian Agricultural Economists Society, Ottawa.

One of the important areas of activity in Canadian agriculture is farm redevelopment and improvement. In 1939 E. W. Stapleford prepared a *Report on Rural Relief due to Drought Conditions and Crop Failures in Western Canada, 1930–1937*, King's Printer, Ottawa, 1939. This report to the Minister of Agriculture laid the foundation for the Prairie Farm Re-habilitation Programme, which has developed widely since 1939.

The rural co-operative movement in Canada has been strong in all provinces, but particularly in Saskatchewan, Manitoba, Ontario, and the Maritimes. *Co-operatives in Canada*, Publ. 1119 of the Department of Agriculture, Queen's Printer, Ottawa, 1962, is a general description of the extent to which these organizations have spread and developed. The Saskatchewan Wheat Pool, a farmer's co-operative, published *The Saskatchewan Wheat Pool and its Accomplishments*, the Pool, Regina, Saskatchewan, 1964, which describes the social, economic, and cultural developments which the Pool has fostered.

Robert L. Jones produced *A History of Agriculture in Ontario, 1613–1830*, University of Toronto Press, 1946, which shows the strength of the rural farm family in the latter part of the eighteenth and the early part of the nineteenth century, and the role it played in early colonization. The Ontario Federation of Agriculture, Toronto, produces an annual *Year Book*, which records the membership of the various agricultural societies which make up the Federation.

Information about farm requirements can be found in the *Canadian Farm Equipment Dealer*, Don Mills, Ontario, published monthly since 1904 and in *Agricultural Chemicals in Canada*, Don Mills, Ontario, issued 5 times a year since 1958.

The monthly *Canadian Journal of Comparative Medicine and Veterinary Science*, Gardenvale, Quebec, was established 1937. Along with the *Canadian Veterinary Journal*, Guelph, Ontario, it covers news and developments in veterinary science in Canada.

Cooking and Furnishings

Bradford Angier has produced a Canadian cookbook entitled *Wilderness Cooking*, Stackpole Co., Harrisburg, Penn., 1961. This work describes the meals which can be prepared from ingredients found in the Canadian wilderness. It also contains information on how to survive in the open. Jehane Benoit has written the *Encyclopedia of Canadian Cuisine* (Fig. 16). Messageries du Saint-Laurent, Montreal, 1963, giving all of the recipes that have

PROCESSING FRUIT

Apples: Wash, peel and remove core. Cut into wedges or dice. Blanch 1½ minutes, cool quickly. Fill chosen sealer or can. Cover with thin hot syrup. Close and process 20 minutes in hot water bath or 10 minutes at 5 lbs. pressure.

Blackberries: Process same as strawberries.

Blueberries: Clean fruit and wash in cold water. Dip in boiling water ½ to 1 minute depending on fruit maturity. Cool quickly in cold water. Pack. Press fruit into container by hitting the sides of the sealer. Cover with a medium hot syrup. Close. Process 16 minutes in hot water bath or 10 minutes at 5 lbs. pressure.

Cherries: Clean the cherries, wash under cold water, remove pits, stem, and pack. Cherries are best when canned in No. 2 cans. The cherries

QUANTITY OF SYRUP REQUIRED PER QUART

Fruit	Cold Pack	Hot Pack
Blueberries	¾ to 1 cup	about 1 cup
Other small fruits	about 1½ cups	
Large fruits	1½ to 2 cups	about 1½ cups

PROPORTIONS FOR SYRUPS

Type of Syrup	Sugar	Water	Approximate Yield
Thin	1 cup	3 cups	3½ cups
Very thin	1 cup	2 cups	2½ cups
Moderately thin	1 cup	1 cup	2 cups
Medium	1 cup	1½ cups	1½ cups
Heavy	1 cup	¾ cup	1¼ cups

APPROXIMATE YIELD OF CANNED PRODUCTS FROM RAW FOOD

Fruits	Quantity, Raw	Approximate Yield, Canned
Apples	1 6-qt. basket or 9 lbs.	3 to 4 qts.

Fig. 16. *Encyclopedia of Canadian Cuisine*, 1963.

originated in Canada and the details associated with the preparation of these. Many of the recipes are traditional ones from France that have been adapted and transformed in 300 years of Canadian practice.

Food in Canada, Maclean-Hunter, Toronto, has been issued monthly since 1941, and provides information on the important canning and food-handling services of the country. The *Canadian Home Economics Journal*, Winnipeg, Manitoba, was established in 1950 and reports on developments in home and institution management. Willson's *Canadian Food and Packaging Directory*, Scarborough, Ontario, has appeared annually, and *Le Fournisseur*, Montreal, is issued monthly since 1935.

Furniture and Furnishings, Don Mills, Ontario, is a monthly publication which first appeared in 1910. It provides current information on trends in Canadian design and decoration.

Canadian Interiors, Toronto, established 1964 and issued monthly, caters to the needs of the home and commercial design industry. The National Industrial Design Committee was formed in 1948 as an extension of the National Gallery of Canada, Ottawa. The Committee gave publicity to improved design in Canada by means of an annual competition and the maintenance of the *Canadian Design Index*, National Gallery, Ottawa, 1947– .

Canadian Designs for Everyday Use, National Gallery of Canada, Ottawa, 1949, was one of the first of a series of publications prepared to document the trends in industrial design in Canada.

In the field of industrial design, a useful source of information is *Design Engineering* and *Product Design and Engineering*, established in 1955 and 1956 respectively and issued monthly.

The *Plastics Directory of Canada*, Don Mills, Ontario, is an annual publication which has appeared since 1959 and provides a guide to the manufacturers of plastic goods. *Progressive Plastics*, Maclean-Hunter, Toronto, is a monthly journal published for the industry since 1959.

The *Canadian Textile Directory*, Scarborough, Ontario, has been issued annually since 1926. Along with the *Canadian Textile Journal*, fortnightly, Montreal, established 1883, it provides a basic source of information on textile developments in Canada. In the field of clothing and fashion, *Style*, and *Men's Wear in Canada*, Maclean-Hunter, Toronto, established 1888 and 1909 respectively, are useful sources. The *Canadian Clothing Journal*, Toronto, covers various aspects of clothing and furnishings.

Printing

The Society of Typographic Designers of Canada, Toronto, was founded in 1956 in order to increase public awareness of the benefits which are derived from good craftsmanship and design in typography and to aid printers and publishers in achieving a high standard in printed communication. The society has printed a series of annual catalogues, *Typography 19–* , Toronto, Montreal, which reproduce the annual award-winning and other entries in national shows of typographical design.

Aegidius Fauteux has written *The Introduction of Printing into Canada, a Brief History*, Rolland Paper Co., Montreal, 1930. This recounts the early history of printing in separate chapters devoted to the Maritime Provinces, Quebec, Montreal, Ontario, and the western provinces. Detailed accounts are given for the early history of printing in Quebec Province. There are 22 facsimiles of early Canadian title-pages. There is no index.

In 1940 the Toronto Public Library, Toronto, prepared *The Canadian Book of Printing* (Fig. 17). This describes how printing came to Canada and the story of the graphic arts. Section I deals with the spread of printing in Canada and includes 44 illustrations and examples of early work. The remainder of the book gives a general history of printing and the practice of printing. There are 96 illustrations and an index.

Presstige Books of Canada has published *The National Publishing Directory: the encyclopedia of the publishing industry*, 1964–5 edition, Toronto. This is a directory of people and institutions concerned with the publishing industry in English and French Canada arranged by type of publishing activity. The encyclopedia includes advertising agencies, periodicals and newspapers, graphic constitutional government in the province. Robson was elected to the provincial legislature where he ultimately (1889) became prime minister, but he continued publishing his newspaper.

Bishop Demers' little press began life anew at Barkerville in the Caribou District. Here in 1865 George Wallace started *The Caribou Sentinel* (a weekly paper at one dollar the copy!) for the gold miners of the district. The old press continued printing in Caribou, then at Emory and Kamloops, till finally it became a museum piece in the Convent of Saint Anne in Victoria. Vancouver, now the largest city and greatest printing centre in the Canadian West, began to grow when the railroad reached across the continent to the coast in 1886. Its printing began with a newspaper of course, *The Vancouver News*, June 1, 1886, whose lineal descendant still appears as *The Vancouver Sun*.

Iron hand press of Bishop Demers.

FIG. 17. *Canadian Book of Printing*, 1940.

art and book publishers, photographers, public relations firms, and press associations. Each section lists addresses and pertinent business information, including advertising rates and circulation figures for periodicals. Biographical sketches of leading Canadian figures in each field are included, and a master index to all biographies is provided. A 49-page account of the history of publishing and journalism in Canada precedes the main body of the work.

Industries and Construction

The Chemical Institute of Canada, 151 Slater Street, Ottawa, was organized in 1921 and has over thirty local sections across Canada. It has published since 1949, *Chemistry in Canada*, a monthly journal devoted to developments in the chemical industry, and chemical research. The Institute also publishes the bi-monthly *Canadian Journal of Chemical Engineering*, which deals with the application of chemistry in Canada and abroad.

The Forestry Branch, Department of resources and development, has prepared *Canadian Woods: their properties and uses*, 2nd edn. (Fig. 18), King's Printer, Ottawa, 1951. This is a well-illustrated account of the commercial use of Canadian wood, including a description of the physical properties of individual types of wood. Information is given on veneers, plywoods, containers, and pulp and paper, as well as the mechanical and physical properties of various Canadian woods. There is a classified list of uses of Canadian woods and an index to the material covered.

Various sections of the wood industries of Canada are represented in the Canadian Hardwood and Veneer and Plywood Association and the Canadian Institute of Timber Construction. Both these organizations produce a variety of studies and reports on the industries of Canada that utilize and manufacture specialized wood products.

Canadian Forest Industries, Don Mills, Toronto, is an important monthly review of the wood-using industries of Canada. The

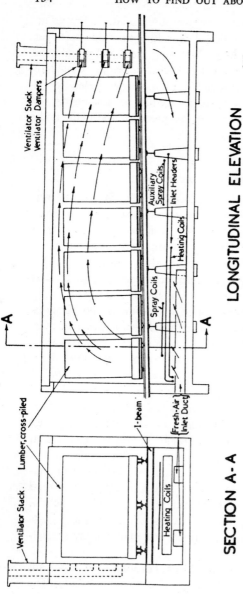

SECTION A - A

LONGITUDINAL ELEVATION

FIGURE 24.—Natural-longitudinal-circulation Progressive Kiln.

The remainder of the circulating air descends and passes longitudinally along the floor of the kiln until it is drawn upward by the hot air currents through the heating system and recirculated.

Figure 25 is a schematic drawing of a natural-cross-circulation progressive dry-kiln. This is very similar to the longitudinal-circulation type. The

the fresh air ducts, heating and spray coils, and ventilators are installed as in the natural-circulation kiln shown in Figure 20.

Advantages and Disadvantages of Each Type

Each type of dry-kiln has its advantages and dis-

Fig. 18. *Canadian Woods*, 1951.

British Columbia Lumberman, Vancouver, BC, is another monthly journal which discusses matters of particular interest to West Coast wood users. "*ABC*" *British Columbia Lumber and Trade Directory and Year Book* is issued from Vancouver on a biennial basis. A general monthly magazine dealing with various aspects of the woodworking trade is *Canadian Wood Products Industries*, Don Mills, Ontario, established 1900.

The Pulp and Paper Magazine of Canada, Gardenvale, Quebec, established 1903, is issued monthly and describes the developments in the industry in general. The Pulp and Paper Research Institute of Canada, Montreal, is a centre of research and learning concerned with virtually every aspect of the production and use of pulp and paper products. It was established in 1913 as a branch of the Dominion Forest Products Laboratories and in 1927 was reorganized under the joint sponsorship of the Canadian Pulp and Paper Association, the Federal Government, and McGill University. The Institute staff carries out fundamental research and some applied research in the fields of woodland operations and pulp and paper mill operations. The projects range from studies of the growing seedling in the forest to the converted pulp and paper product, and fall into seven broad classifications; woodlands, mechanical pulping, chemical pulping, paper making, process control, product quality, and waste utilization. The Institute is regarded as a centre for broad, long-range, and uninterrupted studies of basic principles which individual pulp and paper companies would find difficult to justify in terms of immediate objectives. Since 1927 the Institute has occupied a building on the McGill University campus erected by the pulp and paper industry and, in addition, since 1958, a building at Pointe Claire on the western outskirts of Montreal.

Paper-Making, the Garden City Press Co-operative, Toronto, 1947, is a valuable historic work by George Carruthers. Part I is a general history of paper and Part II deals with the first century of paper making in Canada and recounts the steps which were taken to manufacture and market Canadian paper from the first beginnings in various parts of the country.

A number of studies have been made of the growth of various manufacturing industries in Canada. One of these is *The History of Munitions and Supply in Canada, 1914–1918*, by David Carnegie, Longmans, London, 1925. A particularly important segment of the Canadian manufacturing economy is dealt with in *The Harvest Triumphant* by Merrill Denison, McClelland, Toronto, 1948. This work explains the strategic role which the Massey-Harris firm manufacturing farm implements in Toronto played in opening up the Canadian prairies to settlement, and relates how the farm implement industry developed into one of the major industrial concerns of Canada.

The Elements Combined by William Kilbourne, Clarke Irwin Co. Ltd., Toronto, 1960, is a history of the Steel Company of Canada from its early beginnings in the hand smelting of raw Canadian ore to its rise as a major continental producer of raw and finished steel products.

Lucy Morgan prepared *The Canadian Primary Iron and Steel Industry*, Queen's Printer, Ottawa, 1956, on behalf of the Royal Commission on Canada's economic prospects. This work documents the mergers and consolidations that have occurred in a basic industry of the Canadian economy. An earlier work, still of value in assessing the historical development of Canadian industry, is W. J. A. Donald's *The Canadian Iron and Steel Industry*, Houghton, Boston, 1915. O. W. Main has produced a useful reference work in *The Canadian Nickel Industry: a study in market control and public policy*, University of Toronto Press, 1955.

Leather and furs have always been staple items of Canadian commerce. The *Canadian Footwear and Leather Directory*, Scarborough, Ontario, published annually since 1926, gives an account of this industry, as does the *Shoe and Leather Journal*, Don Mills, Ontario, issued monthly since 1883. *Fur of Canada*, Winnipeg, established 1923, is a monthly publication that provides a review of the main events in the western fur area, while the *Fur Trade Journal of Canada*, Toronto, monthly, has covered fur marketing and manufacturing since 1923.

Building in Canada is well documented in the *Canadian Builder*, Maclean-Hunter, Toronto, published since 1952, and *Daily Commercial News and Building Record*, Toronto, established 1927.

CHAPTER 9

Medicine

THE Medical Research Council of Canada, Ottawa, was established in November 1960 by the Government of Canada. The Council supports research in the broad field of medical science. Such support consists mainly of grants-in-aid of research, carried out by the staffs of Canadian universities, hospitals, and institutes, and of the provision of support for staffs under the fellowship, scholarship, and associateship programmes. In 1965–6 the Council provided $12,000,000 for these purposes.

Health Organizations of the United States, Canada and Internationally, 2nd edn., Ithaca, NY, Graduate School of Business and Public Administration, Cornell University, 1965, lists several hundred voluntary organizations, professional societies, and other groups concerned with health and related fields in Canada. National Canadian associations can be located easily in this directory only if their name begins "Canadian", since no distinction is made between Canadian and United States organizations. Provincial associations are listed separately for each of the Canadian provinces.

The *Canadian Hospital Directory* has been published annually since 1953 by the Canadian Hospital Association, Toronto. It gives information about hospitals, nursing institutions, hospital associations, and allied institutions, and serves as a buying guide for hospitals. Two periodicals dealing with hospitals are *Hospital Administration in Canada*, Toronto, established 1959, and *Canadian Hospital*, Toronto, established 1924, the journal of the Canadian Hospital Association.

The *Canadian Medical Directory* (Fig. 19), Seccombe House, Toronto, annual, is divided into three parts. Part I has an alphabetical list of physicians. It cites diplomas and the year of graduation (MD, CM). It includes retired physicians, internees, hospital residents, and medical officers of the armed forces. Part II includes civilian doctors in active practice arranged by province and town. Part III gives a list of medical officers of the armed forces, some information about hospitals, nursing homes, schools of nursing, poison control centres, health departments, and universities. There is also a "Medical Journals' Guide", an index intended as a selection aid for choosing medical journals. In addition, Section III includes names of the members of the graduating classes in medicine at Canadian universities from the previous year.

The Canadian Medical Association, 150 St. George St., Toronto, with a membership of over 14,000, is organized to maintain and protect the interests of the medical profession. It publishes the weekly *Canadian Medical Association Journal*, established 1911, and the quarterly *Canadian Journal of Surgery*, established 1952. Hugh Ernest MacDermot has written a *History of the Canadian Medical Association*, Toronto, Murray Printing Co., 1935–58, 2 vols. Volume 1 covers 1867–1921 and volume 2 1920–56. A general history of medicine can be found in J. J. Haegerty, *Four Centuries of Medical History in Canada*, Toronto, 1928. This includes a sketch of the medical history of Newfoundland.

The College of General Practice of Canada, 150A St. George St., Toronto, has published a *Journal* since 1952. Each province maintains its own licensing body; the one for Ontario is the College of Physicians and Surgeons of Ontario, 64 Prince Arthur St., Toronto.

D. Sclater Lewis has prepared *The Royal College of Physicians and Surgeons, 1920–1960* McGill Univ. Press, 1962, a history of the development of the College during its first 40 years. The organization was established as a joint college of physicians and surgeons, to set standards for specialist status, and to provide an examining body to see that the standards were met by doctors trained both in Canada and abroad. It was the intention of those

University of Ottawa

Anderson, D.M.
Bradley, J. G.
Brazeau, M.
Camirand, A.
Casserly, J.
Civitella, T.
Courtright, Lucy
DesGroseillers, J. P.
Dupont, F.
Fiorentino, R.
Fong, P.
Germain, M. A.
Hache, A. G.
Harvey, J. H.
Keary, F. V.
Keon, T. P.
Koval, R. J.

Lavallée, A.
Lussier, Jeannette
Lyons, A.
Melanson, A. S.
Merry, G.
Mulvihill, Julia
Munger, L. C.
Nadeau, J. C.
Nazaruk, Eileen
Oliveri, R. A.
O'Neil, G. R.
O'Reilly, G.
Pagé, D.
Paquet, R.
Pastore, L. T.
Petrella, N. J.
Pures, J.

Renaud, L. P.
Robertson, G. T.
Rosman, M.
Schoen, Joanne
Seguin, G. A.
Streater, D.
Surette, G. D.
Swartz, G. J.
Swerdfeger, H.
Tai, J.
Thompson, S.
Ting, L.
Ting-Desaulniers, Monique
Tremblay, N.
Villeneuve, V.
Waszczuk, Madeleine
Webb. G. H.

Queen's University

Adler, Allan, B.A.
Amy, John Van Camp, A.B.
  (Class of 1964)
Barry, Murray Patrick
Beattie, Joan Katharine, B.A.
Brant, Clare Clifton
Brown, Willa Marlene
Buhr, Lois Marilyn
Dowd, Judith Anne
Firth, Sydney Terry, B.A.
Fisher, Mark Murray
Fleming, Sandford Rob
Franko, George
Gray, James Neal
Greenaway, John Robert
Gregor, Ronald Daniel, B.Sc.
Hilton, Donald Richard
Houze, Graham Neal

Kroft, Frederick Earl
Lake, John Richard
Lloyd, Gary Richard
Lockie, John Geoffrey A., B.Sc.
Lugsdin, James Gordon
McGuire, John Joseph
McPhee, Malcolm Scott
McQueen, Thomas Alexander
Marcellus, Edward Ethan
Meyer, Clifford R., B.Sc.
Middleton, Donald George
Mitchell, Winston Murray
Moreland, Stewart Wray
Paskevicius, Lydia
Pickersgill, Jane
Sandomirsky, Stanley Kenneth
  (Class of 1964)
Sanders, Michael Gerald, B.A.

Schlappner, Otto L.A.
Scully, Hugh Edwards, B.A.
Shaffer, Eldon Alan
Smart, Hugh Taylor
Smith, David Fraser
Sparling, James Robert
Stolman, Lewis Peter
Swaye, Paul Sydney
Tayfel, Roy Steven M.
Taylor, Graeme McDonald
Tomka, Brian Edward
Veldhuis, Keimpe
Whetham, John C. G.
Whitfield, Joan A., B.A.
Wigle, Ronald Denis
Wilton, Bruce Wallace
Wynd, Peter Brian
Yam, Diana Elizabeth

FIG. 19. *Canadian Medical Directory*, 1966.

founding the College that its degrees should signify that its fellows have received sound practical training in addition to their academic achievement.

The Canadian Public Health Association has published *The Federal and Provincial Health Services in Canada*, edited by R. D. Davis, 2nd edn., Toronto, the Association, 1962. Articles by Canadian authorities describe the activities in the field of public health of the Federal Department of health and welfare and each provincial department that is responsible for health. There are several appendixes, including "Public Health in Upper Canada, 1791–1867" and a "History of the Canadian Public Health Association from 1910–1959".

Of value for current information is the *Canadian Journal of Public Health*, Toronto, issued monthly since 1910, which provides news and articles dealing with the public health profession in Canada.

In 1961 a Royal Commission on Health Services was appointed by the Federal Government. Its 2-volume report, Queen's Printer, Ottawa, 1964–5, represents the final statement of the Commissioners who were asked "to inquire into and report upon the existing facilities and the future need for health services for the people of Canada and the resources to provide such services, and to recommend such measures, consistent with the constitutional division of legislative powers in Canada, as the Commissioners believe will ensure that the best possible health care is available to all Canadians".

The Commissioners received submissions and heard representatives from 406 organizations or individuals. Public hearings were held in all provinces and the Yukon. Studies were made of the health programmes of the United Kingdom, France, Holland, Sweden, Switzerland, Austria, Italy, the United States, the USSR, Australia, and New Zealand.

Twenty-six research studies are also published "where the information is considered to be of general usefulness and necessary to give a complete background to many of the matters dealt within the report". Volume 1 includes the principles and recommendations;

volume 2 "rounds out the analysis . . . including the quality of health services and the freedom of both providers and users of health services". This report is well documented; it includes many tables of statistical information and is well-indexed.

The monthly *Journal of the Canadian Dental Association* was established in 1935 and is published in Toronto. A further journal is that of the *Ontario Dental Association*, also issued monthly. In the field of pharmacy the *Canadian Pharmaceutical Journal*, Toronto, has appeared monthly since 1868. The Canadian Psychiatric Association, Ottawa, has published its *Journal* 6 times a year since 1956. The *Journal of the Canadian Physiotherapy Association*, Montreal, has been issued quarterly since 1939.

John Murray Gibbon has written *Three Centuries of Canadian Nursing*, MacMillan, Toronto, 1947, which tells the story of Canadian nursing up to and including World War II. There is information on the work of the Canadian Red Cross, on public and mental hospital nursing, and on the Victorian Order of Nurses. The book is illustrated with many photographs of people and places, and there is an index mainly of names and places, including hospitals and training schools.

The Canadian Nurse, Montreal, established 1905, is a monthly publication of the Canadian Nurses Association. A French-language edition *L'Infirmière canadienne* also appears.

Public health nursing in Canada, principles and practice, by Florence H. M. Emoy, revised edition, Macmillan, 1953, outlines the framework within which public health nursing is carried out. The book was prepared originally in 1945 and the revision has added chapters in Part II which deal with industrial hygiene, child hygiene and communicable diseases. The chapters on administration show the organizational framework of public health services in each Province, and in major cities such as Vancouver and Toronto. There are valuable references to various Canadian publications that document the development of public health services in Canada.

CHAPTER 10

Canadian Art

As THE population has grown, there has been a growing interest in the arts in Canada and an increase in the number of official and non-official bodies that are responsible for artistic developments. On the federal level there is the Canada Council whose annual report is a valuable description of cultural and artistic development in Canada. On the provincial level may be found the publications of the Quebec Council for the Arts, the Ontario Arts Council, the Alberta Arts Council, to name only three, as well as the reports of local and municipal art councils in the larger towns and cities.

Related to these are the catalogues and publications of the principal Canadian art galleries. The National Gallery of Canada, Ottawa, provides a wide range of guides, catalogues, brochures, and other publications, as well as its annual report, a valuable source of information on progress made in developing the services of the Gallery. The Art Gallery of Ontario, Toronto, the Vancouver Art Gallery, and the Montreal Museum of Fine Arts issue various illustrated publications dealing with all aspects of Canadian art. Other galleries which publish catalogues and brochures include the Beaverbrook Gallery in Fredericton, New Brunswick, the Musée d'arts contemporain, Montreal, the Norman Mackenzie Gallery, Regina, and several of the private galleries of Montreal and Toronto.

Since 1959 the Canadian Conference on the Arts, an unofficial private group of art supporters and practising artists in all fields, has worked to stimulate the development of community arts organizations. At regular intervals the Conference members meet

Museums and Societies

CANADIAN ARTS COUNCIL—CONSEIL
  CANADIEN DES ARTS*

Louise Barette, Sec.

3936 Parc Lafontaine, Montreal, P.Q.

Est. 1945, to co-ordinate the work of member societies. Ann. meet. Spring. Memb. 22 societies totaling 20,000 artists and patrons in component societies, with an additional 30-40,000 having part-time or indirect affiliation; dues $15 per society. Sponsors exhibitions, competitions, scholarships. Publishes "C.A.C. News".

MEMBERS SOCIETIES

Royal Architectural Institute of Canada; Canadian Authors' Association; La Société des Ecrivains canadiens; Federation of Canadian Artists; Canadian Music Council; Canadian Handicrafts Guild; Canadian Guild of Potters; Sculptors Society of Canada; Canadian Society of Landscape Architects and Town Planners; Canadian Ballet Festivals Association; Canadian Society of Creative Leathercraft; National Ballet Guild of Canada; Guild of Canadian Weavers; Town Planning Institute of Canada; Association of Canadian Industrial Designers; Canadian Council of Authors and Artists; Royal Winnipeg Ballet of Canada; Dominion Drama Festival; Canadian Society for Education Through Art; Opera Fes-

CANADIAN GUILD OF POTTERS

Mrs. Helen Copeland, Pres.

574 St. Clements Ave. Toronto (12)

Mrs. Ruthann Gaerdner, Vice-Pres.

Mrs. Olea Davis, Western Vice-Pres.

Mrs. C. Reid, Eastern Vice-Pres.

Est. 1933, to promote the best in pottery. Monthly meetings. Ann. meet. May. Memb. 250; dues $5.

Activities: Sponsors exhibitions of Canadian pottery in Canada and overseas; conducts yearly workshop at Central Technical School with visiting instructor; presents art shows at its center—100 Ave. Road, Toronto (5).

CANADIAN HANDICRAFTS GUILD

2025 Peel St., Montreal (2) Que.

Tel: 849-1533

Est. 1906 to encourage and revive handicrafts. Ann. meet. Mar. or Apr.; Dues $2 and higher.

Exhibitions: Works through provincial branches and affiliated societies (which pay corporate fees) to arrange exhibitions across Canada. Exhibitions also sent abroad.

Collections: Permanent collection of old and new crafts; also Indian and Eskimo art.

Library: Reference library.

Publications: Monthly "News Letter."

FIG. 20. *American Art Directory,* 1964.

to take stock of existing conditions and to attempt to stimulate an awareness in governmental authorities of the need for a greater place for the arts in Canadian life. Preparations for the 1967 Canadian centennial celebrations were used in many communities to focus attention on the need for a new art gallery or other facility for the arts, and many theatres, galleries, and museums have been constructed as a result of these centennial arrangements.

Much of the current information on Canadian artists and their work is contained in the daily newspapers of the larger centres, particularly Montreal, Quebec, Toronto, Vancouver, Winnipeg, Calgary, Halifax, and Edmonton. The monthly periodical *Arts Canada*, formerly *Canadian Art*, Ottawa, Society for Art Publications, has appeared for over 20 years and provides an excellent source of news about activities and exhibits, as well as articles on and by Canadian artists. *Vie des arts*, published quarterly in Montreal since 1956, includes articles on current and historic developments in art outside Canada in addition to documenting the art scene of French Canada. Summaries in English of the main articles are provided in each issue.

The American Art Directory (Fig. 20), published every 3 years by R. R. Bowker for the American Federation of Arts, has, since 1948, included a separate section on Canadian art institutions. There is concise information on Canadian art galleries, museums, art organizations and societies, and art schools.

Who's Who in American Art (Fig. 21), R. R. Bowker, New York, published every 3 years for the American Federation of Arts, gives a useful coverage of many Canadian artists and sculptors and their work. The 1966 edition contains a section giving short biographical notices on 250 Canadian artists. Information includes principal exhibitions, awards, and representation in public galleries. A $2\frac{1}{2}$-page geographical list of Canadian artists is also included.

The Royal Canadian Academy of Art, Toronto, was established in 1880 to encourage the art of painting, sculpture, architecture, and design in Canada, and includes in its membership distinguished Canadians in these fields. A catalogue for the annual exhibition

Trésor des Anciens Jésuites"; "I Have Seen Quebec"; "Pathfinders in the North Pacific," and many others; volumes in "Canadian Artists" series; and many books and articles on Canadian folklore, art, and anthropology. Contributor: Transactions of the R. Soc. of Can.; Canadian Art; Antiques; Art News; Art Quarterly; Gants du Ciel, etc. Lectures: Pacific Indian Art; French Can. Art, etc. *Teaching:* Univs, Ottawa, Mtl. and Laval, Quebec. Organized: French Can. exhs. at Nat. Mus. of Can.; NGC; AG Tor; AA Mtl.; Detroit Inst. of A. *Position:* Anthropologist and Folklorist, National Museum of Canada; Vice-Pres., Intl. Folk Music Council; Chm., Canadian Folk Music Soc.

BATES, MAXWELL—*Painter, Gr., W., Arch.*
　　640 Beaver Lake Rd., R.R. 3, Victoria, B.C.

B. Calgary, Alta., Dec. 14, 1906. *Studied:* Provincial Inst. Tech. & A.; BMSch., with Max Beckmann; and with Abraham Rattner. *Member:* CGP; CSPWC; CSGA; F.I.A.L.; Alberta Soc. A.; ARCA; Associate Member, B.C. Soc. FA. *Honours:* CSPWC, 1957; Minneapolis, Minn., 1958; Winnipeg A. Gal., 1957 (purchase); CSGA, 1960. *Work:* NGC; AG Tor.; Winnipeg A. Gal.; Norman Mackenzie A. Gal., Regina; Calgary All. A. Centre; Auckland (N.Z.) A. Gal.; London (Ont.) A. Mus. Other work: Bldg., and interior furnishings in marble, bronze, oak, etc., by A. W. Hodges Friba and Maxwell Bates (Archs.), St. Mary's Cathedral, Calgary, Alta., Canada. *Exhibited:* NGC, 1930, 1931, 1953, 1955, 1959, 1961, and traveling exh., 1958-1959; Intl. Biennial of Lith., Cincinnati, Ohio, 1958; Phila. Pr. Cl., 1958; Biennial Exh. A. Minneapolis, Minn., 1958; AFA traveling exh., 1959; Canadian Art, Mexico City, 1960; Biennial Prints, Tokyo, 1960; Coloured Graphics, Grenchen, Switzerland, 1961; one-man: Manchester, England, 1934; London, 1938; Vancouver A. Gal., 1947; Queen's Univ., 1950; Manitoba Univ., 1956; Retrospective exh., Norman Mackenzie A. Gal., Regina, Winnipeg & Edmonton, 1960-61.

BEAMENT, COMMANDER HAROLD—*Painter, Des.*
　　4709 The Boulevard, Westmount, P.Q.

B. Ottawa, July 23, 1898. *Studied:* Osgoode Hall, Tor.; OCA. *Member:* RCA. *Honours:* Jessie Dow Prize, AA Mtl. 1935. *Work:* War Records NGC; Dominion Archives, Ottawa; A. Gal., London, Ont.; MPQ; AA Mtl.; A. Gal., Hamilton, Ont. Commissions: official war artist with R. Can. Navy 1943-46; des. current 10¢ stamp (Eskimo) for Canadian Govt. *Exhibited:* RCA 1922; NGC 1926-33; Wembley, 1924, 1925; Paris 1927; S. America 1929; S. Dominions 1936; Coronation 1937; Tate 1938; WFNY 1939; War art, NG London, NGC 1945, '46; OSA. *Teaching:* AA Mtl. 1936; N.S. Col. A. *Position:* War Artist, Royal Canadian Navy; Hon. Treas., 1958, Pres., 1964, RCA.

BELL, R. MURRAY—*Collector*
　　134 Forest Hill Rd., Toronto 7, Ont.

Collection: Chinese ceramics, with special interest in blue and white Chinese porcelain.

BENTON, MARGARET PEAKE—
　　Miniature and Portrait Painter
　　Wesley Ave., Niagara-on-the-Lake, Ont.

B. South Orange, N.J. *Studied:* OCA under Sir Wyly Grier and Archibald Barnes. *Member:* AG Tor.; Pa. Soc. Min. P.; Min. P. S. & Gravers, Wash., D.C. *Honour:* For best painting, Miniature Painters', Sculptors', Gravers' Soc., Wash., D.C., 1962. *Work:* portraits, Wesley Bldg., Tor.; North Tor. Collegiate Inst.; Nurmanzil Psychiatric Centre, Lucknow, India; King's Col., Halifax, N.S.; PMA; murals, St. John's Garrison Church, Tor. *Exhibited:* OSA, 1933; PAFA 1940, 1941, 1943, 1945-1951; NCFA 1943, 1945-1947, 1951-1964; RCA 1938-1940, 1942, 1948, 1949; Royal Acad. A., London, 1950. Instr., Painting, Niagara-on-the-Lake H.S., 1960-61.

BENY, WILFRED ROLOFF—
　　Painter, Et., L., Eng., Photographer
　　432 13th St. South, Lethbridge, Alta.; also, Lungotevere 3-B, Rome, Italy

B. Medicine Hat, Alta., Jan. 7, 1924. *Studied:* Banff Sch. FA; Univ. Tor. B.A.; State Univ. Iowa, M.A. *Honours:* F., Univ. Iowa; Guggenheim F., 1952. *Work:* St. Hilda's Col., Univ. Tor.; Univ. Iowa; FMA; MMoA; BM; N.Y. Pub. Lib.; Yale Univ.; CM; Wesleyan Univ.;

NGC; A. Gal. Toronto; Oslo Mus., Norway; Bezalel Mus., Jerusalem; Redfern Gal., London. and others. Author, Photographer, "The Thrones of Earth and Heaven," 1958. *Exhibited:* CSPWC 1942-1944; OSA 1943-1945; AA Mtl. 1945; Nat. Print Show, Wichita, Kans, 1946; Phila. Print Cl., 1946; Milan, Italy, 1952; Weyhe Gal., N.Y., 1947; Palazzo Strozzi, Florence, 1949; Knoedler Gal., 1951; Merano, Vicenza, Italy, 1951; one-man: Hart House, Univ. Tor.; Eaton College, Tor.; Univ. Iowa 1946; Librairie Paul Morihien, Paris, 1952; Florence, Italy, 1949; Knoedler Gal., N.Y., 1951, 1954; A. Gal., Toronto, 1954; Robertson Gal., Ottawa, 1954; Waldorf Gal., Montreal, 1954; Contemp. Gal., N.Y., 1955; Western Canada Circuit, 1955, and in Italy and France. Author-Photographer, "A Time of Gods," publ. London, 1962 in 8 Language editions.

BICE, CLARE—*Painter, Mus. Cur.*
　　1010 Wellington St.; Williams Memorial Art Gallery and Museum, London, Ont.

B. Durham, Ont., Jan. 24, 1909. *Studied:* Univ. West Ont., B.A.; ASL; Grand Central Sch. of A., N.Y. *Member:* OSA. *Honours:* RCA; OSA, LL.D. (Hon.); Canadian Govt. F., 1953. *Exhibited:* OSA, 1940- ; RCA 1940- ; CNE 1938-58; WFNY 1939; Western Ont. Exh. 1940-58; NGC Army Art Exh. 1944. Author, Illus., "Jory's Cove"; "Across Canada"; "The Great Island," 1954; "A Dog for Davie's Hill," 1965; "Hurricane Treasure," 1965; also I. of other children's books. Contributor articles on art to Canadian Art, etc. *Position:* Cur., Williams Memorial Art Gallery, London, Ont.

BIELER, ANDRE—*Painter, E., L., Eng.*
　　R.R. #1, Glenburnie, Ont.; Dept. of Art, Queen's University, Kingston, Ont.

B. Lausanne, Switzerland, Oct. 8, 1896. *Studied:* ASL; Ecole du Louvre, Paris, under Maurice Denis; Switzerland under Ernest Biéler. *Member:* RCA; OSA, CGP, CSPWC, CSGA, FCA. *Honours:* Pres. FCA 1942-4; Vice-Pres. CGP 1943; ARCA; Forster award, OSA, 1957. *Work:* NGC; MPQ; AA Mtl.; AG Tor.; Winnipeg AG; Hart House, Univ. Tor.; Queen's Univ.; Aluminum Co. of Canada; mural, East Mem. Bldg., Ottawa; Edmonton A. Gal.; Windsor AA, 1955; Mus. FA, Montreal, 1952; Art Collection Soc., Kingston; mosaics, Chalmer's Church Hall, Kingston; Frontenac Tile Co., Kingston, and others. *Exhibited:* Intl. WC, Chicago; Brooklyn; Coronation 1937; Tate 1938; Chicago 1939; WFNY 1939; Addison 1942; Yale 1944; Rio 1944, '46; DPC 1945; UNESCO 1946; BMFA, 1946; VMFA, 1949; Contemp. Can. Art, 1950; Brazil, 1950; SFMA, 1956; one-man: Mtl. 1924; '26, '45; Paris 1936; Ottawa, 1954; Kingston, 1954, 1955, 1960; Mus. FA, Montreal, 1952; Retrospective, Queen's Univ., 1963; San Miguel de Allende, Mexico, 1964, Glenburnie, Ont., 1964, and others. Contributor: Kingston Conference Proceedings 1941; Maritime Art; Canadian Art. Lectures: Spanish, Mexican, Canadian art on tour of E. Canada; "Modern Art," Windsor and Ottawa. *Position:* Emeritus Prof. FA, Queen's Univ., Kingston, Ont. 1963- ; Dir. Etherington Art Centre.

BINNING, BERTRAM CHARLES—
　　Painter, E., Mus. Cur.
　　2968 Mathers Crescent, West Vancouver; University of British Columbia, Vancouver, B.C.

B. Medicine Hat, Alta., 1909. *Studied:* Vancouver Sch. A.; ASL; Univ. Oregon; in London under Henry Moore, Ozenfant and Meninsky. *Member:* FCA; British Columbia Soc. FA; CSGA; CGP; ARCA. *Honours:* medal, Vancouver, 1951; Carnegie Scholarship, 1936, 1951. *Work:* NGC; AG Tor.; Hart House, Univ. Tor.; Vancouver A. Gal. *Exhibited:* British Columbia Soc. A., 1932-1945; British Columbia Soc. FA, 1935-1946; OSGA, 1941-1946; CGP, 1943, 1944; Rio 1946; BMFA, 1946, 1955; AG Tor., 1949; NGA, 1950; Canadian Biennial, 1954; Venice Biennale, 1954; Sao Paulo, Brazil, 1953; PC (3 Canadians), 1955; Valencia, Venezuela, 1955; Milan Triennial, 1957. *Position:* Assoc. Prof. A., Univ. British Columbia, and Cur. FA Gal., Univ. British Columbia.*

BLOORE, RONALD LANGLEY—*Art Gallery Director, L.*
　　Norman Mackenzie Art Gallery, University of Saskatchewan, Regina Campus, Regina, Sask.

B. Brampton, Ont., May 29, 1925. *Studied:* Univ. Toronto; N.Y. Univ.; Washington Univ., M.A.; Courtauld Inst., Univ. London. *Positions:* Dir., Mackenzie Art Gallery, University of Saskatchewan, Regina, Sask., Canada.

FIG. 21. *Who's Who in American Art*, 1966.

of the Academy has been published since 1880. Current catalogues are generally illustrated and contain a list of living and dead members and associates. Secretary-Treasurer of the Academy for 1966 was Mr. Fred Finley, 63 Warland Avenue, Toronto 6.

The Ontario Society of Artists was instituted in 1872 and is a forum for professional artists in Ontario. An annual exhibition of members' work is held in Toronto and circulated throughout the Province. An illustrated catalogue accompanies the exhibition. The 1965–6 Secretary of the Society is Roy Austin, 407 Birchmount Road, Scarborough, Ontario.

Art Treasures in the Royal Ontario Museum, prepared by T. A. Heinrich and published in 1963 to commemorate the Museum's 50th anniversary, is a picture anthology of artifacts and art objects in Canada's foremost museum, ranging from prehistoric and primitive cultures to nineteenth-century Europe and Canada. It includes much from the Museum's renowned Far Eastern collections. An introduction outlines the history and scope of the Museum's collections, and explanatory text and captions accompany the illustrations. There are 41 coloured and 163 black-and-white illustrations.

Volume 3 of the *Catalogue of Paintings and Sculpture* (Fig. 22), available also in French, published in 1960 by the Trustees of the National Gallery, Ottawa, deals with the Canadian School. It is prepared by R. H. Hubbard, curator of the collections. The body of the work consists of an alphabetical arrangement by artist representing over 1500 paintings and sculptures. Biographical notes on each artist are included. The majority of the works are illustrated by small half-tones. Checklists of the Royal Canadian Academy diploma collection and of Canadian works in the World War I and World War II collections are included. An index to accession numbers, index to genre subjects, index to portraits, topography and landscape, to religious, allegorical, historical, and mythological subjects are provided. A 16-page essay on the development of Canadian painting and sculpture precedes the catalogue portion. Mr. Hubbard has also prepared *The Development of Canadian Art*, National Gallery of Canada, Ottawa, 1963,

G

James Edward Hervey MacDonald, born at Durham (England) of Canadian parents. Came to Hamilton, Ontario, in 1887. Studied at the Hamilton Art School (c. 1890), then for a short time at the Central Ontario School of Art, Toronto, under William Cruikshank and G. A. Reid. Worked as a graphic designer for Grip, Ltd. in Toronto from about 1895 and at the Carlton Studio, London, 1904–7. Returned to Toronto and rejoined Grip Ltd. and began to paint landscape near Toronto. Made his first trip to northern Ontario in 1909 and Georgian Bay in 1910. In 1911 he left Grip and became a full-time painter. Moved to Thornhill, Ontario, in 1912. In 1913, with Lawren Harris, he saw an exhibition of Scandinavian painting in Buffalo. Sketching trip to Algoma with Harris and others in 1918. Original member of the Group of Seven, 1920. Taught at the Ontario College of Art from 1921; principal, 1929–32. A.R.C.A. in 1912, R.C.A. in 1931. Painted in northern Ontario, on the Atlantic coast (1922) in the Rocky Mountains (1924 ff.), and the West Indies. Carried out several murals. Also a poet. Died in Toronto. Founding member of the C.G.P.,

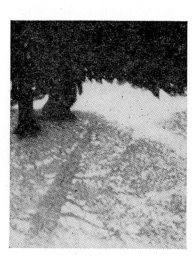

387 IN THE PINE SHADOWS, MOONLIGHT

Canvas, $31\frac{1}{2}'' \times 27\frac{1}{4}''$.

Painted about 1912.

LITERATURE: *Studio*, lvii (1912), reprod. 249 (as 'Early Winter Evening'); Hunter, *MacDonald* (1940), p. 48.

EXHIBITED: C.N.E., 1912, No. 31; N.G.C., *MacDonald*, 1933, No. 1.

Acquired 19

FIG. 22. *Catalogue of Paintings and Sculpture*, vol. 3.

available also in French, which is a brief survey of painting, sculpture, architecture, and the decorative arts from the seventeenth century to the present day. There are 209 black-and-white and 26 coloured illustrations as well as an index of the artists mentioned.

The Arts in Canada: a stock-taking in mid-century, was edited by Dr. Malcolm Ross and published by Macmillan, Toronto, in 1958. In it fourteen Canadian specialists contribute essays on fine arts, creative writing, radio and television, architecture, industrial design, theatre, films, emphasizing post-war developments. Only two of the contributors are Canadians of French origin, and the majority of the contributors concentrate on English–Canadian achievements. Biographical notes on the contributors are included. There is an index and 100 illustrations, 20 of which are in colour.

Graham McInnes has written *Canadian Art*, Macmillan, Toronto, 1950, which is a compact survey of the arts in Canada from earliest times to the present, including a chapter on contemporary film making, industrial design, and architecture. Appendixes list art institutions and public collections in Canada, a chronology of developments in Canadian art from 1535 to 1950, and a select list of Canadian artists—living and dead—with dates. A select bibliography, and an 8-page index are provided. There are 6 colour and 32 black-and-white illustrations.

Coup d'oeil sur les arts en Nouvelle-France, Quebec, by Gérard Morisset, 1941, provides a survey of painting, sculpture, architecture, and the applied arts in Quebec, with particular emphasis on the seventeenth, eighteenth, and nineteenth centuries. Much concise information is included on the work of individual artists and artisans, but the chief value of the work lies in its consideration of the social and cultural milieu and its expression in works of art and craftsmanship. There is a bibliography and 15-page index of names as well as 32 black-and-white illustrations.

F. St. George Spendlove's *The Face of Early Canada*, Ryerson, Toronto, 1958, is a study of paintings, drawings, and prints from the sixteenth to the nineteenth century, bearing upon the history of Canada, illustrated by examples from the Sigmund Samuel

Collection in the Royal Ontario Museum, Toronto. Separate chapters are devoted to such major artist-recorders as George Heriot, W. H. Bartlett, and Cornelius Krieghoff. Minor artists are dealt with in surveys of illustration by regions, provinces, and major cities. Two chapters deal with such specific topics as the War of 1812, the Rebellion of 1837–8, transportation, sports, and caricature. The book contains 122 black-and-white plates and 6 colour plates. There is a general index and index of authors, engravers, and publishers, and a bibliography.

A concise historical survey of Canadian art from the French Colonial period to the present is provided in *The Arts in Canada*, Queen's Printer, 1965, one of the Canadian Citizenship Series prepared by the Department of Citizenship and Immigration, Ottawa. The development of architecture, sculpture, decorative art, and particularly painting, is considered during six chronological periods with the last, contemporary developments since 1930, emphasizing the post-1945 period. Capsule biographies of significant artists are included throughout the text. The arts of Canada's native races are not included. Twenty-three black-and-white and 16 colour illustrations and a 3-page index are provided.

Architecture and Planning

The Royal Architectural Institute of Canada, founded in 1907 to promote the welfare of the architectural profession in Canada, is generally regarded as the official organization of practising architects. A programme of annual awards and scholarships to promising students is maintained, and awards are made for outstanding contributions in such allied arts as mural painting, sculpture, decoration, and industrial design. Since 1924 the Institute has published a monthly *Journal* documenting achievements in the field of architecture, with well-illustrated articles on architectural theory and practice, and the history of architecture with an emphasis on Canadian developments. Other publications include *List of Members*, 1960; *Architectural Directory*, annual; *The Official RAIC Annual Directory and Guide to Services and Products in Building Construction*, 1965; *Report of the Committee of Inquiry into the Design of the Residential Environment*, 1960; and *Historic Architecture in Canada*, 1967. Editorial offices of the Institute are at 160 Eglinton Avenue East, Toronto 12, Ontario.

Urban and regional References urbaines et régionales, Canadian Council on urban and regional research, 225 Metcalfe St., Ottawa, was issued in 1964 containing approximately 1750 references to books, pamphlets, reports, and articles on town planning in Canada, published in the period 1945–62. A *Supplement* appeared in 1966 with a further 1300 items classified into seven subject groups which are further subdivided. A consolidated table of contents and combined author and geographical indexes, covering 3000 items in both issues, is provided in the *Supplement*.

Building Canada: an architectural history of Canadian life (Fig. 23), by A. W. Gowans, Oxford University Press, Toronto, 1966, is a popular account of Canadian architecture considered as an expression of changing patterns of social life and organization from the Indian and pioneer tradition to the industrial structures of the 1960's. 247 plates with extensive captions present a selection of representative buildings of all types. Buildings from all provinces are illustrated and a 3-page geographical index locates them. A 4-page general index is included.

The Ancestral Roof, Domestic Architecture of Upper Canada, was prepared by Marion MacRae and Anthony Adamson and published by Clarke Irwin, Toronto, 1963. It is a social history of domestic architecture in the Province of Ontario from 1783 to 1867 based on a detailed consideration and illustration of important and typical houses, extant or demolished. A major theme of the work is the adaptation of European and American styles to meet Canadian conditions and the development of distinct regional and vernacular variations. It is well illustrated with photographs, plans and drawings, of interiors, and details. There is a glossary and index.

A valuable record of the architectural heritage of the Province of Quebec is provided in publications of the Quebec Historic Monuments Commission. *Les Vieilles églises de la province de*

54. SHELBURNE, N.S. *Ross-Thompson House and Warehouse.* An entirely typical example of the medieval traditions of early New England architecture in Nova Scotia—directly expressing its structure and materials, additive in plan (house and warehouse are contiguous)—and an eloquent testimony to the futility of an attempt by exiled New England merchants to create a New England trading town at Shelburne after the Revolution. It was built shortly after 1784.

55. HORTON, N.S. *Tuzo House.* Originally built in 1763 by one Jonathan Harris (whose tombstone serves as the sill to a pigpen in a nearby farm) for Captain Tuzo, an immigrant from Bermuda via New England. The exterior was remodelled in a more mature American classical manner with vaguely Adamesque storm porch, pilasters, and window-frames; but the additive plan and the directly expressed materials remain.

FIG. 23. *Building Canada,* 1966.

152

Québec, 1647–1800, published in 1925, records the history and architectural significance of thirty-eight notable churches and includes photographs of interiors, exteriors, and details. *Vieux manoirs, vieilles maisons*, 1927, documents houses and mills of historic significance, principally of the seventeenth and eighteenth centuries, and provides an excellent collection of illustrations. Both titles were issued in English and French editions.

Sculpture

Canadian sculptors have made contributions to the arts in Canada for several generations, and the most famous were to be found in the Province of Quebec, working in wood. *Côté, the Wood Carver* by Marius Barbeau, Ryerson Press, 1943, in the Canadian Arts Series, tells how this carver of figureheads for sailing ships turned to the carving of high reliefs illustrating the Scriptures for church decoration. Suzor Côté flourished in the period 1880 to 1900. His work may be found on the exteriors of many churches in Quebec, and he is an acknowledged master among a long line of French-Canadian artists in wood.

Modern Canadian sculpture is best seen in *Canadian Outdoor Sculpture Exhibition, 1962*, National Gallery of Canada, Ottawa, 1962. This collection of biographies of twenty-three contemporary Canadian sculptors is illustrated with an example of the work of each. Included are Gerald Carter, North Vancouver, BC, Jacques Chapdelaine, Châteauguay, Quebec, Gilles Dufour, Île d'Orléans, Quebec, and many others. Some, such as Roy Leadbeater, Augustin Filipovic, and Victor Tolgesy, were born in Europe but have continued their work in Canada. The illustrated catalogues of the Open-air Sculpture Exhibitions held at the Stratford Shakespearean Festival in 1965 and 1966 provide useful surveys of contemporary Canadian sculpture with photographs of all works exhibited and biographical notes. The 1965 exhibition showed the work of thirty-four artists working in English-speaking Canada; the 1966 exhibition showed the work of twenty-four artists from Quebec.

One internationally known aspect of Canadian sculpture is that of Indian and Eskimo carvings, some in wood and some in stone. *Totem Poles* by Marius Barbeau, published by the National Museum of Canada, Ottawa, in 2 volumes in 1950–1, is a definitive work on the art of totem poles, house posts, and grave pillars of British Columbia and Alaska. Volume 1 contains a general introduction on the origin, significance and techniques of totem carving, followed by a comprehensive listing of extant and perished poles, arranged according to crests and topics. A great deal of information concerning the social life, religion, and mythology of west coast tribes is included from accounts of early travellers, oral tradition, and the reminiscences of older tribe members. Volume 2 contains a comprehensive list of poles by original location, including poles destroyed or removed. The work is extensively illustrated with black-and-white reproductions of early and contemporary photographs, engravings, paintings, and drawings.

George Swinton's *Eskimo Sculpture*, McClelland & Stewart, Toronto, was published in 1965. It is a lavishly illustrated exposition of the historic and contemporary sculpture of the natives of Canada's eastern Arctic regions. A general introduction is followed by illustration and discussion of individual sculptures and sculptors, arranged by subject, including such categories as male figures, birds, sea life, and legends. The evaluation of the pieces as works of art as well as their ethnographic interest is noted. Works from public and private collections are illustrated in 16 pages of colour and 200 black-and-white reproductions. An index by name of artist and locality is provided. There is a bibliography.

The *Standard Catalogue of Canadian Coins, Tokens and Paper Money, 1670 to Date* by J. E. Charlton, is published in annual editions by the Canada Coin Exchange, Toronto. It is a manual for dealers and collectors, with values and illustrations of the various coins, tokens, and paper money of Canada issued from the French régime to the present. It incorporates much useful information from Pierre Napoléon Breton's *Histoire illustrée des monnaies et jetons du Canada . . .*, reprint, Winnipeg, 1963, which is available also in English. The *Canadian Numismatic Journal*, Toronto, published since 1956, deals with all matters of interest to collectors of Canadian coins.

John Langdon has prepared *Canadian Silversmiths, 1700–1900*, 2nd edn., Stinehour Press, Lunenburg, Vermont, 1966, which is an authoritative work based on the author's earlier *Canadian Silversmiths and their Marks, 1667–1867*. Over 1500 names are listed and approximately 500 marks are reproduced.

Drawing and Decorative Arts

Canadian Drawings and Prints by Paul Duval, Burns & MacEachern, Toronto, 1952, is a pioneer collection of 100 monochrome reproductions of drawings and prints, all but three produced in the twentieth century. A 10-page introduction surveys the history and development of graphic art in Canada. An index of artists whose works are reproduced is included.

Mr. Duval has also prepared *Group of Seven drawings*, Burns & MacEachern, Toronto, 1965, which contains 70 black-and-white reproductions of the graphic work of the nine Canadian artists who at various times made up the Group of Seven. The drawings include many field sketches for later large-scale paintings. Short biographical notes on the artists are appended.

The style, technology, and use of Canadian furniture in the French traditional manner from the seventeenth to the first part of the nineteenth century are examined in detail from surviving examples, documentary sources, and through socio-ethnographic methods in *The Early Furniture of French Canada* by Jean Palardy, Macmillan, Toronto, 1963, available also in French. A detailed catalogue *raisonné* of surviving pieces arranged by the morphological functional classification developed by G. H. Rivière, Paris, forms the main body of the work. Additional material includes sections on materials and identification, workmanship and the education of craftsmen, and preservation and restoration. A list of French master workers and of British woodworkers and cabinet makers working in Quebec, bibliography, glossary, and

G*

lexicon of French Canadian furniture terms are included. There are 600 black-and-white photographs and 10 colour plates.

Other works of interest are Gerald Stevens's *In a Canadian Attic*, rev. edn., Ryerson Press, Toronto, 1965, which describes common types of Canadian furniture and house wares of the nineteenth century, and Jeanne Minhinnick's *Early Furniture in Upper Canada Village, 1800–1837*, Ryerson Press, Toronto, 1964, a catalogue of the furniture to be found at the reconstructed colonial village on the shores of the St. Lawrence River near Cornwall, Ontario.

Painting

The Growth of Canadian Painting by Donald W. Buchanan, Collins, London, 1950, is the story of Canadian painting told mainly in short essays on individual painters of the twentieth century, from J. W. Morrice (born 1865) to Jack Nichols (born 1921). A chapter on the nineteenth century introduces a principal theme of the work, which is an account of how the Canadian cultural environment affected, and was affected by the achievements of the individual painters considered. There are 26 colour plates and 64 monochrome illustrations. *Painting in Canada: a history* was prepared by J. Russell Harper, University of Toronto Press, 1966. The former curator of Canadian painting in the National Gallery of Ottawa traces the development of Canadian painting from its beginnings in the seventeenth century to the present. Regional painters and their contributions and the influence of French and English continental traditions are considered along with Canadian physical and social environment in the shaping of Canada's artistic history. There are 378 illustrations, 70 in colour.

Alexander Young Jackson, in *A Painter's Country*, Clarke, Irwin, Toronto, 1958, has written a straightforward account of his life and career as one of Canada's foremost painters. The work reveals the force and inspiration which the author devoted to his profession. Jackson's role in the founding and development of the

Group of Seven is documented, and reminiscences and appraisals of his contemporaries provide a highly personal account of the Canadian art world. There are 12 colour reproductions.

A chronological account of painting in French Canada from the seventeenth to the early twentieth century is contained in *La Peinture traditionnelle au Canada français*, Le Cercle du Livre de France, Montreal, 1960, by Gérard Morisset. Separate chapters are devoted to individual artists of importance including Roy–Audy, Plamondon, and Krieghoff. An index of artists' names is provided. There are 48 black-and-white and 8 colour reproductions.

In 1964 the Ministry of Cultural Affairs of the Province of Quebec published *La Peinture moderne au Canada français* by Guy Viau. An exposition of the roots and development of the revival of painting in Quebec is the principal concern of the author. He recognizes two streams as contributing to the revival. The first, which he calls "The Poets of Reality", finds its roots in the nineteenth century and includes such Canadian contemporaries as Lemieux, de Tonnancour, and Goodridge Roberts. The second, "The Explorers of the Imaginary", includes the internationally recognized Borduas and Riopelle. The work of individual artists is carefully evaluated, and both English- and French-speaking artists are considered. There is a bibliography and black-and-white illustrations.

Photography

Canadians have employed photography as a means of exploration, education, and artistic expression since the mid-nineteenth century. *Early Photography in Canada* by Ralph Greenhill, Oxford, 1965, is a history of early photography with special reference to Canada from 1885 to the 1950's. Eight chapters outline the advance of technical processes from sun painting to early photoengraving, and records their use in Canada. An important feature is the reproduction of 106 early Canadian photographs selected for their value as records of the progress of the art, but important, too, for their illustration of the history and social development of the country. There is a selected bibliography and an index.

Canadian Industrial Photography, Toronto, established 1958, deals with industrial applications in Canada and abroad. The bimonthly *Canadian Cinematography*, Toronto, has appeared since 1960 in order to keep Canadian motion-picture photographers aware of developments within the country.

The National Film Board of Canada, Ottawa, was established in 1939 by the Federal Government through the efforts of John Grierson, pioneer documentary film maker, as a national agency to produce and distribute motion picture films dealing with every aspect of Canadian life.

Since that date the Board has made many thousands of films and won more than 500 awards in Canadian and international competitions for its products. The annual report of the National Film Board records the main events of each year. The Board publishes catalogues of its extensive and varied output of educational and documentary films, many of them produced in foreign languages for distribution overseas through Canadian embassies and consulates.

Music

Music in Canada can be divided into the fields of performing, composing, and the manufacture of musical instruments. All of these are included in Helmut Kallmann's *A History of Music in Canada, 1534–1914*, University of Toronto Press, 1960. This book describes the main occurrences for the period 1534–1914. It is concerned with the development of musical taste and institutions against the background of social and political events. Music in New France and among the Indians is briefly documented; more material was available for the eighteenth and nineteenth centuries when Canada was under British occupation, and a review of today's European heritage in Canada concludes the work. Painstaking research has produced a high degree of accuracy, and a judicious selection of material has been provided.

Music in Canada, edited by Sir Ernest MacMillan, Canadian Music Council, Toronto, and the University of Toronto Press, 1955 was written to give a picture of the state of music in twentieth-century Canada. The eighteen contributors were pre-eminently capable of writing on the various assigned topics: Folksong by Marius Barbeau; Composition by Jean-Marie Beaudet; Education in Music by Arnold Walter; Music and Radio by Geoffrey Waddington; and the whole was edited by Sir Ernest MacMillan who probably has been more active in the Canadian musical scene than any other individual. Although a dozen years have passed since the book was published it still provides a useful picture of musical activities in Canada, particularly for the background information contained in the chapters on orchestras, chamber music, competition festivals, and film music. A new book, *Music in Canada*, has been published by the University of Toronto Press, 1967, with a different approach, different contributors, and a different editor, Dr. Arnold Walter. This work brings the account of musical development, which has been very extensive in Canada in the past 15 years, up to date. The 2 volumes provide a basic account of persons and institutions active in the past 40 years.

Edith Fowke and Richard Johnson have prepared *Folk Songs of Canada*, Waterloo Music Co. Ltd., Waterloo, Ontario, 1954. As the first comprehensive collection of Canadian folk songs, this book features more than six dozen songs from Atlantic to Pacific, in English and French, from Indian to Eskimo tunes, with the criteria being those songs native to Canada and suitable for group singing. Edith Fowke has balanced the different regions and aspects of Canadian life and supplied lucid notes which make up half the book. Included are information on sources, a bibliography, and a list of records. Richard Johnson has done the musical adaptations. From a musical standpoint the accompaniments are excellent. There is an index of titles and first lines.

Edith Fowke and Alan Mills prepared *Canada's Story in Song*, W. J. Gage & Co., Toronto, 1965. This is a selection of songs mainly of folk origin from early to modern times. Historical notes accompanying each song and piano accompaniment is provided.

No mention can be made of folk-songs in Canada, and particularly French folk-songs, without paying homage to Marius Barbeau, the venerable dean of Canadian folk-song collectors. Of his many books, *Folk-songs of Old Quebec*, 2nd edn., Queen's Printer, Ottawa, 1963, is perhaps the slightest, but manages in two short chapters the "Origins and varieties of Canadian folk-songs", and "How folk-songs travelled", to give an excellent history of the subject. Fifteen folk-songs are included (melody line only), all with English translations. The illustrations are by Arthur Lismer.

Hélène Baillargeon, a well-known folk-singer, has edited *Vive la Canadienne*, Éditions du jour, Montreal, 1963. This collection of French folk-songs consists of 77 songs divided into 11 categories: "Chansons de l'enfance"; "Chansons d'amour"; "Chansons de mariage"; "Chansons de maumariées" ending with "Pour le temps des fêtes". The melody line and French text only are given for the songs, but for each an indication is given of the collector and the district from which it came. In addition there are two short lists—one of other collections and one of recordings made by the editor.

Among the principle sources of information concerning music in Canada is the Canadian Music Centre, Toronto and Montreal. In 1963 the Centre published a *Catalogue of Orchestra Music at the Canadian Music Centre*, the Centre, Toronto, the first of several that have been planned. In addition to its usefulness as a list of orchestral works by Canadian composers it supplies a wealth of information, such as duration of the work, instrumentation, degree of difficulty, when, where, and by whom first performed, descriptive notes as supplied by the composer, copyright information, and, in addition, a short biographical sketch of each composer; the whole in French and English.

BMI Canada has published *Music by Canadian Composers*, BMI Canada, Toronto, 1962, and *Supplement*, 1963. This pamphlet is one of a series brought out periodically by BMI Canada Ltd., a performing rights society which publishes extensively in the field of Canadian music.

The compositions listed are divided into 13 categories (piano solo, study scores, organ, recorder) listed alphabetically by composer within each category and accompanied by prices.

Although the list includes only those compositions for which BMI has the performing rights, it is, nevertheless, a useful guide and indicates what is available for purchase in music by Canadian composers.

The Canadian Music Library Association has produced *A Biobibliographical Finding List of Canadian Musicians*, the Association, Toronto, 1961. This directory provides a useful list of musicians who have contributed to the growth of music in Canada; this includes those born in Canada whether they lived here or not and those born abroad. It contains over 2000 names, mainly those found in the 124 source books given at the beginning; including in this listing is a number of monographs on Canadian music and musicians. Entered alphabetically, each musician is listed according to full name, birth and death dates, place of birth, musical occupation, and symbols referring the user to the source materials for additional information.

Thirty-four contemporary Canadian composers are included in *Canadian Composers' Biographies*, Canadian Broadcasting Corporation, International Service, Montreal, 1964. This volume was prepared by the Canadian Broadcasting Corporation primarily to give information about composers whose works the corporation had recorded and distributed abroad. The biographies are set up in double columns, in English and in French, and are headed by a photograph and the address of the person described. Each entry concludes with a list of works, date of composition, and publisher where applicable.

Theatre

The Canadian Theatre Centre, Toronto, is a national clearing house for information about developments in theatre and the performing arts in Canada. Its work consists in preparing studies and reports on various aspects of Canadian theatre. It published a

Report of a Survey of Theatrical Facilities in Canada, the Centre, 1962.

Le Théâtre au Canada français by Jean Hamelin was published by the Ministry of Cultural Affairs, Quebec, 1964. This is a survey of the development of amateur and professional French-language theatre in the Province of Quebec over the last 25 years recorded through the history of individual companies. Sections of the survey are devoted to theatre schools, government aid, and radio and television theatre. Twenty pages are concerned with the careers of French Canadian authors writing for the stage. It is illustrated with portraits and production photographs, and there is an index of names, a chronology, and a bibliography. Jean Béraud has produced *350 ans de théâtre au Canada français*, Le Cercle du Livre de France, Montreal, 1958, which is a history of theatre in French-speaking Canada from Lescarbot's performance of *Le Théâtre de Neptune*, in 1606, to the present time, including both indigenous and touring companies. French-language theatre elsewhere in Canada than Quebec is dealt with, and some reference is made to English-speaking theatre in Montreal. Detailed accounts are given of nineteenth and early twentieth-century theatrical enterprises. There is no index, and illustrations include portraits and facsimiles of published plays.

No comparable history of English theatre in Canada exists. The Dominion Drama Festival, 200 Cooper St., Ottawa, has prepared *Canadian Plays in English: a preliminary annotated catalogue*, 1964, which bring together all of the various Canadian plays that have appeared in the past 75 years. For other information on the Canadian theatre it is necessary to consult such works as the *Canadian Annual Review* or the reports of the Canada Council and the provincial arts councils, which have recently begun to give official support to Canadian theatrical activities.

Herbert Whittaker has written *Canada's National Ballet*, McClelland and Stewart, Toronto, to be published in 1967. This describes the origin and development of the National Ballet of Canada.

CHAPTER II

Sports and Pastimes

ALTHOUGH it is a country that has borrowed most of its habits and customs from abroad, Canada has made many original contributions in the field of sports. This is mainly due to a generous winter season which provides abundant ice and snow and bright sunshine in which it can be enjoyed. Native games and sports were originated by the Canadian Indians and Eskimos, and present-day Canadians are still enjoying them.

In *Great Days in Canadian Sport*, Ryerson Press, 1957, Henry H. Roxborough deals with outstanding events and figures of Canadian athletics and games. Significant achievements in sports are recounted from the time of the 1867 tour of the Caughnawaga Indian Lacrosse Team. Starting with a general survey of the sporting scene in 1867, the author then describes Ned Hanlan, the famous sculler, and his most important race against Courtney of the United States in Washington, a race which Hanlan won handily. There are chapters on such famous athletes as Lou Scholes, Bill Sherring, Tommy Burns, Tom Longboat, Percy Williams, Torchy Peden, and the Edmonton Grads, a famous girls' basketball team of the 1930's, the Olympic hockey teams, the sailing ship, the "Bluenose", and Canada's national sport, lacrosse. The book contains black-and-white illustrations of the individuals and teams mentioned but has no index. More recently the same author has expanded this account of Canadian sport in *One Hundred–not out*, Ryerson Press, Toronto, 1966. The Indian, English, and American contributions and pioneer history of Canadian sport are described, and various chapters carry the story of individual sport heroes, famous clubs, and rules, customs, and records of a wide range of sporting activities up to the early twentieth century. Curling, hockey, and other outdoor winter sports are given fairly extensive coverage. Chapters are included on sport journalism and women's role in sports.

In addition to its role in developing performing and spectator games, Canada has paid some attention to the matter of physical fitness. The Canadian Association for Health, Physical Education, and Recreation, Toronto, acts as a clearing house on information for individuals and institutions concerned with physical education, sports, and recreation. It publishes its own material and distributes other material of Canadian and non-Canadian origin. Typical publications made available by the Association are *Canadian Basketball Rules for Girls and Women*, 1966; Canadian Amateur Basketball Association, *Basketball Rules* (*Men*); Canadian Inter-Collegiate Athletic Union, *Football Rules*; Royal Canadian Air Force manuals on such sports as volleyball, hockey, and soccer.

Physical Education in Canada, Prentice-Hall of Canada, Toronto, 1965, is edited by Maurice Van Vliet and sponsored by the Canadian Association for Health, Physical Education, and Recreation. In it twenty authorities record their observations on various aspects of physical education from the elementary school level to professional preparation. Historical background, principles, and objectives, and the interrelationship of agencies in the field are discussed. Eight appendixes contain information on the Federal *Fitness and Amateur Sport Act*, biographical sketches of pioneers in the field, a list of Canadian amateur sports organizations, and a bibliography of graduate theses and research projects by Canadians. There is an index.

In *Football Today and Yesteryear*, Harlequin Books, Winnipeg, 1962, Tony Allan tells the story of Canadian football from the early 1920's, when this game was king, to the present day, with its emphasis on national east–west competitions and the Grey Cup competitions. Written in a popular style by a former sports editor of the *Winnipeg Tribune*, it not only traces the history of the game which originated in Canada but also puts forward some possible reasons for its popularity over its ancestor, soccer. From the beginnings of Canadian football in the powerful university teams formed after World War I to the present days of professional imported players, financial contracts, and all the operations of a big industry, Allan chronicles the developments. An extensive section at the end gives statistics on champions from 1920 to 1960, the names of all-stars of east and west, and other information.

The Department of Health and Welfare, Division of Health and Amateur Sport, has published *Lacrosse*, Queen's Printer, Ottawa, 1965 in both French and English versions. La crosse, or lacrosse in English, is the national game of Canada. It was first played by the Indian tribes and then taken over by the English and French settlers and developed into one of the most popular sports in the colony. In the short introduction to this pamphlet reasons for the popularity of the game are advanced. A history follows and then the rules of the game. There is a section on necessary equipment, stick management, and general principles of playing. A section on trophies is included. It is well illustrated, with many diagrams.

Cricket in Eastern Canada by Colin F. Whiting, Colmur Publications, Montreal, 1963, is a history of cricket in Canada as it has been played since its introduction in Montreal, 134 years ago. The game is still mainly played in the eastern part of Canada. This book is written by an Australian-born, adoptive Canadian, who spent more than 3 years collecting the material. Not only is the book an account of the game in Canada as such, but it is also a report of games played, with the results and names of teams.

The *National Hockey League Guide* (Fig. 24) has been issued annually since 1945 by the National Hockey League, Toronto. It is a detailed source of current and historic information including individual and team records, schedules, club standings, mainly in tabular form. Records of the careers of active players, coaches, and of players recently retired are given. Statistical analysis of games played in the immediately preceding season, and schedules of games in all professional leagues for the current season, may be found as well.

WESTERN HOCKEY LEAGUE

REGULAR SCHEDULE AND PLAYOFF RESULTS

1964-65 SEASON

FINAL STANDINGS

TEAM	GP	W	L	T	GF	GA	PTS
Portland	70	42	23	5	267	216	89
Seattle	70	36	30	4	204	198	76
Vancouver	70	32	32	6	263	244	70
Victoria	70	32	36	2	246	242	66
San Francisco	70	31	37	2	255	283	64
Los Angeles	70	26	41	3	217	269	55

FINAL LESTER PATRICK CUP PLAY-OFF STATISTICS 1964-65

SERIES "A"

	W	L	GF	GA
Portland	4	1	17	11
Vancouver	1	4	11	17

Wed.	Mar. 31	Vancouver	6	at Portland	3 (Duke—13:59—Second Period)
Fri.	Apr. 2	Portland	1	at Vancouver	0 (Hebenton—1:28—Second Period)
Sun.	Apr. 4	Vancouver	3	at Portland	4 (Goyer—8:32 Overtime Period)
Tue.	Apr. 6	Portland	3	at Vancouver	0 (Saunders—9:22—Second Period)
Wed.	Apr. 7	Vancouver	2	at Portland	6 (Saunders—2:53—Second Period)

Portland won Series, 4 games to 1.

SERIES "B"

	W	L	GF	GA
Victoria	4	3	19	17
Seattle	3	4	17	19

Wed.	Mar. 31	Victoria	2	at Seattle	4 (Sabourin—12:05—Third Period)
Fri.	Apr. 2	Victoria	0	at Seattle	3 (Holmes—:52—Third Period)
Sat.	Apr. 3	Seattle	2	at Victoria	5 (Wilcox—6:54—First Period)
Tue.	Apr. 6	Seattle	5	at Victoria	3 (Barlow—14:30—Third Period)
Fri.	Apr. 9	Victoria	3	at Seattle	1 (Sleaver—:59—Third Period)
Sat.	Apr. 10	Seattle	1	at Victoria	2 (Witiuk—16:25—Second Period)
Sun.	Apr. 11	Victoria	4	at Seattle	1 (Redahl—2:44—First Period)

Victoria won Series 4 games to 3.

CHAMPIONSHIP SERIES "C"

	W	L	GF	GA
Portland	4	1	17	8
Victoria	1	4	8	17

Wed.	Apr. 14	Victoria	1	at Portland	5 (Goyer—:18—Second Period)
Sat.	Apr. 17	Portland	3	at Victoria	1 (Jones—14:33—Second Period)
Sun.	Apr. 18	Victoria	4	at Portland	3 (Redahl—4:53—Overtime Period)
Wed.	Apr. 21	Portland	3	at Victoria	2 (Stapleton—5:24—Second Period)
Sat.	Apr. 24	Portland	3	at Victoria	0 (C. Schmautz—6:16—First Period)

Portland won Lester Patrick Cup 4 games to 1.

FIG. 24. *National Hockey League Guide*, 1964–5.

Ken Watson on Curling, Copp Clark, Toronto, 1950, is an account of the other popular Canadian ice sport that attracts tens of thousands of followers and devotees in Canada. It is an introduction for the novice to professional curling techniques, by a recognized player, coach, and participant in Canadian National Championships. From the basic delivery of the stone to the fine points of strategy and psychology, each step is described and illustrated with photographs and diagrams for both skipping and team play.

C. H. J. Snider has written *Annals of the Royal Canadian Yacht Club, 1852–1937*, Rous & Mann Press Ltd., Toronto, 1937. This is the official history of the Royal Canadian Yacht Club written by a long-standing member of that Club from records, fragments, and the memories of the older members. Beginning with the founding of the Club in 1852 through the years of war to 1937, the complete records are given, including officers and significant events of each year. There is also a section on the cups and trophies contended for by the Club, with the history and winners of each. Descriptions of the most important races are also included. The book is illustrated with many black-and-white photographs, but has no index. Norman Hacking and George A. Cran have edited *Annals of the Royal Vancouver Yacht Club, 1903–1965*, Evergreen Press, Vancouver, 1965. This is a history of sail and power boat activities on Canada's west coast compiled from records of the Club and from the personal reminiscences of members. The story of the Club's founding and biographical sketches of prominent early yachtsmen are included. A list of early sail yachts from 1903 to the 1930's and detailed accounts of races and records are presented. A 70-page section illustrates the Club's trophies and lists the history of these awards. Photographs of historic and contemporary activities, and portraits of vessels and their owners, are among the many illustrations provided.

Water sports have always been a prominent part of Canadian life, and marathon swimming probably heads the list in public interest and enthusiasm. Ron McAllister, a well-known Canadian sportswriter and broadcaster, in *Swim to Glory*, McClelland &

Stewart, Toronto, 1954, recounts the story of Marilyn Bell, a young Canadian schoolgirl, and her remarkable feat. He tells the story of Marilyn Bell's swim across 32 miles of cold Lake Ontario in a race in which she was not officially entered, then backtracks to what led up to these events. A brief history of the Lakeshore Swim Club, Toronto, and its work with crippled children, is given followed by separate chapters on Cliff Lumsden, George Young, and other Canadian swimming champions. Included also is an account of the 1954 Atlantic City Marathon and the events leading up to the 1954 Canadian National Exhibition swim at which Marilyn Bell achieved her victory.

In the Canadian horse-racing world, the running of the Queen's Plate in Ontario is an institution comparable to that of the English Ascot. Trent Frayne's *The Queen's Plate, 1860–1959*, McClelland & Stewart, Toronto, 1959, traces the history of the Plate from its first running on 27 June 1860, by permission of Queen Victoria, to its 100th anniversary, 30 June 1959, when the 50 guineas were presented by Queen Elizabeth II. Beginning with a general history of the race, the book then continues with an account of each individual year of the running, and the winning horses, jockeys, and owners. The work is lavishly illustrated, with both black-and-white photos, 4 colour plates, and drawings.

A final indication should be given of the books that provide information on Canadian hunting and fishing. *Hunting in Canada: a brief description of Canada's resources of big and small game*, Canadian Government Travel Bureau, Queen's Printer, Ottawa, 1965, is a province-by-province account of native and introduced species sought for game, designed as a guide for sportsmen. Information is given on recommended methods of travel to hunting locations, particularly those in sparsely settled parts of British Columbia, Yukon, and the North-west Territories. This last location is one of the largest wilderness areas in the world, covering more than one-third of Canada, and is almost half the size of the United States (not including Alaska). *Le Petit almanach du chasseur et du pêcheur* is published by John de Kuyper & Son (Canada) Ltd., Montreal, 1965. It contains articles written by various authorities on individual species for hunting and fishing. Calendars are included indicating the best months and time of day to secure particular animals or fish, and information on camping and on game and fish cookery is provided.

Harry Symons has written *Playthings of Yesterday*, Ryerson Press, 1963. This is a valuable illustrated guide to a collection of antique toys and dolls, played with by Canadian children, which is now displayed at Pioneer Village, operated by the Metropolitan Toronto and Region Conservation Authority, Woodbridge, Ontario.

CHAPTER 12

Literature

BECAUSE well-prepared surveys to the whole of Canadian literary output are available, very little mention of individual authors will be made in this chapter. In a country that has two official languages, there can be no lack of Canadian writing. If anything, Canada suffers from the production of too many ephemeral books and periodicals and too few of originality. These facts can be explained by the high degree of popular literacy in Canada in both French and English for the past 100 years, abundant resources for publishing and printing, but the lack of a critical audience. Any brief review of Canadian literature can only list the standard guides to Canadian literary criticism without attempting to enumerate the works of Canadian writers themselves.

French

The highest standards of imaginative writing in Canada have been reached in French, although the total number of works has not been great. This has occurred because in this part of Canada there has been greater need for the cultivation of a national literature than in English-speaking Canada. This is particularly apparent in poetry, theatre, and essays, and less true in the novel. English-Canadian writers, on the other hand, have had the advantage of a steady market in the United States of America and Great Britain. This has meant that they wrote in terms of a foreign market rather than for Canadian readers. While not a bad thing in itself, it has delayed the cultivation of a deep and sympathetic exchange between writers and readers in English-speaking Canada.

LITERATURE 171

Canadian Writers; Écrivains canadiens, 2nd edn., revised and enlarged, Ryerson Press, Toronto, 1966, is a useful source of information on over 300 Canadian writers, both living and dead. The articles on French-Canadian authors are in French; those on English-Canadians are in English. Information on many of the authors is not otherwise readily available to the general reader. Each article, usually from 50 to 100 words, provides vital statistics about the author and sketches his educational background and literary milieu. His work is summarized and his chief published works are briefly annotated, often with concise critical evaluations or comparisons. Critical or biographical studies about the author are listed at the end of the article. A chronological table at the beginning of the volume provides a record of important Canadian literary events from 1608 to 1960. A bibliography of source materials (anthologies, bibliographies, and critical studies) is provided together with a title index of the books mentioned in the text.

In February 1964 the Department of Sociology and Anthropology at Laval University organized a discussion on the general topic of French-Canada and its literature, both past and present. Fernand Dumont and Jean-Charles Falardeau have edited the papers in *Littérature et société canadiennes-françaises*, published by Les Presses de l'Université Laval, Quebec, 1964. Among the papers presented were the following: "The place of the writer and the spread of literature", "Cultural alienation and the Canadian novel", "Religion in contemporary French-Canadian literature", and "Feelings of revolt as shown in recent French Canadian literature". A valuable paper dealt in a critical manner with the history of French-Canadian literature. A bibliography of novels and collections of poetry cited in the various papers and the discussions is included in the work as well as an index to the names of authors mentioned. This book is the best critical guide to French-Canadian literature—both past and present—that has appeared to date.

An authority on French literature in North America, Auguste Viatte, has written *Histoire littéraire de l'Amérique française*, Les

Presses Universitaires de France, Paris, 1954, which is a detailed and fully documented handbook. It surveys all aspects of literature in the French language from the beginning until the mid twentieth century, describing briefly the developments and trends of each period and place. Part I of the book deals entirely with Canada. Since the early colonists directed their writings to readers in France, all the work of the seventeenth and eighteenth centuries could be called a "literature of action", of which a typical example is the well-known *Jesuit Relations*. There were no printing presses in the colony, and after the conquest by the British in 1759, literature in French virtually disappeared. Gradually it reappeared, still dependent upon the parent culture, and following literary movements in France.

Gérard Tougas's *History of French-Canadian Literature*, 2nd edn., Ryerson Press, Toronto, 1966, is a comprehensive and up-to-date compilation by a professor at the University of British Columbia. The author presents a complete account of French-Canadian writing by offering detailed individual profiles of authors. The inclusion of an author is determined entirely by the importance of that author at the time of writing. After a brief introduction dealing with the beginning of writing in Canada, Tougas divides Canadian literary history into 20-, 30-, and 40-year periods. Each period is subdivided by literary forms, e.g. poetry, criticism, novel, drama, and others, and, under each form, authors and their most important work are discussed clearly and concisely.

According to Tougas no evaluation of French-Canadian literature can be made without taking into account the important part played by literary criticism of which Casgrain (1831–1904) was the chief representative. Tougas is silent about the extent to which the guide lines of Casgrain are still valid, but he makes a point of mentioning that writers who in their early days liberated the Canadian novel have now become fossilized (Langevin and Desrosiers), and he predicts their virtual disappearance from the world of letters. A special appendix is devoted to the poet Albert Lozeau, another to a manifesto by Paul Emile Borduas on the destiny of French Canada. This book is the best survey in English of French-Canadian writing to 1963. It has an author and title index and a useful list of pseudonyms, but no bibliography.

Séraphin Marion has edited *Les Lettres canadiennes d'autrefois* in 9 volumes, University of Ottawa, 1939–52. Each volume of this carefully documented series deals with a different aspect of the literary history of French-Canada. M. Marion has subtitled his work, "Journalism, the cradle of Canadian literature", and in the first 3 volumes, covering the period 1764–1837, he illustrated this thesis by a thorough examination of the material in early Quebec newspapers. To compensate for the lack of foreign news during the long winters, the editors printed poems and stories, stimulating the growth of a native literature. This dependence of literature on journalism for an audience ended in the first half of the nineteenth century with the emergence of the novel as a distinct form. The fourth volume in the series deals with this stage, and the next 5 are concerned with the important themes and movements in French-Canadian letters during the formative years. An accurate reflection of the nineteenth century, these include the "The Humanist quarrel", "Men of letters and moralists", and the "The Romanticist battle". M. Marion has delved extensively into newspapers, journals, and books, and by methodical investigation has compiled a valuable history of ideas and letters in French Canada. He has included an abundance of notes and also quotes extensively from the source material—one volume containing the complete text of a three-act play. For students and researchers this series is made less useful by the absence of any index to the contents.

The *Bibliographie du roman canadien-français, 1900–1950*, Presses Universitaires Laval, Quebec, 1955, by Antonio Drolet, lists 886 separate titles of novels by French-Canadian writers, not including reprints and re-editions of earlier issues. The arrangement is by author with a chronological arrangement for each author's work. There is an index to the titles. This list represents the best survey of French-Canadian novels written during the first half of the twentieth century.

Adrien Thério has issued *Livres et auteurs canadiens, panorama de la production littéraire de l'année* (Fig. 25), Chez L'Auteur,

LITTERATURE

Barbeau, Marius : *Folklore*. Cahier no 9 de l'Académie canadienne-française. Montréal, 180 p.

Caselais, Clément : *Conseils à mon grand-père*, La cité des Livres, Montréal.

Collet, Paulette : *L'hiver dans le roman canadien*, Les Presses de l'Université Laval, Québec. 282 p.

Duhamel, Roger : *Lecture de Montaigne*, Editions de l'Université d'Ottawa, Ottawa, 175 p.

Fournier, Jules : *Mon encrier*, Nénuphar, Fides, Montréal. 350 p.

Gagnon, Marcel-A. : *Le ciel et l'enfer d'Arthur Buies*. Les Presses de l'Université Laval, Québec. 362 p.

Harvey, Jean-Charles : *Des bois, des champs, des bêtes*, Editions du Jour, Montréal. 130 p.

Kempf, Yerri : *Les trois coups de Montréal*. Déom, Montréal.

Lebel, Maurice : *Un plaidoyer pour la poésie*, (traduction) Les Presses de l'Université Laval, Québec, 185 p.

Pellerin, Jean : *Le calepin du diable*, Editions du Jour, Montréal. 128 p.

Pagé, Pierre : *Anne Hébert*, Coll. (Ecrivains canadiens d'aujourd'hui) Fides, Montréal.

Ringuet : *Confidences*, Editions Fides, Montréal, 198 p.

Shortliffe, Glen : *Gérard Bessette, l'homme et l'oeuvre*, Edition de la Faculté des Lettres de l'Université de Montréal, Montréal. 40 p.

Simard, Jean : *Nouveau Répertoire*, Editions H.M., Montréal, 420 p.

Robert, Guy : *Roussil*, Musée d'art contemporain, Montréal.

Roussil : *Manifeste*, Editions du Jour, Montréal.

HISTOIRE ET GÉOGRAPHIE

Arsenault, Bona : *Histoire et généologie des Acadiens*. Québec. Le conseil de Vie française en Amérique. 1118 pages, en 2 volumes.

Brault, Lucien : *Histoire des Comtés Unis de Prescott et de Russell*, L'orignal, Ontario, Conseil des Comtés Unis. 377 p.

En collaboration : *Les Cahiers des Dix*, no 29 (1964). Montréal, Les Dix. 259 p.

Castonguay, Jacques : *Le fort Saint-Jean. Trois siècles d'histoire*. Montréal, Les Editions du Lévrier. 95 p.

Costisella, Joseph : *Peuple de la nuit. Histoire des Québecois*, Montréal. Editions Chénier. 126 p.

Daveluy, M.-Claire : *La Société de Notre-Dame de Montréal, 1639-1663, Son histoire. Ses membres. Son manifeste*. Montréal et Paris, Fides. 326 et 127 p.

Drolet, Antonio : *Les bibliothèques canadiennes 1604-1960* Montréal, Le Cercle du Livre de France. 234 p.

Giry, Danielle : *A la recherche des traditions bancaires de l'Occident méditerranéen: Du monde antique au monde médiéval*. Le Centre de Psychologie et de Pédagogie, Montréal. 172 p.

Hamelin, Jean; Hamelin, Marcel; Huot, John: *Aperçu de la politique canadienne au XIXe siècle*,

FIG. 25. Livres et auteurs canadiens.

Montreal, as an annual review of current writing, beginning in 1961. The work covers only titles published during the year and gives lengthy critical reviews of each. It excludes technical and scientific works, but includes essays, criticism, children's books, and the main categories of *belles-lettres*. There is a brief summary of the most important English-language books of the year as well.

Lectures, revue de culture et de bibliographie critique is published monthly by Fides, Montreal, since 1946. It examines the current French-language publications of Canada and abroad from the point of view of the Roman Catholic Church. Four or five principal sections of the review are in each issue, and to them is added leading articles of a critical nature. The sections give bibliographical details, résumés, lists of new publications, as well as moral judgements on the value of the publications. There are two separate cumulated annual indexes, one listing the contents of the sections and the other the authors of the works noted and reviewed during the year.

The fourth edition of Guy Sylvestre's *Anthologie de la poésie canadienne-française*, Beauchemin, Montreal, appeared in 1964. First published in 1942, this collection brings together all of the major French-Canadian poets of the nineteenth and twentieth centuries. The introduction to the anthology provides a valuable critical résumé of the development of French-language poetry in Canada. Laura Rièse has edited *L'Âme de la poésie canadienne française*, Macmillan, Toronto, 1955. This contains selections from the works of twenty French-Canadian poets of the nineteenth and twentieth centuries, with critical evaluation, a complete list of their works, and biographical information for each poet. The introduction reviews the history of French-Canadian poetry.

English

English-Canadian literature has been greatly affected by the attention which French-Canada has been giving to its literary output. This has resulted in a number of scholarly studies and comparative works. Most recent of these is the *Oxford Companion to Canadian History and Literature*, Oxford University Press, Toronto, 1967, by Norah Story. A systematic review has been made of the whole range of literature of English and French Canada from the very first days of colonization. This work provides detailed information on the literary output of Canadians and is an indispensable volume for the study of Canadian writing.

Reginald E. Watters has prepared *A Checklist of Canadian Literature and Background Materials, 1628–1950* (Fig. 26), University of Toronto Press, 1959. This is a comprehensive list of the books which constitute Canadian literature written in English, together with a selective list of other books by Canadian authors which reveal the background of Canadian writing. There are approximately 6000 entries listed by author and divided into poetry, fiction, biography, and other headings. The subjects range from scholarly works on the classics to handbooks for immigrants.

The bibliography is compiled in two parts: Part I gives all the known titles by English-speaking Canadians up to 1950 without any attempt at evaluation; Part II is a selection of works which seem to have some value to anyone studying the literature and culture of English-speaking Canada. Each entry is coded to show a library or libraries in Canada in which the work can be found. Publishers, dates, and paging are also given when possible, and an author index is provided. This bibliography, which is complete up to 1958, provides an unparalleled survey of the written resources of English-speaking Canada.

Professor Watters has followed his *Checklist* with a briefer guide to critical studies of English-Canadian literature, in collaboration with I. F. Bell, entitled *On Canadian Literature, 1806–1960*, University of Toronto Press, 1965. This list of articles, books, and theses on English-Canadian literature, its authors and language, provides an index of critical and scholarly material exclusive of that which is contained in standard reference works. It is arranged in two parts: Part I deals with subjects such as Canadian culture, literature, poetry, fiction, literary criticism, song, and folklore; Part II lists criticism of individual authors. Over 100

SAMUEL, Sigmund, 1868–

A CATALOGUE OF THE SIGMUND SAMUEL COLLECTION, CANADIANA AND AMERI-
CANA. . . . Comp. and Annotated by Charles W. Jefferys. Toronto,
Ryerson, 1948. 180p [BVaU LC OTP

SMITH, Lillian H.

BOOKS FOR BOYS AND GIRLS. Ed. by ——. Prepared at Boys and Girls House,
Toronto Public Libraries. 2nd ed. Toronto, Ryerson, 1940. 367p
[OTP

STATON, Frances M., 1863–1947

A BIBLIOGRAPHY OF CANADIANA. Being Items in the Public Library of Toronto,
Canada, Relating to the Early History and Development of Canada [. . .
1534–1867]. Ed. by Frances M. Staton and Marie Tremaine. Toronto,
Public Library, 1934. 828p [BVaU LC NSHD OTP QMM

THE CANADIAN NORTH WEST. A Bibliography of the Sources of Information
in the Public Reference Library of the City of Toronto in regard to
Hudson's Bay Co., the Fur Trade and the Early History of the Canadian
North West. Comp. by ——. Toronto, Public Library, 1931. 52p
[BVa LC OTP QMM

STEWART, Sheila I.

A CATALOGUE OF THE AKINS COLLECTION OF BOOKS AND PAMPHLETS. Comp.
by ——, under the direction of D. C. Harvey. . . . Halifax, Imperial Pub.
Co., 1933. [Publications of the Public Archives of Nova Scotia, No. I]
[BVaU LC OTP QMBM

FIG. 26. *A Checklist of Canadian Literature*, 1959.

Canadian and foreign periodicals have been indexed, including both scholarly and ephemeral material. Entries are brief with no description and the paging is not always given. Most of the items listed are from the last few decades, but there are some listings from articles that were written over 100 years ago.

The aim of the compilers is to facilitate the study of English-Canadian literature and thereby promote its understanding and enjoyment. The focus is on *belles-lettres* with the more serious student in mind. The relative inaccessibility of the material indexed is a determining factor in the ultimate usefulness of the list. It is an excellent reference tool for those who have the resources of a large library at their disposal.

Dr. C. F. Klinck and a group of distinguished Canadian scholars have prepared the *Literary History of Canada* (Fig. 27), University of Toronto Press, 1965. The maturity and scholarship of the editors and contributors of this history have ensured a high standard in the style and organization of the material. Under the heading of literature the editors have included not only poetry, drama, fiction, essays, and historical writing but also philosophical, theological, scientific, travel, nature stories, folk-songs, and children's books. Over forty essays by thirty specialists make this the most comprehensive and up-to-date work on Canadian literature in English that has been published. It is the nearest approach that Canada has to the type of literary histories available for various European countries and the United States.

The book has four main divisions: covering the early voyage and exploration literature; discussing the settlers and their writers from 1715 to 1880; dealing with the era of the immigrant from 1880–1920; and covering the fertile years between 1920–60 where for the first time Canadian literary editors could afford to be more descriminating. Each main division has an introductory chapter and the writers are studied in relation to the burgeoning Canadian communities of their period. Thoroughness is the key to these studies, and because so much is covered the dangers of seeming to be a mere catalogue of names and events has not entirely been avoided. However, because of this completeness, the work is an

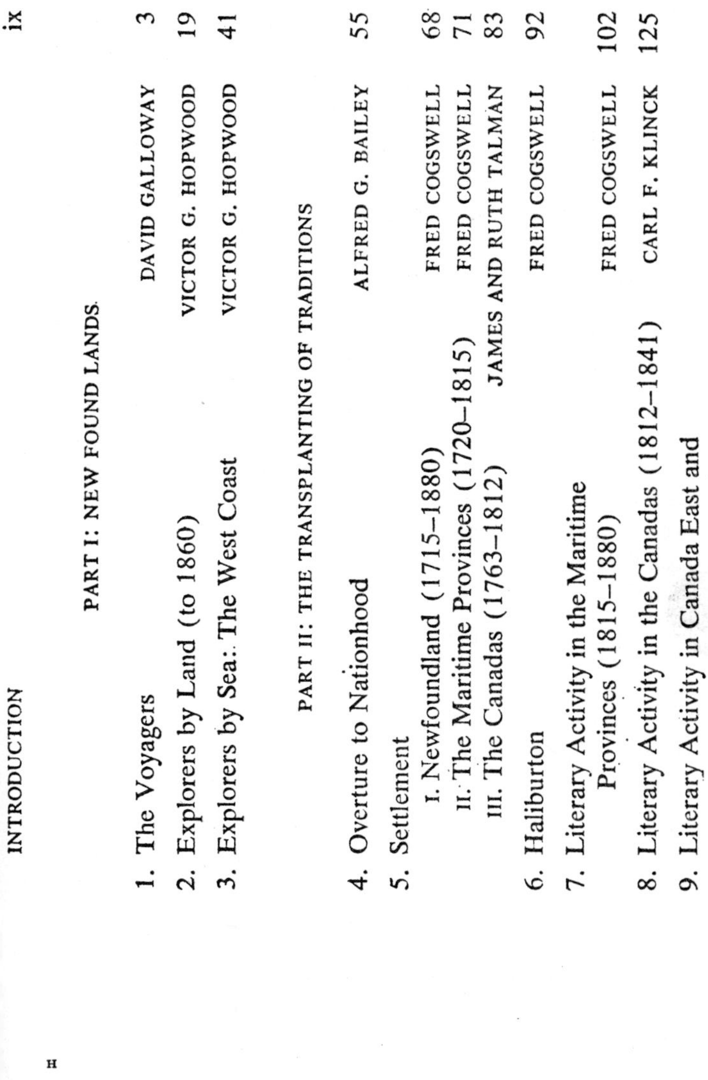

FIG. 27. *Literary History of Canada*, 1965.

indispensable aid to the study of Canadian literature, and a challenging guide to further research.

Canadian Literature, published since 1959 by the University of British Columbia, Vancouver, is a quarterly magazine which critically examines creative writing in Canada, past and present, and reviews Canadian books. It is the only English-language Canadian journal devoted exclusively to Canadian literary criticism. It acts as a unifying force for Canada's diffuse and thinly spread literary community, and provides a continuing expression of Canada's literary heritage. It is saved from being a short-lived *coterie* publication by the liberalism of its editorial policies, by the authoritativeness of its many contributors, by the wisdom of its editor, George Woodcock, and by the prestige and financial support of its publisher. The editor and contributors (and often the writers under review) are concerned with the problem of defining Canadian culture and with the Canadian search for a national identity. Since the output of creative writing is small some quite minor works often receive critical attention. However, there is never any tendency to over-praise. The useful annual *Canadian Literature Checklist*, which is a feature of the winter issue, includes theses and periodical articles as well as the year's output of books. French-Canadian books are listed separately.

Creative Writing in Canada by Desmond Pacey, Ryerson Press, 1961, is essentially one man's opinion of the literary scene in Canada. The first edition of this book in 1952 stirred up enough controversy to promote a healthy revival of interest in Canadian literary criticism after a drought of nearly 25 years. In 1961 popular demand led to a second edition which was revised to include a consideration of such contemporary writers as Mordechai Richler, Irving Layton, and Leonard Cohen. This short history of English-Canadian literature is basically a selective survey which concerns itself with the quality of Canadian writing rather than trying to prove that Canada has a distinctive literature. The emphasis is on poetry, humour, fiction and *belles-lettres* from their origins in the colonial Maritimes and their development is related to the social and cultural growth of Canada. The index and a bibliography of the major Canadian critical writing is an invaluable aid to the serious student.

The New Canadian Library series is an important collection of Canadian literary works reprinted in paperback format by the publishing firm of McClelland & Stewart, Toronto. The general editor for the series is Professor Malcolm Ross, Trinity College, Toronto, and there are special introductions to each volume by Canadian scholars. Works reprinted range from Ralph Connor's *The Man from Glengarry* (1901) and Stephen Leacock's *Sunshine Sketches* (1912) to Morley Callaghan's *More Joy in Heaven* (1936), and there are more than fifty other titles.

Since 1956 the *Tamarack Review*, a quarterly magazine, has published new Canadian writing in both French and English, as well as interviews with writers, literary criticism, and extensive reviews of Canadian and other works. The *Canadian Forum*, published in Toronto since 1920, has carried original short stories and poetry, as well as reviews of new Canadian books for many years, and has been one of the leading magazines of literary and political criticism in English-speaking Canada. *Saturday Night*, published in Toronto for over 60 years, has been a regular source of information on Canadian literature, and continues this tradition. Mention has been made on page 19 to the *University of Toronto Quarterly*.

The Canadian Authors Association, Toronto, and the Societé des Écrivains, Montreal, have existed for many years. The *Canadian Author and Bookman*, Toronto, is published by the former as a national review of activities of the branches of the Association.

Anthologies of Canadian poetry, short stories, and other writings are a useful source of information on Canadian writers, and often contain information about each author. Some of the recent poetry anthologies include Louis Dudek and Irving Layton, *Canadian Poems 1850–1952*, 2nd edn., Contact Press, Toronto, 1952; Ralph Gustafson, *The Penguin Book of Canadian Verse*, Harmondsworth, Toronto and New York, 1958; and A. J. M. Smith, *The Oxford Book of Canadian Verse in English and French*, Oxford University Press, Toronto, 1960. Short-story anthologies have been prepared by George E. Nelson, *Cavalcade of the North*, Doubleday, New York, 1958; Robert Weaver, *Canadian Short Stories*, World's Classics edition, Toronto, Oxford, 1960; and *Ten for Wednesday Night*, McClelland & Stewart, 1961. In addition Mr. Weaver has edited *The First Five Years: a selection from the Tamarack Review*, Toronto, Oxford, 1962.

CHAPTER 13

Geography

THE geography of Canada, not just its physical geography, but its economic and political geography as well, is well described in *Canadian Regions: a geography of Canada*, edited by Donald F. Putnam, the seventh edition of which was published by Dent, Toronto, 1965. This is an invaluable source book for every region of Canada. The book divides Canada into Newfoundland and Labrador, the Maritimes, Quebec, Southern Ontario, Northern Ontario, the Prairie Provinces, British Columbia, and the Canadian Northland, giving all aspects for each. The Maritimes include the provinces of Nova Scotia, New Brunswick, and Prince Edward Island. The Prairie Provinces are Manitoba, Saskatchewan, and Alberta. The Canadian Northland consists of the Yukon Territory, the North-west Territories, and the Canadian Arctic.

The Geographical Branch of the Federal Department of Mines and Technical Surveys produces the National Topographic Series of maps of Canada covering the country on a grid pattern. There is a series of scales, the basic one being 1:25000. These maps are indispensable for economic information and for camping, canoe, and hiking trips, as well as for general exploration of the less inhabited portions of the country. The Department of Mines and Technical Surveys also produces the *Hydrographic Charts* for Canada's navigable waterways.

It would be impractical for an individual to compile a complete set of detailed maps covering every area of Canada, and therefore one must turn to atlases. The Canadian North is habitually ignored in foreign atlases, and to look for maps of the northern half of the country is often a frustrating task.

The same government department has also published *The Atlas of Canada* in 1957 and 1958, Queen's Printer, Ottawa. This is the most authoritative atlas of Canada and was compiled with the help of the Dominion Bureau of Statistics. It is a specialized socio-economic atlas mapping physical features, climate, vegetation, natural resources, the growth of the economy, and social and cultural growth, and contains a large amount of data on the natural resources of Canada. Even though its statistical data is not up to date, it will be a reference tool for years to come.

Two Oxford University Press publications, *Canadian Oxford Atlas*, published in 1951, and its second edition, the *Canadian Oxford Atlas of the World*, published in 1957, are excellent works of their kind. The 1957 edition is divided into two parts—Part I: Canada; and Part II: the world. Part I contains distribution maps, regional maps, and a gazetteer of Canada. The maps are prepared by the Cartographic Department of the Oxford University Press.

Such topics as exploration, spread of settlement, development of trade and transportation routes, drawing of boundary lines, are all fully explained in *A Historical Atlas of Canada*, edited by Donald G. G. Kerr, 2nd edn., Thomas Nelson, Toronto, 1966. It is unique among historical atlases in that it includes its text juxtaposed with its maps. It also includes statistical diagrams and political charts plus other drawings and diagrams illustrative of developments in Canadian life.

Another excellent historical atlas is the *Atlas historique du Canada français des débuts à 1867*, edited by Marcel Trudel and published in Quebec, Les Presses de l'Université Laval, 1961. This atlas contains 93 maps of New France and Quebec from their origins to the beginning of the English régime, classed in chronological order, and presenting a vivid pictorial history of Lower Canada from the fifteenth century to Confederation. The first charts show the Atlantic Ocean as a tremendous barrier to exploration, then gradually, century by century, the wilderness is opened and the volume ends with town plans. Many of the maps extend beyond Canada in the scope of their coverage, and together portray varied aspects of Canadian history. There are records of exploration and settlement, battle plans, and population maps, the latter both Amerindian and colonial. The organization of the early settlements is amply documented in maps divided by parish and seigneurie. The provenance of each map is given.

Three books disclose the geography of Canada in its grandeur and beauty. One is John W. Fisher's *Canada: as seen by the camera of Yousuf Karsh and described in words by John Fisher*, published by Thomas Allen, Toronto, 1960. All aspects of Canadian life and people from the Atlantic to the Pacific are shown in photographs taken by one of the world's most famous photographers, with text by the man nicknamed "Mr. Canada".

A second work is Sylvia Seeley's *Mirror of Canada*, compiled for the Royal Canadian Geographical Society and published by the Ryerson Press, Toronto, 1960. This depicts pictorially the varied face of the Canadian nation.

Thirdly, there is *Image of Canada: compiled for the Canadian Geographical Society*, edited by Malvina Bolus and published by the Ryerson Press of Toronto in 1955. This is a cultural, geographical, economic, and recreational portrayal of Canada in excellent photographs from the collection of the Canadian Geographical Society, now the Royal Canadian Geographical Society. The Society publishes the *Canadian Geographical Journal* which appears monthly devoted to all aspects of geography relative to Canada.

One source for place-names is the *Gazetteer of Canada* (Fig. 28), produced by the Canadian Geographic Board and published by the Queen's Printer, Ottawa, between 1952 and 1962. Each province has a volume to itself with the territories, the Yukon and the North-west Territories, being combined in one. Within a volume all place-names are listed alphabetically, giving each its geographical designation—whether lake, mountain, city, or village, followed by its latitude and longitude. The *Gazetteer of Canada* is geared to the National Topographic Series maps mentioned above and provides a place-name index to these maps. A further piece of information given with each place-name in the *Gazetteer* is that locality's relation to other localities, thus making it possible to determine a

NAME	FEATURE	LOCATION	POSITION
Graham Centre	Settlement	E. side of Masset Inlet, Q.C. Dist.	53° 132° NE.
Grahame, Mount	Mountain	N. of Davis Cr. and E. of Fort Grahame, Cassiar Dist.	56 124 NE.
Grail Point	Point	E. side of Lancelot Inlet, N. of Theodosia Inlet, New Westminster Dist.	50 124 SW.
Grain Creek	Creek	Flows SE. into North Arm, Quesnel L., Cariboo Dist.	52 121 NE.
Grainger, Mount	Mountain	E. of Kootenay R. and Canal Flats P.O., Kootenay Dist.	50 115 SW.
Gramophone Creek	Creek	Flows W. into Bulkley R., NE. of Doughty, Rge. 5, Coast Dist.	54 127 NE.
Granby Bay	Bay	W. side of Observatory Inlet, W. of Larcom I., Cassiar Dist.	55 129 SW.
Granby Peninsula	Peninsula	Observatory Inlet, W. of Larcom I., Cassiar Dist.	55 129 SW.
Granby Point	Point	N. end of Granby Pen., Observatory Inlet, Cassiar Dist.	55 129 SW.
Granby River	River	Flows S. into Kettle R. at Grand Forks city, Similkameen Dist.	49 118 SE.
Grand Canyon	Canyon	Fraser R., W. of Toneko L., Cariboo Dist.	53 121 NW.
Grand Canyon of the Liard	Canyon	Liard R., W. of Toad R., Peace River Dist.	59 125 SE.
Grand Canyon of the Stikine	Canyon	Stikine R., E. of Tuya R., Cassiar Dist.	58 130 SE.
Grand Canyon		See Nechako Canyon.	53 124 NW.
Grand Creek	Creek	Flows SW. into Indian Arm near head, New Westminster Dist.	49 122 SW.
Grand Forks	City	On C.P.R. and G.N.R., at jct. of Kettle and Granby Rs., Similkameen Dist.	49 118 SE.
Grand Glaciers	Glaciers	W. of hdwtrs. of Beaver R., Kootenay Dist.	51 117 SE.

Fig. 28. *Gazetteer of Canada*, 1958.

place's position without actual reference to a map. There is a series of supplements to the *Gazetteer of Canada*, and as they grow in size the respective volumes will be revised and reprinted.

All of the provinces are covered by the *Gazetteer* with the exception of the Province of Quebec. This disadvantage is offset by the existence of the *Dictionnaire des rivières et lacs de la province de Québec* published by the Département des terres et fôrets, Quebec, 1925. This dictionary is a revision of the first edition published in 1914, and lists in alphabetical order the majority of lakes and rivers which were explored or visited up until 1925. With each description of a lake or river the reader is given information on the nature of the soil in the vicinity, the species of trees to be found in the neighbouring region, the possibility of hydroelectric power development on selected waterways, and the resources offered in each area for hunting and for fishing.

Further information on the geography of Quebec can be found through the *Bibliographie du Nouveau-Québec* produced by the Service de géographie du Ministère de l'industrie et du commerce, Quebec, 1955. This is an introduction to geographical research bearing upon the problems of physical geography, economics, cartography, and human resources of Nouveau-Québec. It is classed in alphabetical order by author with an index by region, by subject, and according to the nature of the documents.

The *Origin and Meaning of Place Names in Canada*, was compiled by George H. Armstrong and published by Macmillan, Toronto, 1930. Since its publication, this work has been the standard reference source for place-names of Canada. Now out-of-print, it was the first attempt, and the only one extant, to deal with the place-names of Canada as a whole. Numerous other books dealing with Canadian place-names exist, such as those issued since 1898 by the Canadian Board on Geographical Names, Ottawa, and W. F. Moore's *Indian Place Names in Ontario*, but none are as inclusive of language and territory as Armstrong. A useful list of the sources consulted is found on the first page. In alphabetical order, each entry locates the place concerned and the date of designation or settlement. Then follows a brief

H*

description of the locality which includes not only the language and origin of the name but also quite often tales and myths which surround its beginnings. The study of place-nomenclature is one of the more exciting methods of approach for the student of history and geography, often proving a stimulus to inquiry as well as being a field of legitimate research for the serious scholar interested in the tides of migration and waves of settlement. One example of the oddity of place-names is the Île-aux-Coudres in the St. Lawrence River. Because Jacques Cartier discovered it covered with hazel nuts he named it "Île-aux-Coudres", meaning "Island of Nuts".

Another work dealing with Canadian place-names is Joseph E. Guinard's *Les Noms indiens de mon pays: leur signification, leur histoire*, published in Montreal by Rayonnement in 1960. It consists of an alphabetical word-list of Amerindian place-names, principally Iroquois, Micmac, Algonquim, Cree, and Eskimo. The author gives a scientific translation of each word, followed by a brief historical summary of the localities, animals, and things chosen as the designation of each name. A missionary priest, Père Guinard, o.m.i., spent 10 years with the Amerindians of the James Bay region and then 30 years with the missions to the Crees and Algonquins. He is a foremost authority and acknowledged expert on Amerindian languages.

A further work on place-names, more regional in character, is Hormidas Magnan's *Dictionnaire historique et géographique des paroisses, missions et municipalités de la province de Québec*, Arthabaska, Imprimerie de l'Arthabaska, 1925. Parishes, missions, and municipalities are given in alphabetical order, with reference from each civil entity to its corresponding religious entity. The date of its original establishment is given for each parish, along with the dates for the opening of the parish register, the construction of the church, etc., as well as historical notes on the origin of the name of the site.

A compilation of early maps and discussion of early voyages that is indispensable for the study of a Canadian history is the monumental and scholarly *The Discovery of North America: a critical, documentary and historical investigation, with an essay on the early cartography of the new world, including descriptions of two hundred and fifty maps or globes existing or lost, constructed before the year 1536, to which are added a chronology of one hundred voyages westward projected, attempted, or accomplished between 1431 and 1504, biographical accounts of the three hundred pilots who first crossed the Atlantic, and a copious list of the original names of American regions, caciqueships, mountains, islands, capes, gulfs, rivers, towns and harbours* of Henry Harrisse, published by H. Welter in Paris in 1892. A critical exegesis of all voyages of discovery, this work, with its wealth of additional information, is an invaluable source for all students of the discovery and exploration of North America. The work is divided into 5 parts. Part I deals with the voyages and is a minute discussion of their respective claims and a searching assessment of the evidence both for and against. Part II is a discussion of the methods and techniques of early cartography. Part III—Cartographia Americana Vetustissima—consists of lists of maps, charts, globes, and portolani, divided into two sections: (i) pre-1492; (ii) 1493–1536. Part IV is a chronology of voyages in two sections: (i) 1431–92; (ii) 1492–1504. Part V is biographies of pilots and cartographers from the period 1492–1550. For students of late fifteenth- and early sixteenth-century discovery and exploration of North America, Harrisse's study is a critical discussion of primary sources, treatise on early map making, biographical dictionary, and gazetteer all in one.

Another equally valuable work in this same field is *Crucial Maps in the Early Cartography and Place-name Nomenclature of the Atlantic Coast of Canada*, edited by William F. Ganong and published in 1964 by the University of Toronto Press in co-operation with the Royal Society of Canada. To the avid student and well-informed general reader, this volume provides an excellent source of reference. The book consists of a series of papers in 9 parts originally written by the author for the *Transactions* of the Royal Society of Canada between the years 1929 and 1937. The work was a pioneer effort in Canada in the history of discovery and early cartography: some of the essays have become classic examples of the presentation and evaluation of cartographical data. It is primarily a detailed analysis, grouping and description of the maps of the early explorers of north-eastern North America from John Cabot through Jacques Cartier to Champlain. Specific maps are presented, and are correlated with the explorers' reports of their discoveries: this, then, leads to a critical interpretation of the language used on the maps and their varying spellings and changes since initial discovery. One essay concerns the "La Cosa Map" and the accompanying theory that Cabot landed in Cape Breton and not in Newfoundland. However, in consideration of this piece of scholarship, it must be remembered that new discoveries of cartographical materials have been made since Ganong's day, and thus his study is dated. Theodore Layng, the editor of the 1964 edition, fortunately supplements each essay with notes on errors and new data which have come to light since 1937. *The Road Across Canada* by Edward A. McCourt, published by Macmillan in Toronto in 1965, is a travel account of the journey undertaken by Canadian writer Edward McCourt and his family along the Trans-Canada Highway, describing the route and giving their own personal reflections and opinion on the Canadian nation as it exists in the mid 1960's.

The annual *Canada: vacation manual and tariff, compiled and edited by the travel consultants of Canadian Outdoor Vacations, Ltd.*, is published by Canadian Outdoor Vacations Ltd. of Winnipeg, the latest edition being 1966. This is, so to speak, a "Canadian almanac" of description and travel in Canada. It contains just about any type of information possibly required by a traveller or vacationer. There are lists of tours, historic sites, camping places, and provincial and national parks, etc., as well as a hotel–motel directory.

Another useful guide is *Wrigley's Hotel Directory: official directory of the Hotel Association of Canada* (annual), Wrigley Directories Ltd., Vancouver (53rd edn., 1963), 554 pp., which devotes 136 to Canada, dealing mostly with hotels (though some motels are listed), providing the number of rooms and the address of each. Entries are made for each province under cities and towns which are located on railway lines.

It is possible to go from St. John's, Newfoundland, to Victoria, British Columbia, across Canada, by water, with less than 50 miles to portage overland. Canada is geographically fortunate that the majority of her major rivers run east–west, and these rivers provided the route from coast to coast. They facilitated westward penetration and enabled the Pacific to be reached across Canada long before the United States route was used. The Pacific was the lure that drew the explorers—Alexander Mackenzie (the first white man to cross North America from the Atlantic to the Pacific), Simon Fraser, and David Thompson; and the rivers dictated their paths of destiny. For those interested in the role the rivers played in Canada's history, there are *The St. Lawrence* by William Toye, Oxford University Press, Toronto, 1959; Marjorie W. Campbell's *The Saskatchewan*, Clarke, Irwin, Toronto, 1965; Bruce Hutchinson's *The Fraser*, Clarke, Irwin, Toronto, 1950; and *The Mackenzie* by Leslie Roberts, Rinehart & Co., New York, 1949.

CHAPTER 14

Biography

Canadian Who's Who: with which is incorporated "Canadian men and women of the time", a biographical dictionary of notable living men and women, Trans-Canada Press, Toronto, has been published since 1910, and is the only one of the pair of Canadian "Who's Who" which publicly claims that absolutely no one has paid for inclusion. It is published triennially, and is kept up to date by additional booklets. Each volume is accompanied by a supplement containing the important changes in biographies received during the course of printing, and including biographies received too late for inclusion in the main volume, thus ensuring substantially correct biographical information to within 10 days of the date of printing. Four supplementary booklets incorporating all the latest changes, together with new biographies, are issued at 6-month intervals for 2 years following the main publication. Then all is incorporated into the next triennial volume and the cycle is repeated. The biographies are arranged alphabetically by surname, and there are no accompanying photographs. There is a classified index by profession to the main text. It is especially useful for biographies of Canadians prominent in the arts and letters.

Another "Who's Who" is *Who's Who in Canada: an illustrated biographical record of men and women of the time* (Fig. 29), International Press, Toronto, published since 1914. This is primarily a directory of and for Canadian businessmen. There is an alphabetical-by-surname table of contents which is actually an index to the biographies in the main text, since they appear in no discernible order. Each is accompanied by a photograph of the subject.

TORNO, Philip — Vice President, Jordan Wines Limited, est. 1920, 146

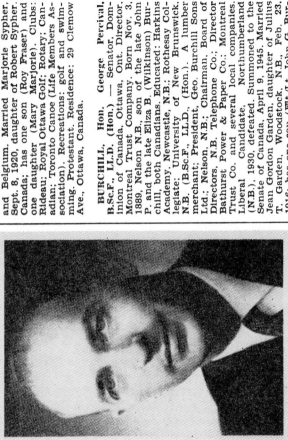

PHILIP TORNO

Bloor Street West, Toronto 5, Ont. Born Toronto, Ont., Oct. 9, 1917, son of Fred and Sophie Torno.

Carlton College, Ottawa. Served in World War I, Officer, 7th Battery, 2nd Brigade, 1st Div., Canadian Field Artillery, France and Belgium. Married Marjorie Sypher, Sept. 8, 1920, daughter of Robert Sypher, Canada; has one son (Roy Fraser) and one daughter (Mary Marjorie). Clubs: Rideau; Royal Ottawa Golf; Rotary; Canadian; Toronto Canoe (Life Members Association). Recreations: golf and swimming. Protestant. Residence: 29 Clemow Ave., Ottawa, Canada.

BURCHILL, Hon. George Percival, B.Sc.F., LL.D. (Hon.) — Senator, Dominion of Canada, Ottawa, Ont. Director, Montreal Trust Company. Born Nov. 3, 1889, Nelson N.B., son of the late John P. and the late Eliza B. (Wilkinson) Burchill, both Canadians. Educated: Harkins Academy, Newcastle, N.B.; Rothesay Collegiate; University of New Brunswick, N.B. (B.Sc.F., LL.D., (Hon.). A lumber merchant; President, Geo. Burchill Sons Ltd.; Nelson, N.B.; Chairman, Board of Directors, N.B. Telephone Co.; Director Bathurst Power & Paper Co.; Montreal Trust Co. and several local companies. Liberal Candidate, Northumberland (N.B.), 1930, defeated. Summoned to the Senate of Canada, April 9, 1945. Married Jean Gordon Garden, daughter of Julius T. Garden, Woodstock, N.B., Feb. 23, 1916; has one son (Flt./Lt. John G. Burchill, married to Jean McDonald). Clubs: St. James, Montreal; Rideau, Ottawa; Miramichi Golf; Union (St. John, N.B.). Societies: A.F. & A.M. (Grand Master for N.B., 1933-35); Member, Senate, Univer-

FIG. 29. *Who's Who in Canada*, 1965.

Another source for biographical details of contemporary Canadians is the *National Reference Book*, edited by H. E. Durant, Montreal, Canadian Newspaper Service, published biennially since 1963. It contains sections on (a) Facts and figures re: Canada; (b) Administrative functions of the Federal Government; (c) Business directory; and (d) Personalities in business. It has a detailed classified index.

The standard French-Canadian "Who's Who" is *Biographies canadiennes-françaises*, published by L'Eclaireur in Montreal since 1920.

More important for biographical information of prominent French-Canadians is *Vedettes* (*Who's who en français*), 4th edn., Montreal, La Société Nouvelle de Publicité, 1962. The entries are arranged alphabetically without portraits. The previous editions were 1st (1952), 2nd (1958), and 3rd (1960). The earlier editions contain sections which trace the history and describe the activity and organization of religious communities, universities, seminaries, classical colleges, normal schools, hospitals, and social service associations.

Another more specialized source for biographical information is *Le Dictionnaire de nos vedettes* (*de TV, radio, théâtre, cabaret, music-hall, et cinéma*), Montreal, Janin Productions, 1961. This contains the names of about 1100 leading personalities, classed in alphabetical order, and each accompanied by a photograph.

Additional biographical information can be found in *Biographies françaises d'Amérique*, 2nd edn., Sherbrooke, Journalistes Associés, 1950. This collective biography first appeared in 1927 and was reissued in 1942. It gives a page to each person, with a photograph. It mentions nearly 900 living personages who have played an important role in all parts of the country and in all spheres. It is classed by professions, with an alphabetical index by name.

Another work of this type is the *Social Register of Canada*, 1st and 2nd editions, Montreal, published for the Social Register of Canada Association by the Social Register of Canada Ltd., 1255 University St., 1958, 1960. The only such venture to attempt to list on an ambitious scale the "society" of Canada, arranged alphabetically by province and subdivided by major urban areas with an added "non-metropolitan" group for each. Listings show surname, title, rank, given names, honours, degrees, professional status, clubs, family, and telephone number. A glossary lists abbreviations used for honours and clubs and there is an index giving provinces with their urban subdivisions.

Another very important source for biographical data of prominent Canadians is the *Who's Who in Canadian Jewry*, published by the Jewish Institute of Higher Research, Central Rabbinical Seminary of Canada in Montreal in 1965.

The first volume of *The Dictionary of Canadian Biography* (Fig. 30) was issued by the University of Toronto Press in 1966. The *DCB*, as it is commonly called, is one of the principal compilations of biography, the standard reference source for information. The plan of publication is to include all Canadians of note. They do not have to have been born in Canada, but they must have played some part in Canada's history or to have been Canadian-born but achieved prominence abroad. Unlike its two counterparts, *The Dictionary of National Biography* and *The Dictionary of American Biography*, its arrangement is not alphabetical throughout a main set and kept up to date with supplements, but rather it is basically chronological. One volume has appeared to date: vol. 1, 1000–1700. Vol. 2 will cover 1701–40. Anybody with any claim to fame who had a hand in the shaping of Canada during either of these periods and who died before the close-off date is listed in alphabetical order. The volumes will continue to be issued, the periods covered becoming smaller as more people are included. Supplementary volumes are planned to include names omitted in the chronological sequence. A French-language edition is published simultaneously by Laval University.

Another source of retroactive biographical data is a *Standard Dictionary of Canadian Biography: Canadian who was who*, published in Toronto by the Trans-Canada Press in 2 volumes between 1934–8: vol. 1, 1875–1933, covers the lives of over 400 men whether Crignon wrote the "Discorso . . ," published by Ramusio, and of the validity of the evidence for a North American voyage by Parmentier, see Henri Harrisse, *Découverte et évolution cartographique de Terre-Neuve et des pays circonvoisins, 1497, 1501, 1769* (Paris, 1900); Hoffman, *Cabot to Cartier*, 149, 169; and *Les voyages de découverte et les premiers établissements, XVe, XVIe siècles*, éd. Ch.-A. Julien (Colonies et Empires, 3e série, Paris, 1948).

PASQUINE (Paquine), French engineer of the department of Marine, who prepared plans for the re-fortification of Port-Royal (Annapolis Royal, N.S.); fl. 1681–88.

Pasquine, experienced in the mapping of the Mediterranean coasts of France and Spain, was sent to Acadia in 1688 at the request of Des Friches* de Menneval. His instructions, dated 10 April 1688, stated he was "to have an examination made of the posts which it is particularly necessary to occupy and fortify for the defence and conservation of the colony in case of war with its neighbour. . ."

Pasquine arrived in Acadia aboard *La Friponne*, commanded by Barthélemy de Beauregard*. He drew a detailed plan of the river and country surrounding Port-Royal and visited the other posts on the Bay of Fundy (Baie Française).

example of one aspect of the European impact on Indian culture. In 1620 he was taken as a child to France by the Recollets, baptized, and given the name Pierre-Antoine, with the Prince de Guémenée acting as his godfather. The latter supervised his studies for the next five years and Pastedechouan became proficient in both Latin and French.

He was persuaded to return to Canada in 1626 with the Recollet Father JOSEPH DE LA ROCHE Daillon, who arrived in August of that year. Pastedechouan lived for a time with the Recollets at Quebec but did not mix with the Indians, probably because he had almost forgotten his own language. He was, therefore, advised to return to his own district near Tadoussac and to live with his three brothers, CARIGOUAN (a famous medicine-man who had great influence over him), Mestigoît, and Sasousmat, so that he might again become fluent in his native tongue.

Here he was found in 1629 by the English, who, under the command of the KIRKE brothers, had come to invade Canada. At first Pastedechouan pretended that he could not understand the English who questioned him in both French and Latin but a French deserter exposed this feigned ignorance. The English held Pastedechouan as an interpreter, supplied him with goods to trade with

Fig. 30. *Dictionary of Canadian Biography*, vol. 1, 1966.

and women including those born abroad who were active in Canadian affairs or were born in Canada and achieved distinction elsewhere and who died between 1875–1933; vol. 2, 1875–1937, lists persons who were Canadian and who died between 1875–1937. Included in these volumes were poets, statesmen, engineers, educationalists, scientists, physicians, businessmen, etc.

An additional source is William S. Wallace's *The Macmillan Dictionary of Canadian Biography*, 3rd edn., revised and enlarged, Macmillan, Toronto, 1963. This is the best general dictionary of Canadian biography of all periods and all classes, exclusive of living persons. It contains concise biographical sketches with bibliographies.

A more literary retrospective biographical compendium is the Makers of Canada Series, Oxford University Press, 1926, 25 vols. in 12. Prominent Canadian men of letters contributed the biographies to this series. Its contents are: vol. 1: N. E. Dionne, *Champlain*; H. A. Scott, *Bishop Laval*; vol. 2: W. D. Le Seur, *Count Frontenac*; H. R. Casgrain, *Wolfe and Montcalm*; vol. 3: A. G. Bradley, *Lord Dorchester*; J. N. McIlwraith, *Sir Frederick Haldimand*; vol. 4: D. C. Scott, *John Graves Simcoe*; Lady M. (R.) Edgar, *General Brock*; vol. 5: S. B. Leacock, *Mackenzie, Baldwin, Lafontaine, Hincks*; A. D. De Celles, *Papineau, Cartier*; vol. 6: A. Shortt, *Lord Sydenham*; W. P. M. Kennedy, *Lord Elgin*; N. Burwash, *Egerton Ryerson*; vol. 7: J. Lewis, *George Brown*; Sir G. R. Parkin, *Sir John A. Macdonald*; vol. 8: J. W. Longley, *Joseph Howe*; J. W. Longley, *Sir Charles Tupper*; J. Hannay, *Lemuel Allan Wilmot*; J. Hannay, *Sir Leonard Tilley*; vol. 9: G. Bryce, *Mackenzie, Selkirk, Simpson*; R. H. Coats and R. E. Gosnell, *Sir James Douglas*; vol. 10: J. MacNaughton, *Lord Strathcona*; W. Vaughan, *Sir William Van Horne*; vol. 11: Sir J. S. Willison, *Sir Wilfrid Laurier*; vol. 12: L. J. Burpee (ed.), *The Oxford Encyclopaedia of Canadian History*. The last volume, the *Oxford Encyclopaedia of Canadian History*, is an invaluable reference tool, being the only source for tables showing governors, premiers, etc., with tenures of office, of the various French and

British colonies and provinces that went to make up the Canadian nation.

A more specialized historical-biographical source-book is J.-B.-A. Allaire's *Dictionnaire biographique du clergé canadien-français*, Montreal, Impr. de l'École Catholique des Sourds-muets, 1908–34, in 6 vols. Vol. 1: *Early Clergy*; vol. 2: *Contemporary clergy*; vol. 3: *Supplement*; vol. 4: *Review of the Role of the Clergy*; vol. 5: *Additional Clergy*; vol. 6: *Supplement*.

Outstanding Canadian genealogical works have been produced but with the possible exception of those dealing with people of Icelandic origin, they have for the most part dealt with individual families and not with a national group. Much has been done on geneology in French Canada. Beginning with a small body of settlers, the settlers from France spread forth across the continent and consequently have a nucleus to return to for their origins. Another reason facilitating genealogical research among this group is the fact that there were no significant influxes of French-speaking settlers after French North America passed to the control of the British. An additional factor was their common bond of language and religion, as well as continuous parish records.

The definitive and monumental work on French-Canadian genealogy is Cyprien Tanguay's *Dictionnaire généalogique des familles canadiennes, depuis la fondation de la colonie jusqu'à nos jours*, Eusèbe Sénécal, Quebec, 1871–90, 7 vols. 1st series—vol. 1: 1608–1700; 2nd series—vols. 2–7: 1701–63. The 2nd series includes some entries later than 1763 belonging to a projected third series. Tanguay's work is an extensive genealogical dictionary of French-Canadian families including those from the beginnings of settlement to the year of British domination and a few items beyond. Only two of the projected series were complete in the existing 7 volumes.

So important is Tanguay's work that it has not been allowed to languish but has been revised and supplemented since its original publication. From 1955 to 1959 Archange Godbout, OFM, published in Quebec *Nos ancêtres au XVIIe siècle: dictionnaire généalogique et bio-bibliographique des familles canadiennes* in

5 vols. This is a revision of the first volume of Tanguay's *Diction-naire généalogique*, but worked out according to a different plan. The work includes the families founded before 1700 and still having descendants at the present time. The work was done in collaboration with généalogiste Rolland-J. Augé, past director of the Bureau des Recherches Historiques in Montreal. Abundant and varied documentation is the foundation of this study. Vol. 1 is the bibliography: manuscripts, cartography, printed books, and proper names.

Tanguay's work has been continued by La Société Généalogique Canadienne-Française in Montreal. Since 1957 they have been publishing, under the editorship of J. Arthur Leboeuf, the *Complément au dictionnaire généalogique Tanguay*.

Further genealogical information dealing with French-Canadian families can be found in La Société Généalogique Canadienne-Française, *Mémoires*, Montreal, 1944 to date.

There are many first-class biographies of individuals. Choosing one at random as an example, there is Hugh MacI. Urquhart's *Arthur Currie: the biography of a great Canadian*, J. M. Dent & Sons Ltd., Toronto, 1950. This is a scholarly and eminently readable biography of Sir Arthur William Currie, the first man to be made a full General in the Canadian Army. He was not only one of Canada's greatest soldiers but he was also one of the ablest commanders in the Allied cause during World War I. Under his leadership the Canadian Army gained its immortal name at Second Ypres and Vimy Ridge.

One of the most important aspects of a country's history is its political history, and one way of tracing this is through the biographies, journals, diaries, and memoirs of its political leaders. Since its creation under the British North America Act in 1867 Canada has had fourteen prime ministers. Of these, two—Sir John Joseph Caldwell Abbott (1821–93) and Sir Mackenzie Bowell (1823–1917), have not yet been delineated by an historian, but for the others, material exists.

Canada's first prime minister, Sir John A. Macdonald, one of the Fathers of Confederation, is recorded in Donald G.

Creighton's *John A. Macdonald*, Macmillan, Toronto, 1955–6; vol. 1: *The Young Chieftain*; vol. 2: *The Old Politician*. Following in chronological order by tenure of office there are Dale C. Thomson's *Alexander Mackenzie: clear grit*, Macmillan, Toronto, 1960; the *Life and Work of the Rt. Hon. Sir John Thompson, Prime Minister of Canada* by John C. Hopkins, United Publishing Houses, Toronto, 1895; and Edward M. Saunders's *The Life and Letters of the Rt. Hon. Sir Charles Tupper, Bart., K.C.M.G.*, Cassell, London, 1916, supplemented by *Supplement to the Life and Letters of the Rt. Hon. Sir Charles Tupper, Bart., G.C.M.G.*, compiled by Sir Charles H. Tupper, Ryerson Press, Toronto, 1926.

Next came one of Canada's greatest prime ministers, Sir Wilfrid Laurier. There are two outstanding biographies available, John W. Dafoe's *Laurier: a study in Canadian politics*, McClelland & Stewart, Toronto, 1922, 1963, and Joseph Schull's *Laurier: the first Canadian*, Macmillan, Toronto, 1965.

His successor, Sir Robert Borden, has had no biographer, but left *Robert Laird Borden: his memoirs*, Macmillan, Toronto, 1938.

Next came Arthur Meighen, who held office briefly in 1920–1, taking over from Borden, and again, from 29 June to 25 September 1926, and who has been discussed in Roger Graham's *Arthur Meighen: a biography*, Clarke, Irwin, Toronto, 1960–5; vol. 1: *The Door of Opportunity*; vol. 2: *And Fortune Fled*; vol. 3: *No Surrender*.

Arthur Meighen was succeeded by William Lyon Mackenzie King, who held office as prime minister of Canada for an un-precedented and unequalled 21 years. More has been written about Mackenzie King than about any other Canadian prime minister. A good 1-volume biography is Bruce Hutchison's *The Incredible Canadian: a candid portrait of Mackenzie King, his works, his times, and his nation*, Longmans, Toronto, 1953. A more scholarly and detailed work is Robert MacGregor Dawson's *William Lyon Mackenzie King: a political biography*, University of Toronto Press, Toronto, 1958–63; vol. 1: *1874–1923*; vol. 2: *1924–1932, the Lonely Heights* by H. Blair Neatby.

Mackenzie King's sojourn in power was broken, with the exception of Meighen's brief appearance in the 1920's, only once, by R. B. Bennett, from 1930 to 1935, who has been dealt with in *R. B. Bennett: a biography* by Ernest Watkins, published Kingswood House, Toronto, 1963.

Mackenzie King's terms of office spanned 1921–46. He was followed by Mr. L. St.-Laurent, described in *Louis St.-Laurent* by Dale Thomson, Macmillan, 1967. Then came John George Diefenbaker, who has been written about by Peter G. Newman in *Renegade in Power: the Diefenbaker years*, McClelland & Stewart, Toronto, 1963.

And though there is as yet no satisfactory biography of Lester Bowles Pearson, some information may be secured from *The Pearson Phenomenon* by John R. Beal, Longmans, Toronto, 1964.

All fourteen of Canada's prime ministers are discussed and analysed in Bruce Hutchison's collective biography *Mr. Prime Minister*, Longmans, Toronto, 1964.

One of the other Fathers of Confederation, and the bitter political opponent of Sir John A. Macdonald, George Brown, founder of the *Toronto Globe*, now the *Globe and Mail*, may be studied in James M. Careless's excellent *Brown of the Globe*, Macmillan, Toronto, 1949–63; vol. 1: *The Voice of Upper Canada, 1818–1859*; vol. 2: *Statesman of Confederation, 1860–1880*.

Newfoundland did not become a province of Canada until after World War II; before that it was a Crown Colony and one time independent Dominion. The story of its own prime ministers may be read in Michael F. Harrington's *The Prime Ministers of Newfoundland*, St. John's Evening Telegram, 1962.

Biographical information about Canada's Governors-General since Confederation can be found in *Canada's Governors-General: Lord Monck to General Vanier*, 2nd ed., revised and augmented, York Publishing Co., Toronto, 1965, by John Cowan.

Canada has also had her rebels. There was William Lyon Mackenzie, who is written up in William M. Kilbourn's *The Firebrand: William Lyon Mackenzie and the rebellion in Upper Canada*, Clarke, Irwin, Toronto, 1956, which could have been a good historical biography but is flawed by the author's deliberate twisting of fact in order to get a better story, and Mackenzie's compatriot, Louis Joseph Papineau, who can be studied in Fernand Ouellet's *Papineau*, Presses Universitaires Laval, Quebec, 1959, and in *Papineau* by Robert Rumilly, Éditions Bernard Valiquette, Montreal, 1944.

Another rebel was Louis Riel who has had his biographers in Edmund B. Osler's *The Man who had to hang: Louis Riel*, Longmans, Toronto, 1961, and in George F. Stanley's *Louis Riel*, Ryerson Press, Toronto, 1963. A fuller account of Riel and his times is told in G. F. G. Stanley's *The Birth of Western Canada: a history of the Riel rebellions*, University of Toronto Press, Toronto, 1963.

There are several good collective biographies of outstanding Canadians; one such is R. L. McDougall's *Our Living Tradition*, University of Toronto Press, 1959. In this collection eminent Canadian scholars analyse various aspects of the Canadian heritage. Twelve biographical studies serve to illustrate Canadian themes contributing towards a distinctive national identity. The men and women discussed have played vital roles in the development of Canadian literature, politics, and the visual arts. They include such disparate personalities as Thomas Chandler Haliburton, humorist, satirist, and creator of the immortal Sam Slick; Louis Joseph Papineau, patriot and leader in Lower Canada; and Frederick H. Varley, outstanding Canadian artist and one of the Group of Seven. The main concern throughout is "to secure a creative view of the ideas and values of the past from the vantage point of the present". This book which recognizes both a French- and English-speaking culture is meant to be read and enjoyed. It is only, incidentally, a source of information for the student who will find these brief but vital biographies very useful.

Another interesting collective biography is Herbert F. Wood's *Forgotten Canadians*, Longmans, Toronto, 1963, discussing in brief but interesting sketches some lesser-known Canadians, such as Jean Oliver Chenier; William Alexander Smith who expressed his philosophy by changing his name to Amor de Cosmos, "Lover of the World"; the Denisons, Canada's foremost military family; Gabriel Dumont; James Fitzgibbon, whose contribution to the freedom of Canada has been overshadowed by the propaganda and legend surrounding Laura Secord; and others, all of whom played an important part in making up the fabric of Canada.

CHAPTER 15

History

THE best overall all-round history of Canada is William L. Morton's *The Kingdom of Canada: a general history from earliest times*, McClelland & Stewart, Toronto, 1963. This is the first history of Canada to take into consideration all the varied threads that make up Canada's beginnings and weave them into a comprehensive pattern. Professor Morton is the foremost exponent of what may be termed the "Western school" of Canadian historiography as opposed to the "University of Toronto school". The Western school, so called because its leaders came from the University of Manitoba and other prairie universities, takes a broader perspective of the Canadian scene than was evident in the work of earlier historians.

Two first-class 1-volume histories of Canada are James M. S. Careless's *Canada: a story of challenge*, revised edn., Macmillan, Toronto, 1965, and Donald G. Creighton's *Dominion of the North: a history of Canada*, new edn., Macmillan, Toronto, 1962. Both of these works are important for an interpretation of Canada and the emergence of the Canadian nation out of scattered colonies.

There unfortunately is not a good 1-volume history of Canada by a French-Canadian historian—Canada, that is, in terms of the nation as a whole. Canada, to French-Canadian historians, means, understandably, New France, and many histories end with 1759. The classic nineteenth-century history of French Canada is Francois-Xavier Garneau's *Histoire du Canada* (Fig. 31), 5th edn., revised Éd. de l'Arbre, Montreal, 1944, originally published in 1850 in 8 volumes and covering the history of Canada (i.e. French

FRANÇOIS-XAVIER GARNEAU

HISTOIRE DU CANADA

CINQUIÈME ÉDITION, REVUE,

ANNOTÉE ET PUBLIÉE

AVEC UNE INTRODUCTION ET DES APPENDICES

PAR SON PETIT-FILS

HECTOR GARNEAU

Préface de M. Gabriel HANOTAUX, de l'Académie française.

TOME I

PARIS

LIBRAIRIE FÉLIX ALCAN

108, BOULEVARD SAINT-GERMAIN, 108

1913

FIG. 31. *Histoire du Canada.*

North America) from the time of its discovery until the union of
Lower Canada with Upper Canada in 1840–1. It exists in both a
French-language and English-language edition.

Another early twentieth-century history is Lionel Groulx's
Histoire du Canada français depuis la découverte, 4th edn.,
Fides, Montreal, 1960. L'Abbé Groulx was the spokesman for
the clerical-nationalist view of French-Canadian history, but his
history is still important even though most of his ideas are now
challenged.

There are at present two schools of French-Canadian historiography. The one, containing for the most part the older French-
Canadian historians, is a "passive" school, interpreting the history
of French-Canada as a result of its own problems and viewing the
transition from French to English domination with objectivity. It
is best represented in Gustave Lanctôt's *A History of Canada*,
Clarke, Irwin, Toronto, 1963–5, vol. 1: *From its Origins to the
Royal Régime, 1663*; vol. 2: *From the Royal Régime to the Treaty
of Utrecht, 1663–1713*; vol. 3: *From the Treaty of Utrecht to the
Treaty of Paris, 1713–1763*. The Clarke–Irwin edition is a simul-
taneous English-language edition of the original French-language
edition published in Montreal. This is an excellent history of the
early years of Canada from the French point of view.

The other school of French-Canadian history can be called the
"activist" school, centred at Laval University. It is the spokesman
in the field of history for what has been called Quebec's "Quiet
Revolution", an upsurge of French-Canadian nationalism, radic-
ally different from the old nineteenth-century French-Canadian
nationalism. This latter was an isolationist provincialism, and dis-
satisfaction with Quebec's place in Confederation and her position
vis-a-vis English Canada.

It is best represented by Marcel Trudel's *Histoire de la Nouvelle-
France*, Fides, Montreal, 1963; vol. 1: *Les Vaines tentatives 1524–
1603*; vol. 2: *Du comptoir à la colonies, 1604–1632*, a projected
multi-volume history of French North America now in progress.
This is an attempt to give as complete a history as possible of the
years 1524 to 1763 when France occupied North America.

One can only understand present-day Quebec by tracing the intellectual and cultural history of French Canada from its beginnings. A good start in this direction was made by Mason Wade's *The French Canadians, 1760–1945*, Macmillan, Toronto, 1955, an attempt to explain why the French Canadians live, think, act, and react differently from English-speaking North Americans. It tries to give an explanation of *le fait français en Amerique*—the French fact in North America. Wade's work must be read with the realization that it was published just as the new nationalism in Quebec became vocal.

Another standard multi-volume history of French Canada is Thomas Chapais's *Cours d'histoire du Canada*, Garneau, Quebec, 1919–34, in 8 vols.

The outstanding multi-volume history of Canada, covering all aspects of its early years and rise to nationhood, will be, upon its completion, the *Canadian Centenary Series: a history of Canada*, McClelland & Stewart, Toronto, 1963– , in 17 vols., with William L. Morton as Executive Editor and Donald G. Creighton as Advisory Editor. Each historian has been given leeway to interpret his assigned period as he sees fit. The volumes are models of scholarship and historical writing. Each volume is complete in itself, and together, they will form a definitive history of Canada, superseding all multi-volume, multi-authored, historical series previously published. The volumes in the series are: vol. 1: Tryggvi J. Oleson, *Early Voyages and Northern Approaches, 1000–1632*; vol. 2: Marcel Trudel, *New France, 1524–1662*; vol. 3: W. J. Eccles, *Canada under Louis XIV, 1663–1701*; vol. 4: Jean Blain, *New France, 1702–1743*; vol. 5: G. F. G. Stanley, *New France, 1744–1760*; vol. 6: Hilda Neatby, *Quebec, 1760–1791*; vol. 7: Gerald M. Craig, *Upper Canada, the Formative Years, 1784–1841*; vol. 8: Fernand Ouellet, *Lower Canada, 1792–1841*; vol. 9: W. S. MacNutt, *The Atlantic Provinces, the Emergence of Colonial Society, 1712–1857*; vol. 10: J. M. S. Careless, *Canada, 1841–1857*; vol. 11: E. E. Rich, *The North, 1670–1857*; vol. 12: W. L. Morton, *The Critical Years, the Union of British North America, 1857–1873*; vol. 13: P. B. Waite, *Canada, 1874–1896*;

vol. 14: G. R. Cook, *Canada, 1897–1921*; vol. 15: F. W. Gibson, *Canada, 1922–1939*; vol. 16: Morris Zaslow, *The North, 1870–1965*; vol. 17: D. G. Creighton, *Canada, 1939–1967*. Of this series, several volumes have not yet been published; the titles given here are indications as to each volume's region and period covered.

A useful source of primary documents is James J. Talman's *Basic Documents in Canadian History*, L. Van Nostrand, Toronto, 1959, providing a selection illustrating the development of Canada from an unexplored geographical region to an independent world power, beginning with an extract from Jacques Cartier's narrative of his second voyage and ending with a quotation from the *Debates of the House of Commons*.

Another excellent compilation of documents is Michel Brunet's *Histoire du Canada par les textes*, revised edn., Fides, Montreal, 1963; vol. 1: *1534–1854*; vol. 2: *1855–1960*. This is a revision of the 1952 edition. Vol. 1 was compiled and edited by Guy Frégault and Marcel Trudel, vol. 2 by Michel Brunet. It is a collection of documents relating to the history of Canada from the French point of view.

A very useful special collection is *Documents concernant l'histoire constitutionnelle du Canada, 1759–1828*, King's Printer, Ottawa, 1911–35, in 3 volumes, compiled by the Archives of Canada. The study of constitutional history is especially necessary because political unification and autonomy were requisite before Canada could gain the position she has achieved in the world today.

There are two other very valuable collections of documents, journals, etc., indispensable to the student of Canadian history.

The first of these are the *Publications* (Fig. 32) of the Champlain Society of Toronto, comprising three series, and first appearing in 1907. The Champlain Society was founded in 1905 by the President of the Canadian Bank of Commerce with 525 elected members as a private publishing company specializing in rare Canadiana and previously unpublished material, available to members only. The 1st series ran from 1907 to 1936, and contained such works as the journal of Samuel Hearne's journey, David Thompson's narrative,

THE

PUBLICATIONS OF
THE CHAMPLAIN
SOCIETY

THE DIARY AND SELECTED PAPERS
OF CHIEF JUSTICE WILLIAM SMITH
1784-1793

VOLUME II

TORONTO
THE CHAMPLAIN SOCIETY

Fig. 32. Champlain Society, *Publications*.

documents relating to Seigneurial tenure, and a definitive 6-volume edition of Champlain's writings. The policy of the organization has always been to issue well designed volumes edited by competent scholars. The Society's 2nd series was the *Publications* (Hudson's Bay Company Series), Champlain Society, Toronto, 1938–49, 12 vols. done in conjunction with the Hudson's Bay Company.

The Society's present series, *Publications* [Ontario Series], Toronto, 1957– , is on regions of Ontario and is being done at the expense of the Province of Ontario. At present it comprises: vol. 1: E. C. Guillet, *The Valley of the Trent*; vol. 2: Léopold Lamontagne, *Royal Fort Frontenac*; vol. 3: R. A. Preston, *Kingston before the War of 1812*; vol. 4: E. J. Lajeunesse, *The Windsor Border Region*; vols. 5 and 8: Edith G. Firth, *The Town of York, 1793–1834*; vol. 6: F. B. Murray, *Muskoka and Haliburton, 1615–1875*; vol. 7: C. M. Johnston, *The Valley of the Six Nations*. These are all scholarly collections of documents each pertinent to their subject, and introduced by an historical study placing the documents in their proper context.

The other important set of documents relating to the history of Canada is the *Publications* of the Hudson's Bay Record Society, London, 1938– . The series at present consists of 23 vols., vols. 8–23 being in print and available to members of the Society. Vols. 21–22 are especially valuable in that they are a 2-volume *History of The Hudson's Bay Company*, vol. 1: *1670–1763*; vol. 2: *1763–1870*, written by E. E. Rich, until his retirement in 1959 General Editor of the series. The early volumes of this series are duplicated by the Champlain Society's *Publications* [Hudson's Bay Company Series]. Each volume of documents has a historical introduction giving its background and tieing the series together.

The history of a country is read not only in written and printed records but in pictures as well. One of the best collections for Canada is Charles W. Jefferys's *The Picture Gallery of Canadian History*, Ryerson Press, Toronto, 1942–50; vol. 1: *Discovery to 1763*; vol. 2: *1763 to 1830*; vol. 3: *1830 to 1900*. These 3 volumes present accurate drawings and imaginative pictorial reconstructions, correct in detail, of historical events in Canada's history and Canadian social life and customs, from the pen of one of Canada's most famous artists. The pictures are accompanied by an historical commentary.

Two other equally valuable collections of pictures and drawings representing Canadian life of the past are in the Toronto Public Library. One is the J. Ross Robertson historical collection; the other the Toronto and Early Canada Picture Collection. Between them they represent one of the most extensive pictorial collections illustrative of the Canadian heritage, and are constantly being called upon to provide reproductions of their contents for use as illustrations in Canadian books and for other purposes. Their scope and content can be discovered through the Toronto Public Library's publications *Landmarks of Canada, what Art has done for Canadian History: a guide to the J. Ross Robertson historical collection in the Public Reference Library, Toronto, Canada*, reprinted edition, 1967; and *Toronto and Early Canada: a catalogue of the Toronto and early Canada picture collection in the Toronto Public Library*, Baxter Pub. Co., Toronto, 1964 (Fig. 33). The J. Ross Robertson collection was a gift to the Toronto Public Library and is a static collection; the Toronto and Early Canada Picture Collection is the Library's own and is continually growing. Each collection consists of oil paintings, water-colours, etchings, engravings, prints, and photographs depicting every aspect of the Canadian scene from the past, and presenting an invaluable reference source to the historian and artist.

The histories of particular regions and of periods count for much and can go a long way toward filling in the gaps left in general histories. Of special value to anyone interested in the Province of Quebec is Philip Garigue's *A Bibliographical Introduction to the Study of French Canada*, Department of Sociology and Anthropology, McGill University, Montreal, 1956. This is the basic bibliography for anyone approaching a study of the social sciences as they relate to the Province of Quebec and French-Canadians. It is arranged by nine major topics of major

I

1061. *Wigwam, an Ojibway half-breed, 1858. Photo by H. L. Hime.*

FIG. 33. *Toronto and Early Canada,* vol. 3, 1964.

1076. 'John Bull making a new batch of ships to send to the lakes.' 1813?
Cartoon engraved by William Charles, Philadelphia, published and sold wholesale by Wm. Charles. 11 x 17. A.

NORTHWEST REBELLION

1077. The Battle of Cut Knife Creek . . from topographical sketches by Capt. Rutherford . . .' (and others).
Chromolithograph by Toronto Lithographing Co. Grip Publishing Co., Toronto, 1885. 18½ x 24½. A.

1078. 'Battle of Fish Creek . . . sketches by Mr. F. W. Curzon . . .'
Chromolithograph by Toronto Lithographing Co. Grip Publishing Co., Toronto, 1885. 18½ x 24½. A.

1079. 'Capture of Batoche, by the special artist of the 'Canadian Pictorial and Illustrated War News', Sgt. Grundy. . .' (and others).
Chromolithograph by Toronto Lithographing Co. Grip Publishing Co., Toronto, 1885. 18½ x 24½. A.

Sports

1080. BASEBALL. 'Varsity baseball club, 1887.' *Photo.* E3:53a.

importance towards an understanding of French-Canada—general historical studies; the human geography of French Canada; the social institutions of French Canada; French-speaking groups outside the Province of Quebec; social changes and social problems; cultural characteristics; the educational system; special problems in the study of French Canada; and bibliographies.

For those who have read Longfellow's *Evangeline* and who have wondered about the Acadians, the basic authority is Bona Arsenault's *Histoire et généalogie des Acadiens*, Conseil de la Vie Française en Amérique, Quebec, 1965, 2 vols. This is a revision and expansion of the author's earlier *L'Acadie des ancêtres: avec la généalogie des premières familles acadiennes*, Conseil de la Vie Française en Amérique, Université Laval, Quebec, 1955. Largely genealogical in content, the *Histoire et généalogie des Acadiens* is the standard work on the French in Acadia, that part of eastern North America now comprised of Nova Scotia, New Brunswick, Prince Edward Island, Îles de la Madeleine, plus part of Maine, that was lost to France by the Treaty of Utrecht in 1713. Arsenault's work is an impressive synthesis of Acadian history and genealogy from the founding of Port Royal to the Disperson. Some of the Acadians became the "Cajuns" of Louisiana, others returned eventually to their homes in Acadia where their descendants still eke out an existence, proudly considering themselves different from the Québécois.

Provincial histories and the history of individual cities can contain useful information not found in general histories and can often throw considerable light on early beginnings in Canada. A selective list of provincial histories is given here for those who wish to delve deeper into Canada's history.

NEWFOUNDLAND. Albert B. Perlin, *The Story of Newfoundland: comprising a new outline of the island's history from 1497 to 1959, a brief account of the social and economic life of the province and of its resources, natural history, public services and culture, and a description of some of its* principal industries, public utilities, and commercial institutions, St. John's, Nfld., 1959.

NOVA SCOTIA. G. G. Campbell, *The History of Nova Scotia*, Ryerson Press, Toronto, 1948.

NEW BRUNSWICK. William S. MacNutt, *New Brunswick: a history, 1784–1867*, Macmillan, Toronto, 1963; and *New Brunswick and its People: the biography of a Canadian province*, New Brunswick Travel Bureau, Fredericton, 1952.

PRINCE EDWARD ISLAND. Francis W. Bolger, *Prince Edward Island and Confederation, 1863–1873*, St. Dunstan's University Press, Charlottetown, 1964; and Lorne C. Callbeck, *The Cradle of Confederation: a brief history of Prince Edward Island from its discovery in 1534 to the present time*, Brunswick Press, Fredericton, 1964.

QUEBEC. Robert Rumilly, *Histoire de la province de Québec*, Éditions Bernard Valiquette, Montreal, 1940– . 34 vols., the latest having appeared in 1963.

ONTARIO. Joseph M. Scott, *The Story of Ontario*, J. M. Dent & Sons (Canada) Ltd., Toronto, 1949.

MANITOBA. William L. Morton, *Manitoba: a history*, University of Toronto Press, Toronto, 1957; and D. W. Friesen, *Manitoba: the birth of a province*, Altona, Man., 1965.

SASKATCHEWAN. James F. Wright, *Saskatchewan: the history of a province*, McClelland & Stewart, Toronto, 1955.

ALBERTA. Alberta Publicity Bureau, *Alberta through the Years*, Edmonton, Alta., 1963.

BRITISH COLUMBIA. Margaret A. Ormsby, *British Columbia: a history*, Macmillan, Toronto, 1958.

For the cities, the following might be noted:

HALIFAX, N.S. Thomas H. Raddall, *Halifax: warden of the North*, McClelland & Stewart, Toronto, 1948.

MONTREAL, QUEBEC. Camille Bertrand, *Histoire de Montréal*, Beauchemin, Montreal, 1935–42. Stephen B. Leacock, *Leacock's Montreal*, McClelland & Stewart, Toronto, 1963.

OTTAWA. Wilfrid Eggleston, *Queen's Choice: a story of Canada's capital*, Queen's Printer, Ottawa, 1961.

TORONTO, ONTARIO. Jesse E. Middleton, *Toronto's 100 Years*, Centennial Committee, Toronto, 1934. Percy J. Robinson, *Toronto During the French Régime: a history of the Toronto region from Brulé to Simcoe, 1615–1793*, 2nd edn., University of Toronto Press, Toronto, 1965.

VANCOUVER, BC. Alan Morley, *Vancouver: from milltown to metropolis*, Mitchell Press, Vancouver, 1961.

The Amerindians, to use the anthropological term for the "Indians" of North America, play an important role in the history of Canada both in their own right and in contribution to the general development of the Canadian nation. The most exhaustive and definitive work on Canadian Amerindians is Diamond Jenness's *The Indians of Canada*, 6th edn., Queen's Printer, Ottawa, 1963. Compiled by one of Canada's foremost scholars and anthropologists, this work covers every phase of Amerindian and Eskimo life and culture—political, social, and economic. It is interesting, informative, authoritative, and valuable. The work is copiously illustrated and contains extensive sections on the history of the Amerindians in Canada and on recent archaeological exploration into their past.

Local historical societies in Canada are a useful source for information and materials. Quite often they maintain a local museum, and sometimes publish an historical journal or booklets concerning their locality and its prominent citizens. They can also sometimes be of assistance to the aspiring genealogist. A very useful guide to such organizations is the American Association for state and local history's *Directory of Historical Societies and Agencies in the United States and Canada*, the Association, 132 Ninth St., Nashville, Tenn., USA, 1967. The arrangement is, first, by the states of the United States, then the provinces of Canada in alphabetical order. Within each state or province section, historical societies and agencies are listed in alphabetical order by name, giving the address of each, their major field of interest, and other sundry details.

The most important historical association in Canada is the Canadian Historical Association. It grew out of the Historical Landmarks Association of Canada and became the Canadian Historical Association in 1922. Its function is to work for the preservation of landmarks and to promote historical research. It publishes a series of historical booklets, of which there have been 12 so far, as well as the *Canadian Historical Review*, University of Toronto Press, Toronto, 1920– . The *Review* is quarterly and contains two long articles per issue of a specialized nature devoted to scholarly research. In addition about one-half of each issue is used for reviews of recent historical publications, especially those bearing on Canada, and a bibliography of new books in the fields of history, travel, biography, etc. This bibliography, "Recent publications relating to Canada", is subject arranged and is the successor to the "Review of historical publications relating to Canada". A further source of historical articles dealing with Canada is the annual report of the Canadian Historical Association containing papers read at the annual meeting.

The Canadian Catholic Historical Association Société Canadienne d'Histoire de l'Eglise Catholique, Ottawa, is a bilingual society, founded 3 June 1933, which annually publishes French and English volumes. It has produced a separate index to its materials for 1933–59.

A number of other Canadian periodicals are either devoted exclusively to Canadian history or carrying articles of an historical interest. Two valuable journals are the *Recherches historiques: bulletin d'archéologie, d'histoire, de biographie, de numismatique,* . . ., Pierre-Georges Roy, Levis, PQ., 1895–1961, and the *Revue d'histoire de l'Amérique française*, L'Institut d'Histoire de l'Amérique Française, Montreal, 1947– . *Recherches historiques* is no longer published and will be sorely missed; the *Revue d'histoire de l'Amérique française* is equivalent to the *Canadian Historical Review* and is concerned not only with the French in Canada but in the United States as well.

Other historical periodicals of local coverage of interest are:
the *Collections* of the Nova Scotia Historical Society, Halifax,
printed at the Morning Herald Office, Halifax, NS, 1879 to date;
the New Brunswick Historical Society's *Collections*, Barnes & Co.,
Ltd., Saint John, NB, 1894 to date; *Cahiers d'histoire*, Société
d'Histoire Régionale de Québec, Quebec, 1947 to date; the
Ontario Historical Society's *Papers and Records*, William Briggs,
Toronto, 1899 to date (since 1947 has appeared as *Ontario History*); the *Papers read before the Historical and Scientific Society
of Manitoba, Winnipeg*, Advocate Printers Ltd., Winnipeg, 1945
to date; *Saskatchewan History*, Saskatchewan Archives Board,
Saskatoon, Sask., 1948 to date; the *Alberta Historical Review*
(quarterly), Historical Society of Alberta, Edmonton, 1953 to date;
the *British Columbia Historical Quarterly*, Victoria, BC, 1937 to
date; and the *Vancouver Historical Journal*, Archives Society of
Vancouver, Vancouver, 1958 to date.

Index of Subjects, Authors and Titles

The following symbols are used to show various editions of a work:

* indicates published both in French and English.
** indicates published in a bilingual English/French edition.

K

K*

A MESSAGE TO PARENTS

It is of vital importance for parents to read good books to young children in order to aid the child's psychological and intellectual development. At the same time as stimulating the child's imagination and awareness of his environment, it creates a positive relationship between parent and child. The child will gradually increase his basic vocabulary and will soon be able to read books alone.

Brown Watson has published this series of books with these aims in mind. By collecting this inexpensive library, parent and child are provided with hours of pleasurable and profitable reading.

This edition first published 2001 by
Brown Watson, England
Reprinted 2003, 2005
© 2001 Brown Watson, England
Printed in China

Snow White
and the Seven Dwarfs

Text by Maureen Spurgeon

Brown Watson
ENGLAND

Long ago, a queen sat sewing at a palace window. Looking out at the white snow drifting against the black window frame, she pricked her finger and three drops of blood fell. "If only I had a daughter with skin as white as snow, blood-red cheeks and hair as black as the window frame," she sighed, "I would call her Snow White."

Before long, the queen's wish was granted. Everyone celebrated the birth of her baby daughter. And, as the years passed, Snow White became more and more beautiful.

But the happy times were not to
last. Suddenly, the good queen
became ill and died. Within a
year, Snow White's father had
taken another wife, as hard-
hearted as she was beautiful.

The new queen was also very vain. Her greatest treasure was a magic mirror, and every day she asked it the same question. "Mirror, mirror on the wall, who is the fairest one of all?"

The answer from the magic
mirror was always the same.
"In all the land,
'Tis thou, oh queen!
Thou art the fairest
To be seen!"

Then, one day, the mirror gave
a different answer.
"No maiden was more fair
Than thou!
But Snow White is
The fairest, now!"

The queen flew into a terrible
rage, screaming for a palace
guard.
"Take Snow White into the forest!"
she stormed. "Put her to death!
Then bring me back her heart!"

The guard was shocked. He knew he had to do as the queen said. But, by the time he and Snow White reached the forest, he had made up his mind that he could never do such a wicked deed.

He told her of the danger she was in. "Run away, as far as you can," he begged Snow White, "so the queen will not find you! I shall take back a deer's heart and pretend it is yours!"

Poor Snow White! She would never have thought anyone could hate her so much. On and on she ran, strange shadows looming everywhere, and thorns

and brambles seeming to reach
out, clawing at her. How long
she kept running, she hardly
knew. It seemed like a dream
when, quite suddenly, she came
across a little cottage nestling in
the very heart of the forest.

"Anyone at home?" she called, stepping inside. How dusty and untidy it was in that little cottage! But Snow White was so glad to have somewhere to rest, she did not mind.

She set to work, feeling much happier as she laid a fire, ready to cook some broth.
"I wonder who lives here?" she thought, dusting the seven little chairs set around the table.

By the time she had washed seven little plates, seven mugs, seven knives, spoons and forks, then made seven little beds, Snow White was feeling very tired. She only meant to rest a little while . . .

When she woke up, there were the faces of the seven dwarfs smiling at her. How pleased they had been to return to a warm, clean cottage, and find a meal waiting for them, cooked by a pretty girl!

As soon as they heard what had
happened to her, the dwarfs
said she could stay with them.
Snow White had not been so
happy for a long time. She loved
looking after the seven dwarfs.

"Do not open the door to anyone
while we are out," they told her.
"If ever the queen should hear
where you are, she will surely
try to harm you again." Snow
White knew this was true.

At that very moment, the magic
mirror was telling the queen,
"In the seven dwarfs' cottage,
Snow White lives now.
She is, dear queen,
Still fairer than thou!"

The queen went white with rage! Determined to put an end to Snow White, she disguised herself as an old pedlar woman, then put poison into the rosiest apple she could find . . .

With her magic powers, the queen soon found the cottage in the forest and tapped at the door. "Lovely apples!" she croaked, as Snow White came to the window. "Try one, my dear."

Snow White did not want to hurt
an old woman's feelings. One
bite of the poisoned apple and
she fell to the floor. Cackles of
wild laughter from the wicked
queen echoed all through the
forest.

The dwarfs were heartbroken when they found dear Snow White. Wanting to keep her with them for always, they put her in a crystal casket and set it down in her favourite part of the forest.

As time passed, the story of the beautiful young princess asleep in a crystal casket began to spread. One day, a handsome young prince decided to discover the truth for himself.

The moment he saw Snow White, he had to lean over and kiss her. Her eyelids fluttered, and as she looked into the face of the young prince, she knew she loved him as much as he already loved her.